D1287612

DISCARDED
UNIVERSITY OF WINNIPEG
PORTAGE & BALMORAL
WINNIPEG 2, MAN.   CANADA

DISCARDED

BIRDS
OF TOWN AND SUBURB

by the same author

BIRD MIGRANTS (1952)

THE SONGS AND CALLS OF BRITISH BIRDS (1955)

VOICES OF THE WILD (1957)

WITHERBY'S SOUND GUIDE TO BRITISH BIRDS (1958)
(with Myles North)

WOODLAND BIRDS (1971)

WILD LIFE IN THE ROYAL PARKS (1974)

QL
690
.G7S54

BIRDS

OF TOWN AND SUBURB

ERIC SIMMS, D.F.C., M.A.

COLLINS
ST JAMES'S PLACE, LONDON

TO
THOMAS, WILFRID AND MARGARET

First published 1975
© Eric Simms 1975
ISBN 0 00 219126 1
Made and printed in Great Britain by
William Collins Sons & Co Ltd Glasgow

Contents

List of Text Figures

Photographs

Foreword

'THE English are town-birds through and through,' wrote D. H.
Lawrence, and it would seem that at least eighty per cent of them
actually do live in towns and cities. Yet deep down in the consciousness
of many of them still smoulders a keen regard for their rural origins.
How else could we account for the gracious city squares, the avenues
of trees only too often mangled by ignorant municipal authorities, the
plots of allotments, the garden suburbs and even the soulless blanket
of villas flung around so many town centres? Of more than eighteen
million British households nearly four fifths – some fourteen and a half
million – have a private garden, each a potential and vital link in a chain
of unofficial wildlife reserves. Watching birds is a pursuit that gives
positive pleasure to many thousands and I sincerely believe that many
more accept the presence of birds with their attractive plumage, varied
behaviour and melodious voices as an essential part of the backcloth
of life; their disappearance would impoverish them beyond belief.
Many people may accept their existence because they are so familiar
and only some special event will remind them of the birds who share
their environment with them. It may be the sudden earthward plunge
of a flock of feral pigeons from a tenement roof, a couple of sparrows
dust-bathing on a parched lawn or flowerbed, or a blackbird singing
on a chimney-pot.

I have lived on a typical inter-war estate for more than two decades
and have derived both pleasure and satisfaction, not from the faceless
rows of pebble-dashed houses but from the opportunity of pursuing a
continuous study of a group of birds that had not been investigated in
depth before. And I speak as one who came to suburbia from a delightful Warwickshire village on the Avon! I was able to find my research
material in or on the roof of my home, feeding in my garden, nesting
in my trees and bushes, bathing in my pond and flying overhead on its
way to nearby roosts or farther afield on its migratory journeys. A
local park and reservoir, old disused pits and a sewage farm, playing
fields and bits of waste ground, factory sites, river banks and ponds all
fitted with the houses and gardens into a nature conservation pattern
and offered a range of habitats in a small and easily accessible area that
was unique. The late Sir Dudley Stamp in his authoritative book,

Nature Conservation in Britain, wrote: 'The local zoo, the town park, the large town garden, the urban common all become part of the open-space network vital to wild life conservation.' This may be some compensation for those who feel that much of suburbia is 'a no-man's-land' halfway between the town and the country with all the worst and none of the redeeming features of either.

There are, of course, various types of suburb as well as different ways of suburban living. Some of the inner ones are poor in garden space and parkland where only the hardiest and most adaptable of our birds can survive. Others are richer in parks and commons and more spacious gardens where one can see a far wider range of bird species. Generally the outer suburbs have more open space, bigger gardens, larger sheets of water, more scrub and woodland and here, where the environment is varied and richer, the birds will undoubtedly benefit. As I wrote in a letter to *The Times* in February 1972 about the wildlife of north-west London, 'if so many animals can find the region still a favoured habitat – and woodland birds do better at Dollis Hill than in real woodland – then man could do a lot worse.'

I have written this book in two halves. The first opens with a history of suburban growth and then traces the bird life through the concentric rings formed by the inner and outer suburbs to the edge of the country-side and the 'green belt' zones where these exist. The second half of the book is concerned with an examination of some of the more interesting and specialized habitats and aspects of bird behaviour. Chapters 6 and 7 are devoted to urban and suburban wetlands – rivers, swamps, reservoirs and gravel pits, natural and artificial lakes, estuaries, coastal zones and lagoons. Not always perhaps as scenically attractive as the beauty of natural marshlands and open skies, many of these habitats can provide a sanctuary for wildlife as well, in the words of the International Union for Conservation of Nature, as 'one of the most popular, varied and valuable outlets for leisure activities.' Another chapter looks at birds and various sporting activities involving playing fields, game-keeping and shooting; in this last pursuit which is growing in popularity in Britain there may be mutual collaboration between the shooters and conservationists, but this is not always the case. The last two chapters deal with two interesting aspects of bird behaviour – that of roosting and migration – both of which can provide enormous interest since birds may roost in gardens and roofs as well as pass over on roosting or migration flights. Other migrants may drop in for an hour or so to rest and feed, even into quite small suburban gardens. The local reservoir, sewage farm or park lake may prove astonishingly rich in other migrants.

A great deal of this book is based inevitably on original observations but where I have been able to find parallel records from other localities or detailed notes on species and habitats I have incorporated these where they seemed relevant. I have relied considerably in this respect on county avifaunas and reports, especially those of the London Natural History Society and the West Midland Bird Club. I would be more than satisfied if this account of my studies, and I believe it to be the first book devoted entirely to suburban birds, were to inspire more suburban bird watchers to resist the understandable temptation to go too often tally-hunting after rarities when they might be adding to our knowledge of the ways in which the birds of our suburbs live and behave.

I would like to thank the editors of *British Birds*, the *London Naturalist*, the *London Bird Report*, the *West Midland Bird Report*, *Bird Study* and *Bird Notes* whose journals have provided some of the material included in this book. I must also express my appreciation to *The Observer* for permission to quote from an article by Stephen Gardiner, to *The Willesden and Brent Chronicle* in which some of my original observations were first published, to Messrs Faber and Faber for allowing me to quote from David Thomas's book *London's Green Belt*, and to Putnam and Company for approving an extensive quote from my own book, *Voices of the Wild*. The late Terry Gompertz also kindly agreed to my reproducing a quotation and two illustrations from her paper in *Bird Study* on the feral pigeon. Acknowledgement is also due to the Nature Conservancy and HM Stationery Office who published the table which is included as appendix 5.

I have also had very special help from Dr Jeffery and Dr Pamela Harrison, Mr L. A. Batten, Mr Kenneth Williamson, Mr David Glue, Mr Ronald Peal, Mr T. W. Gladwin and Mr D. Parr who have most kindly allowed me either to quote very fully from their scientific papers or to reproduce illustrations from various journals. My own researches have been very greatly aided by Mr J. T. Gillett, formerly Chief Librarian of the Borough of Brent, who undertook numerous pieces of research for me and loaned me manuscripts and maps and Mr J. G. Green, formerly Public Relations Officer of the same borough who assisted me in many practical ways in my investigations. The Brent Council itself has also granted me many generous facilities and I am grateful to them.

And lastly I must also pay a tribute to my many neighbours, friends, acquaintances and previously unknown informants who have kept me posted of events in the bird world which I would have missed or which I have subsequently been able to confirm.

CHAPTER I

The Rise of Suburbia

THE process of town growth is often complex and varied but the character of towns and cities, their plans and styles of architecture, their changing forms and activities can all affect the wildlife to be found there. In this introductory chapter I propose to trace in broad terms the continuing development of towns and their environs.

How did cities first come into being? It seems very likely that it was the change in neolithic times from man's well established practice of hunting and looking for food to the rather more static occupation of food growing that led to the setting up of towns. Early man with his agricultural economy and domesticated animals chose to live in fixed settlements – the first villages, in fact. Such early peasant communities arose not only in the Middle East but also in the Indus Valley, China and Central America. The new way of life was able to produce more than its practitioners needed and this, in its turn, released members of the community for other jobs besides just producing food. There was now opportunity and room for development for groups of leaders, priests, traders, manufacturers and craftsmen.

The first cities began to take shape about 5000 years ago. In Sumeria their populations ranged from 7000 to as many as 20,000 inhabitants. The first suburbs probably appeared in even these early times for the ancient city of Ur had an overspill settlement outside its boundary. Early urban man was no longer just an agriculturalist; he was now a specialist gathering in the surplus production of the region, developing trade, forming hierarchies in the community, planning towns and erecting public buildings. Thus early towns were often tight, well populated settlements protected by an outside wall. By Roman times they were noteworthy for their simple geometrical plans inside a fortified, defensive curtain of stone or brick. Even during the Roman occupation of Britain a suburb was built at Southwark outside the city walls and London itself preserved its irregular walled core as late as the Great Fire of 1666.

With the fall of Rome the urban way of life in Europe almost disappeared and towns did not begin to live again until the early Middle Ages; these amorphous organisms grew up often with churches at their very heart. Now the town was a centre of trade with its own market but it still remained a defensive unit. Edward the First's scheme for Conway in North Wales was an ambitious one and his military engineer, James of St George, produced a design that linked the new castle with a series of town walls; these were some 1400 yards long with 21 towers and 3 double-bastioned gateways which threw a strong defensive arm right round the town itself. On the whole medieval towns were not very big and most of their populations were around the 10,000 mark; fifteenth-century London with 40,000 inhabitants was quite exceptional. Outside these cities suburbs began to take shape and they were basically of two kinds. The first was to provide luxury villas for the more affluent city dwellers and the second was to accommodate the merchants and traders. Sir George Clarke has described the competition that grew up between the residents of the towns and the inhabitants of these new suburbs of the thirteenth and fourteenth centuries. Many of the suburban dwellers became the equals in skill of those living inside the city but they had such positive benefits as lower taxation, cheaper food and freedom from the guilds. It is true of course that for the towns built in alien territory by its conquerors the original and defeated inhabitants were made to live outside the walls in a distant kind of suburb, a feature, for example, of the towns in North Wales built after the Edwardian subjugation. Medieval towns were often cluttered and the pressure on space might lead to the high buildings that characterize Edinburgh. The streets were unpaved and foul with excrement and household refuse so that crows, jackdaws, ravens and kites found varied pickings in them while in the suburbs and outskirts of the town predatory buzzards and hawks, foxes, wild cats, martens and polecats menaced the lambs and poultry chicks.

It is possible to divide English towns between 1500 and 1700 into three groups. There were firstly some half a dozen cities, besides London, which were big enough to function in many ways as regional capitals. There were also about a hundred corporate towns with quite high population densities and flourishing economic and political lives. And, lastly, there were several hundred towns which had a low density of population, no real political significance but quite often a very active and lively market. During these two centuries there was a fairly steady rise in population and London itself, after the unsettled times of the Wars of the Roses, began to grow and prosper until modern times. A peak was reached in the late sixteenth century and there was a slackening off in the seventeenth. It was a period in which material wealth, influence and political power were increasingly attracted to a growing oligarchy which preferred to dwell in mansions situated in suburbs far away from the city centre. Coincident with this flow away from the town was another of an entirely different character; the urban poor, tradesmen looking for cheaper land and lower rents and aliens not allowed to work in the city were also moving into areas beyond the city limits. We have already seen how Southwark was a Roman suburb; now it was fast becoming a compact and unhealthy aggregation of tenements and cheap housing.

So far town growth had been slow and unspectacular. Now it was to be revolutionized in a far-reaching and fundamental way by the industrial upheaval that began in Britain towards the end of the eighteenth century and which was to reach its peak late in the nineteenth. This was a revolution that came at a much later period to the rest of Western Europe and to the United States. Previously the needs of the community had been met by small, scattered industries that had been absorbed with little difficulty into a rural landscape. The new industrial revolution demanded coal and iron and so people began to move in from the countryside to settle on the coalfields and in the thinly populated moorland valleys. As there was also a contemporary rise in home food production, and then a wide exploitation of the Australian and American grasslands, the new industrial masses could be fed from the surpluses gathered in by the farming communities.

In addition to being fed they also needed homes. 'The new England they built was housed not so much in towns as in barracks. These were grouped round the new factories, on the least expensive and therefore most congested model attainable.' This stricture by Sir Arthur Bryant reflects an era in the early and middle part of Victoria's reign when the working class population toiling in the mills, mines and factories was housed by small speculators and jerry-builders in back-to-back dwellings, erected on the cheapest sites and without drainage or sanitation. Rows of dingy tenements packed with people stretched towards the horizon under a grim pall of smoke that issued from the tall chimneys of the new industrial Britain. In Preston some 442 such dwellings housed 2400 individuals who shared 852 beds between them. In Belfast in the twentieth century 280 people live to each acre of the oldest working class districts compared with 1 person per 2 acres in the area of upper class villas. The spacious upper and middle class suburbs built in the fresher air of the countryside contrasted strangely with the homes of the workers. The new industrial houses went up at a phenomenal rate, erected by what Wilkie Collins called the 'modern guerilla regiments of the hod, the trowel and the brick kiln'. There were no parks or open spaces at this time to relieve the deadly monotony. Victorian towns lacked amenities and often grew up without planning and this inevitably meant a harsh treatment of the natural environment.

An important factor in urban growth was the development of a new transport system and the building of a network of railways to link the new cities also speeded up their expansion. This was the era of steam and gas, of dirt and noise and of town growth that Professor Asa Briggs described as 'impressive in scale but limited in vision'. A blanket of terrace housing enveloped the town centres. With better transport and new commercial enterprises the upper and a new and flourishing middle class demanded large modern houses with plenty of open space and, of course, no industrial developments. They opted for 'pure and invigorating air' and 'charming scenery' away from the urban environment. The new middle class tried to create in their suburbs a countryside in miniature and their grand villas were designed with country estates in mind. Most towns of any size soon developed suburbs of this kind.

Early in the nineteenth century semi-detached houses began to appear in St John's Wood in north-west London. They were designed to look like a single villa in a fair-sized bit of ground but they were intended to serve the needs of two families. 'In a way, then,' wrote Emrys Jones in *Towns and Cities*, 'the small suburban house, and even the semi-detached, are the final stage in the devolution of the country house, and the smallest lawn is the last remnant of the stately demesne.' Much of St John's Wood remains largely unchanged today and its gardens provide a sanctuary for the wildlife of the nearer suburbs. What a contrast this offers to the centres and inner suburban rings of most of the new nineteenth-century towns! Here the habitats for wildlife were usually barren and uncompromising with a few small and grimy public gardens or churchyards supporting only the toughest forms of plant growth. In these deserts of asphalt, stone, brick and mortar a few mosses, some slimy grass and a small tally of man's commensals – rats, mice, sparrows, pigeons, spiders and a few insects – were able to survive. Lack of sunlight, polluted air and vandalism all played a part. The new towns and cities had offices, municipal buildings and shops at their hearts while around them sprang up the houses and manufacturing premises. Birkenhead was the first to get a public park and Manchester, which was the first large provincial city to be given one, had to wait until 1846 when three were, in fact, formally opened.

It is interesting to see how Victorian towns developed in a variety of ways. Some just grew from the nucleus of smaller and older towns while others were the product of a fusion of small centres into larger urban units. A few towns associated with railways, industry and trade such as Middlesbrough, Barrow-in-Furness, Crewe and Rugby were actually new foundations.

The houses that were built in the nineteenth-century middle-class suburbs followed no very fixed design and, like many of the public buildings of the period, they illustrate what has been called 'the battle of the styles'. There tended to be a swing away in opinion from the formalism and even predictability of the old Georgian style and its critics felt that it lacked both imagination and invention. The 'battle' itself took place between the old Classical traditions and Gothic ideas.

SPARROWS. *Above*, male house sparrow drinking; *centre*, female house sparrow on gutter; *below*, tree sparrow nesting in drainpipe – a scarce suburban species.

SWIFT and HOUSE
MARTIN, inner suburban
birds. *Right*, male swift
clinging to wall near
nest site in house roof;
below, house martin
approaching its mudcup
nest with food.

The former expressed themselves with cornices, pediments, hipped roofs and sashed windows while the latter appeared in a welter of roofs, gables and chimneys. No final solution emerged from the battle but we do find many Gothic churches and Classical public buildings. In Victorian times there was, in fact, a great deal of plundering of architectural ideas from previous ages and styles. Oxford can offer some fair examples of incongruous styles while North Oxford, where I lived for a time, has been called 'the most quintessentially Victorian of all England's suburbs'.

As transport improved towards the end of the nineteenth century, there came a new surge in speculative building which created for the first time the mass suburb. In London this phenomenon was different in character between the east and west ends of the city. In *Ann Veronica* H. G. Wells reported how along the road from Surbiton there appeared 'a sort of fourth estate of little red-and-white rough-cast villas, with meretricious gables and very brassy window blinds' which emerged from the fused complex of shopping centre, workers' dwellings and big brick villas. In Rugby the new suburbs did not have the attractive gardens, the flowering shrubs or the trees that could be found in the south and west of the town. Their streets lacked trees until plantings were carried out at the start of the twentieth century. The country's population was still rising and, in the ring of development around the county of London, the number of inhabitants went up from 414,000 in 1861 to over 2 million in 1901. London was beginning to lose its shape and it was increasingly difficult to tell where it started and ended. Avenues and roads 'embowered in lilacs and laburnums' pushed out from the centre into Middlesex, Kent and Surrey and soon old villages and churches were engulfed by the tide of suburban growth.

One of the factors that may have helped to shape the new suburbs was the construction of local and suburban railway lines. As early as 1836 a line linked Greenwich with London while the Metropolitan Railway, which was established in 1863, offered cheap early morning fares to travelling workers. The Cheap Trains Act of 1883 was designed to encourage the emigration of the working classes into the suburbs to ease the pressure on housing in the more central areas. Companies differed in the way that they provided cheaper fares but it has been suggested that there could well be a correlation between the spread of working-class suburbs along the Great Eastern Company's line and their generous provision of cheap travelling facilities. Some authorities think that the part of the railways has been overplayed and that their greatest contribution was the making possible of longer distance commuting to areas which kept their middle-class character. In some cities the distance between town and suburb was not sufficient to warrant a railway at all. Trams certainly brought new areas and the towns and cities closer together and these 'gondolas of the people', as

Richard Hoggart called them, marked a new and much more mobile period in the activities of suburban and urban man. Buses were also to have a part to play after they had recovered from the increase in the trains.

Towards the end of the nineteenth century a new kind of community began to take shape. This was the factory estate designed to provide the work force with reasonable living accommodation, gardens and recreational space. Practically all the previous developments in that century lacked this kind of planning. Experimental building was carried out in 1888 by Lever Brothers at Port Sunlight and in 1895 by Cadbury's at Bournville. It was in this period that Ebenezer Howard, who was to have a profound influence on suburban growth, published his book *Tomorrow, A Peaceful Path to Real Reform*. This was a reaction against the uncontrolled growth of the industrial town with its random straggle into a formless suburbia. In his book Howard outlined his own ideas of town planning and schemes for such garden cities as Bedford Park near London which was designed in 1875 by Norman Shaw. Although to many it seemed rather a romantic idea to combine 'all the advantages of the most energetic and active town life, with all the beauty and delight of the country', there were many practical plans to underpin the idealism of 'this joyous union'. The town had to be economically viable and its size was to be so limited that it would make no room available for any expansion of the population; any surplus numbers would have to be accommodated in a new city.

Outside the new garden cities there was to be a ring of farmland. In the very heart there would be a large park and the rest of the region was to be divided into planned sectors with public buildings and places of amusement near the centre, factories on the outside and the shops in the middle. Places of work and homes were to be handy for each other but the houses were to vary in design, all were to have gardens and there were to be plenty of parks. Provision was also to be made for a kind of inner green belt some 400 feet wide and here the schools, playing fields and churches were to be situated.

In 1899 Ebenezer Howard formed his Garden City Association. Later the company that he was able to set up in 1902 began to look for a site where his ideas could be put into practice. In the following year Howard, his associates and supporters decided to buy the 3900 acres of the Letchworth Estate in Hertfordshire. Planned by Raymond Unwin the new Letchworth was to be a town fully designed before it was built. The work was finished before the First World War and the present population is just under 30,000 of which about 40% work in the local zoned light industries. The family houses and gardens at Letchworth provided for a population density of twelve to the acre – a figure that was to set a density pattern for a great deal of the building after the 1914-18 War. Another garden city was built at Welwyn in

1920 and since then the idea has been translated with varying degrees of success into the suburbs of many towns as well. Hampstead Garden Suburb, which was founded by Mrs Henrietta Barnett and planned by Unwin and Barry Parker, forms an organic whole with a varied street plan and detached, semi-detached and terraced houses, set in plenty of trees and open space and with a great sense of community.

One consequence of Howard's ideas has been the adoption of watered down conceptions of 'garden suburbs' and these often took a strong hold in the inter-war years. And his belief in the 'garden city' was to have its effect on the thinking behind the later New Towns. Attempts were made to produce more pleasing suburban areas on the outskirts of many towns and cities but, just as one suburb was completed, so another was begun farther out and the protective belt of countryside was continually eroded away. The Wythenshawe suburb of Manchester which was purchased by the City in 1926, had well-grouped houses and open spaces but the area was later developed to provide accommodation for nearly 100,000 people. Roe Green Village in the London Borough of Brent is a small estate of about 250 houses built between 1918 and 1920 for the aircraft workers at the nearby factory. It was planned as a 'garden village' with small houses and flats and medium-sized gardens. To preserve the character of this estate the local council has declared it to be a Conservation Area.

The period that straddled the nineteenth and twentieth centuries saw progress being made in many technological fields. The advent of the car was to have a profound effect as it further encouraged the spread of towns from their Victorian centres out into a fast-growing suburbia. As town and country were brought nearer to each other, areas of land could no longer be classified as either primarily urban or rural in character. They became what American sociologists call 'rurban' areas.

Development was temporarily halted by the First World War but cars, trams and trains were soon to have a deep effect on suburban growth. The railways turned much of the Middlesex landscape into its present form – a series of suburbs linked either by the network of London Transport's electrified rail system or by local branch lines. After the 1914–18 War the Metropolitan Railway Company issued brochures advertising 'Metro-land' in order to sell and lease off the estates that they owned along their line across the countryside of Middlesex, Hertfordshire and Buckinghamshire. The company endeavoured by cheap season tickets and the promise of rural bliss to encourage more people to live 'on beautiful residential estates' in 'picturesque and healthy localities'. And what about *this* seductive appeal from one of their brochures? 'The song of nightingales for which the neighbourhood is renowned; its mingled pastures, woods and streams; its gentle hills clothed with verdure, crested by copse and thicket; the network of translucent rivers traversing the peaceful valley render Rickmansworth a Mecca to the city man pining for country and pure air'. But the internal combustion engine has changed the original dreams, and the car has made it all so much closer to London now. The outward growth of suburbia through Neasden, Wembley, Harrow, and Northwood has only failed to reach Rickmansworth and its translucent river because a golf course intervenes. Now there are traffic jams and the needs of the insatiable car have required more motorways, underpasses and flyovers.

In 1919 there was a very serious shortage of houses and new building schemes were put in hand. These, however, lacked real central planning and were carried out by speculative builders on any land that they could get hold of. This became increasingly widespread after 1932 when local authority building was slowed down as a result of changes in government subsidies. After 1930 lower deposits on houses were required and it became possible for the lower middle class to move into the small three-bedroomed semi-detacheds which were primarily intended for the young married couple with only one or two children. Thomas Simms in *The Rise of a Midland Town. Rugby 1800–1900* recorded this expansion that occurred between the two world wars; 'the semi-detached house and the council estate, symptoms of a revolution in social attitudes, stamped a quality upon the new areas different from those of the earlier periods of expansion.' The houses were often of reddish or rustic brick, covered or partly covered with pebble-dash and with tiles or slates on their roofs. Many had window bays at the front of the façades and some were ornamented with gables. Land was also provided for a small plot in the front and a larger garden in the back.

The steady rise in motor traffic led to the construction of new arterial roads and as house building often tended to follow these links there arose the phenomenon known as 'ribbon development'. Subsequently many of these arterial roads were widened to meet a rising flood of traffic which was now brought even closer to the front door. A great deal of industry was redistributed, taking advantage of the road arteries and so workers, encouraged by the new availability of mortgages, came to live on estates near the factories and industrial sites. Some of these outer suburbs merge into the more open countryside but they bring to it urban attitudes and ways of life. Around London the development grew along the North Circular Road and Western Avenue. There were large industrial settlements at Watford and Slough while smaller dormitory and commuter towns arose at Dorking, Gerrard's Cross, Radlett and even Rickmansworth. But the effect was still one of a vast number of houses, some built by private enterprise, others in municipal estates moulded by current economic circumstances. As Lewis Mumford would say, they have all been fashioned as 'a collective attempt at private living'. These tend to form suburbs with no plan and no heart. Their air of inconsequence and irrelevance is often reinforced by a curious variety of building styles; even the arrangements of crescents, closes and avenues which distinguish the middle-class suburb from the planned working-class one do little to offset their facelessness. It is difficult to find anything properly to focus on and in Neasden, close to where I live and celebrated by *Private Eye* for years, the vistas in this faceless dormitory just lead from pebble-dash to pebble-dash. Nearby Willesden has been called by its former chief librarian, John Gillett, a 'vast transit camp' with 15% of the population leaving every year. Some of these suburbs are also beginning to change their character with the arrival of many immigrants from the West Indies, Africa and Asia who bring different cultures and customs to the areas.

Not far from Neasden is Dollis Hill which was largely developed between 1928 and 1932 from existing farmland and a golf course; now it carries rows of terraced or semi-detached houses. Here the birdlife was changed abruptly from one of farmland to another that was more characteristic of woodland or scrub. The new estate, built by Costains, is typical of many that arose between the wars. There were 3600 houses built on 330 acres, giving a density of 11 houses to the acre – a figure that Ebenezer Howard would have approved of. This comparatively low density is comparable with that of the Garden Cities but today it makes these areas vulnerable to compulsory purchase orders and higher-density development. In fairness the current developments in 1973 do suggest a desire for middle-density housing so that such areas are likely to carry fewer people than they might. Twelve was the actual number agreed by the Walters Committee of 1918, indicating a general reaction against high-density housing. In these new suburbs the houses have small front gardens, bordered by privet hedges, fences, walls or railings. Many have small plots of grass in the front as well but in the case of many terraced and some semi-detached houses the front gardens have been paved or concreted to hold the family car for which no garage space was originally provided. In Brent in 1950 there was one car to every six households but by 1972 the rate of ownership had become one car for every two households. The back gardens are separated from their neighbours by wooden fences or palings, chain link and, more rarely, walls. Many of the estate roads are planted with trees and sometimes large elms, oaks and ashes are allowed to remain from the open country which preceded the estate. There are often factories, shopping parades, public houses, schools and their environs, accommodation for public utilities and perhaps a park as well as tennis courts and playing fields for recreation. On some estates there are still allotments – known today as 'leisure gardens' – which provide valuable wildlife habitats; but with the present policy of in-filling open spaces near to town centres many of these are now being developed. Some local authorities are not only putting high or middle density housing on most of their remaining open spaces but they may also be trying to acquire land outside their existing boundaries by compulsory purchase in other boroughs.

Whereas suburbs once used to be a kind of epibolic growth on a town, they now have a tendency to become more urban in character, engulfing smaller settlements, linking communities and forming 'conurbations'. Manchester's suburban sprawl has swallowed three large towns and half a dozen smaller ones. So an amorphous mass of former villages, newer estates and industrial complexes which may be random or planned begins to grow.

One feature of the inter-war era was the development of 'cottage estates' among the various kinds of housing prepared for the working class. The London County Council built a large one of this type between 1921 and 1934 at Becontree in Essex after acquiring the land outside the existing London boundaries. The numbers living on this estate were in the neighbourhood of 90,000 who were accommodated in 27,000 houses. At that time this was not only the largest housing estate in the world but it was also the biggest planned working-class suburb.

After the Second World War it could be seen that unrestrained growth was taking place around London and other big centres of population. The great increase in car ownership was making suburban communities much less dependent on public transport. One serious attempt to control this run-away tendency was to maintain a so-called 'green belt' around the town which could act as a strait-jacket against urban sprawl. David Thomas, who has investigated the London green belt in some depth, has summed it up as follows: 'The pattern which emerges in an idealised transect of the green belt is of a fairly clean edge to built-up London followed by a narrow settlement-free zone. Beyond this lies a band of dense settlement, perhaps commuters' towns and villages which, but for the green belt, might have already become part of the London conurbation. Through the remainder of the green belt there is a fair scatter of settlement but as the outer edge is approached the amount increases to match the peak of the inner zone. This outer fringe of settlement is composed of rapidly growing towns and villages, including new towns, which have been forced to grow at some distance from London by the green belt, and which accommodate much of London's current overspill.' There appears to be some tendency for building to jump over green belts and its real function is still very much a subject for discussion.

The planners of the green belt recognize three types of land use within it. The first is an undesirable one and this includes housing, commerce and manufacturing. The second is an undesirable but nevertheless inevitable one and involves gravel diggings, sewage works and water-pumping stations. The final use is an approved one and satisfies the needs of agriculture, forestry, education, hospitals, cemeteries and recreational pursuits.

The London green belt covers nearly 2000 square miles in a broad strip lying between 12 and 20 miles from the city centre. A White Paper in 1963 made it clear that the then Minister of Housing and Local Government did not regard all the green belt around London as sacrosanct or inviolable. However, more land was added to the belt and in August 1972 the Government declared its intention of approving another 170 square miles in Surrey and the Minister for Local Government and Development announced that 'there is much more to come in other counties'. In the following month another 127 square miles – this time in Buckinghamshire – were added to the metropolitan green belt and at the same time more than 130 square miles in Kent were safeguarded under the development plan for that county. The green belt was also being extended some 11 miles into the Chiltern Hills. To set against these positive proposals is the Government White Paper published in April 1973 which indicated that some expansion in green belts would be permitted and the Secretary of State for the Environment said that it might be possible to make 2000 acres in London's green belt available for housing because this land made little or no contribution to amenity.

The Department of the Environment is anxious to preserve those wedges of open land that stretch from the countryside towards the town as well as the surrounding region. Southampton is a good example of an urban area with just these features. The intention is to give the countryside the protection where it is most needed and to concentrate the efforts of developers and builders in growth areas elsewhere. Building within the present green belt has been fairly well controlled and there are restrictions on development. Strong pressures are always being applied by developers who wish to establish footholds and even bridgeheads inside it. The belt is fairly rich in woodlands, farmland and sports grounds and, besides having a positive value for recreation, may have to some extent a negative one in which it helps to hold back a struggling city in danger of bursting its bonds. Green belts can also be found at Bristol, Huddersfield, Sheffield, Stoke-on-Trent, Gloucester, Leeds, Manchester and Newcastle while there are also proposals for Southampton, Oxford, Cambridge, the Wirral, Liverpool, York, parts of Berkshire and the West Midlands.

The conception of the green belt was not the only sign of reaction against town sprawl. A constructive effort was made to decentralise industry and move populations into new towns or growth areas. This new idea was first explored in the 1940 Barlow Report and the first

New Town Act became law in 1946. Eight new towns were planned for London outside the green belt, including Crawley, Stevenage and Basildon, while other towns farther from London were to be expanded. Each town was to be a viable unit with its own industries and estates and so self-contained that the old pattern of commuting into and out of towns could be broken. Such plans obviously owed a great deal to Ebenezer Howard. Harlow New Town, which lies some 40 miles north of London reflects the traditional English way of living in small houses with proper garden space. By the late 1960's the total population of the new towns was about 400,000. They have also increased their independence and David Thorns believes that they should no longer be regarded as suburban areas since they have no dependence upon a city. From the point of view of their bird life they resemble many of the newer planned suburbs.

One of the present-day and very obvious features of many suburbs is their massive blocks of flats. These were firstly an inter-war phenomenon made possible by the introduction of such new materials as structural steel and reinforced concrete. Their building was also made easier by the use of pre-fabricated components. New architectural styles evolved with sharp vertical and horizontal lines, simple outlines and the wide employment of glass and curtain walling. Blocks of flats offered a solution to desperate housing shortages. I can remember Highpoint Flats being built at Highgate in 1935 and also the working-class housing scheme at Kensal House in Ladbroke Grove in London which was finished in the following year. Other designs were employed for Loughborough Park in Brixton and Quarry Hill Flats in Leeds where it was intended to provide homes for literally thousands of people.

After the last war blocks of flats and high-rise towers began to transform the old suburban skylines out of all recognition. Many of them were built on the sites of Victorian properties and have kept some of the mature trees already growing there. One of the most interesting examples is the Roehampton Estate in south-west London which has tried to combine buildings with a strong suggestion of nature. It was constructed between 1952 and 1959 and is made up of some two dozen point blocks in three groups, some parallel high slabs, a number of five-story blocks of flats and some terraces formed from small houses. There is a great deal of variety in the siting of the buildings and, since the whole imaginative complex stands in an area once occupied by large Victorian villas and their gardens, the estate is enhanced by the original trees and a lot of grass between the blocks and houses. It was described by Sir Nikolaus Pevsner as 'the best housing estate to date'. The mixture of giant block and smaller units was tried at Cumbernauld where huge boxes in the style of the old city tenements tower over smaller constructions. For me one of the least attractive schemes was that at Chalkhill in Wembley where large houses and gardens were replaced by vast uncompromising cliff-like slabs of grey concrete and many rows of small houses and flats which provided a couple of thousand living units. London's new town of Thamesmead is also a mixture of what is called high- and low-rise building. With so many of these schemes there seems a deadly grey sameness and a shortage of trees, flowering shrubs, bushes and areas of water.

An unusual experiment in urban living is to involve some 60 square miles of land in Nottinghamshire and Derbyshire on either side of the M1 motorway. It concerns the growth-zone towns of Alfreton, Mansfield, Sutton-in-Ashfield, Kirkby-in-Ashfield and Mansfield Woodhouse; it is hoped to form a kind of open-plan city from this group of towns and villages. In this way an urban area is supposed to possess the advantages of a city but without the crush of buildings and heavily jammed roads that most cities suffer from. Some of the villages will remain in what are to be designated 'conservation areas'. Part of the variety of the London conurbation is provided by the villages that have been obsorbed within it but, as Nicholas Taylor, author of *The Village in the City*, has warned, grave assaults are being made on these virtues of many suburbs by the erection of tower blocks that dominate regions graced by commons and open spaces and by rows of unpretentious Victorian and Edwardian terraces.

Nevertheless high-density housing and high-rise flats are part of the contemporary British urban scene. Their flat roofs may afford a temporary perch for pigeons, crows, starlings and gulls and I have even seen goldfinches looking for grit on their garage roofs. The trodden grass swards may be visited by an occasional pied wagtail, crow or party of foraging starlings but our birds of scrub – robins, wrens, hedge-sparrows and thrushes – are often missing because there are literally no nesting places for them. For those who live high in the tower blocks the only wildlife they see may be a circling swift or two in the summer, gulls, crows and starlings in the winter and perhaps some of the bird migrants that in the autumn cross suburban areas at about their eye level. Trevor Stroud (*in litt.*) tells me that from his seventeenth-floor flat in a south-east London tower block he has watched kestrels on the top of a chimney stack a hundred yards away and he can see swans flying over the River Thames. In Peckham kestrels have been known to breed in a window box on the sixteenth floor of a tower block. Over the last seventy years the suburban movement was against dense housing conditions and this naturally favoured the growth of subtopia and all its attendant evils but it meant that open spaces and gardens were available as quite rich habitats for birds. Now it seems that life in giant blocks may have a stultifying effect upon the human spirit. According to Pevsner the present styles are 'eminently suitable for a large anonymous clientele'. A sign of the growing concern was the calling in Tokyo in 1972 of the first summit conference in history to discuss the problems of cities.

In addition to the new towns there are also 'growth' areas planned for different parts of the country. One example is provided by a region of Hampshire not far from Southampton and Portsmouth; this embraces Totton, Chandler's Ford, Horton Heath, Park Gate, Lock's Heath and Waterlooville. Between 1966 and 1972 the population of this region grew from 818,000 to 890,000. By 1991 the number is expected to reach 1,161,000. The scheme included new segregated transport systems since the dispersed twentieth-century city has to rely on highly modernized and efficient methods of communication. There are also plans in Hampshire to conserve the countryside, particularly along the coastline and on the downs, to put a brake on mineral workings and to restrict any straggling developments that might lead to subtopia.

It might now be useful to summarise the types of suburb; the classification follows that suggested by David Thorns and others.

TYPES OF SUBURB

(A residential suburb is one in which the greater proportion of people commutes to work than works within it. An industrial suburb is one in which the greater proportion lives and works within it, rather than commutes.)

Residential

1. Middle-class planned residential	archetype of suburbia, usually from private development. A laid out estate or tract suburb with rows of single-family semi-detached houses. Typical of Wales and England but recent in Scotland. Has some variety in street lay-out and well-supplied with gardens and trees.
2. Working-class planned residential	usually a product of local authority as overspill and rehousing scheme. Rows of identical houses in straight lines with wide roads, small gardens and very few trees.
3. Middle-class unplanned residential	complex form taking a long time to develop. In it small housing developments grow up unplanned, of low density with a village centre. The existing community has to accept an immigrant one. Known as the commuter village or the reluctant suburb.

Industrial

4. Working-class planned industrial	Similar to type 2 but has employment facilities within the suburb – Saltaire, Bournville, Port Sunlight.
5. Working-class unplanned industrial	a mixture of industrial and residential growths formed in a random and piecemeal way, e.g., West Ham. Also unplanned middle-class suburbs like Camberwell, Paddington, Kilburn, which are now working-class areas in the inner ring and show both residential and industrial features.

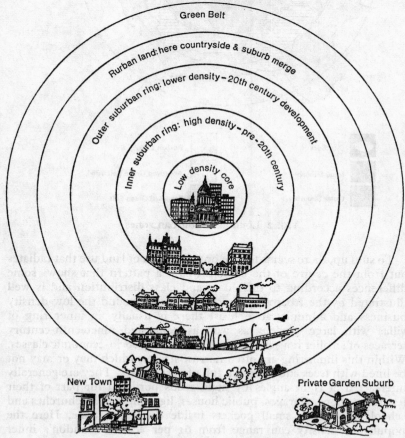

Green Belt

Rurban land: here countryside & suburb merge

Outer suburban ring: lower density – 20th century development

Inner suburban ring: high density – pre-20th century

Low density core

New Town

Private Garden Suburb

FIG. 1 Stylized diagram of suburban ecology.

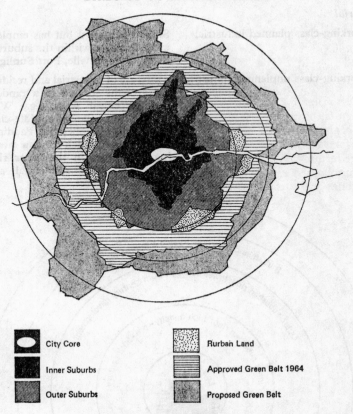

	City Core		Rurban Land
	Inner Suburbs		Approved Green Belt 1964
	Outer Suburbs		Proposed Green Belt

FIG. 2 London's suburban zones.

To sum up, there seems to be a broad pattern of land use that radiates out from the centre of the older towns – a pattern that shows some differences according to their date and class distribution and is well illustrated by the Abercrombie Plan of 1945. Around the low-density business and administrative heart there is usually an inner ring of villas with large gardens as well as congested nineteenth-century terraces of smaller houses occupied by differing socio-economic classes. Within this inner ring are often narrow streets, which may or may not be lined with trees and are often full of parked cars. They are generally intersected at right angles by main roads bordered for part of their length by shops. Garages, public houses, light industries, churches and schools may form small pockets inside this inner zone. Here the population density can range from 61 per acre in London's inner suburbs to 64–127 in Liverpool and, as we have already seen, to nearly

300 in Belfast. These older properties are often difficult to maintain and so may be demolished to make way for tower blocks, flats and other housing developments.

Beyond these nearer suburbs lies an outer ring of twentieth-century estates of terraced or semi-detached dwellings, factories, new parks, allotments, small open spaces, rubbish dumps, reservoirs, arterial roads and perhaps old village centres. The human density here is much lighter than in the inner ring. On its further limits the outer ring itself then begins to merge into open countryside with its pieces of woodland, farms, orchards, market gardens, private parklands, commons, sewage farms, gravel pits, motorways, airfields, green belts and middle-class unplanned residential housing. Finally there may be true green-belt zones and the countryside itself.

CHAPTER 2

The Nearer Suburbs

CLOSE to the nucleus or heart of many of our older towns lies a ring
of inner suburbs formed from rows of nineteenth-century terraced
houses, mansions and villas. The ornithology of the tightly packed small
terraces with their tiny gardens or backyards, sometimes ornamented
with sour-looking laurels and privets is a very restricted one. House
sparrows and starlings may succeed in nesting in the less well-main-
tained roofs and, if there are mud, water and insects at hand, perhaps a
few house martins will build their mud cup nests beneath the cornices.
You may also find a few blackbirds and feral pigeons, while the lopped
and grimy trees in the streets, often planes, sycamores, limes or trees-
of-heaven, can provide possible nesting sites for occasional pairs of
woodpigeons or short-term roosts for sparrows. In these terraced
areas there are few secure nesting places and hardly any sources of
natural food while the disturbance from traffic, children and cats may
be of a very high order indeed. Often the most exciting spectacle is that
of a grimy sparrow tucking himself in behind a pigeon's or starling's
wing and then carrying out some remarkable flying manoeuvres
around the chimney pots. In winter a few gulls may forage over the
backs and a wandering tit or wren drop in to search for food in the
sparse and unpromising vegetation. Where the gardens behind the
terraces are larger, then perhaps a few more nesting species may be
encountered; these might include blue tits, hedgesparrows and even
a song thrush. For nineteen months I lived in a terraced Victorian
house in Rugby and, although I observed 31 species in or over its
pocket-handkerchief garden, only house sparrow and jackdaw were
breeding.

To the north-west of Regent's Park in London lies St John's Wood,
once part of the Forest of Middlesex and the property of the Knights
Hospitallers of St John of Jerusalem. It was thickly wooded in medieval
times and held deer, boars and wild bulls. After Henry VIII's dissolu-
tion of the monasteries the area became part of the Royal Hunting
Grounds. After changing hands a number of times it was sold in 1732
by the Earl of Chesterfield to Henry Samuel Eyre, a City of London
wine merchant. By now the estate had become farmland and occupied
about 500 acres. Towards the end of the eighteenth century Eyre's

descendants began to see the possibilities of developing an area within handy reach of the expanding city nearby. In the 1820's and 1830's speculative builders began to put up detached or semi-detached villas standing in quite large gardens. They varied in style from gabled and castellated Gothic to the porticoed and graceful Classical while the gardens were rich in flowering trees, and in some of them grass swards sloped gently down towards the new Regent's Canal. Today this open and gracious environment can be well seen in the width of Hamilton Terrace and the elegant rise of Clifton Hill. You can still find in this middle- and upper middle-class suburb the harmony and balance that were possible with proper planning and construction and it continues to show its character in spite of the tide of Victorian building and twentieth-century flats and tower blocks that finally engulfed it.

The large gardens in St John's Wood have provided an important sanctuary for birds. Here the regular breeding species include carrion crow, starling, blackbird, song thrush, robin, hedgesparrow, great and blue tits, house sparrow, and woodpigeon. Such a list is typical not only of St John's Wood, Kensington and Brondesbury in London but also of many other inner suburban areas with large houses developed in the mid-Victorian period. Immediately after the last war, as a result of German bombing and subsequent neglect, some of the gardens became overgrown with a kind of semi-natural scrub under the tall and mature trees. There are many instances in which old houses are cleared in inner suburban zones and the empty sites left for months or even years before building operations are started. When this happens it is possible to watch the different stages in plant succession, and this I was able to do in one inner suburb: 'After the blitz of 1940 I examined a basement floor in a bombed house in London colonised within the first year by Oxford ragwort, rose-bay, groundsel and Canadian fleabane. All these plants, like the coltsfoot and bracken which came in the second year, were wind dispersed. By the third year elder seedlings had taken hold, probably from seeds excreted by birds like starlings which had been feeding on them elsewhere. The elders were followed by sallows and finally by sycamores which in a few years had become the dominant plants well over twenty feet tall'. On some sites in St John's Wood I also found balsam, hawthorns and berry-bearing shrubs that attracted thrushes as well as seed-bearing weeds that brought in the finches. Sites such as these can be found in many other inner suburban areas of Britain.

In 1968 P. J. Grant watched a 40–50 acre site which had been cleared in Deptford for housing redevelopment and had acquired 'an abundant weed growth'. A count that he made on 11 January revealed the astonishingly high totals of 280 linnets, 110 tree sparrows, 35 chaffinches, 20 bramblings, 12 greenfinches and 6 goldfinches. There was also a single redwing and two kestrels which hunted linnets. By

16 February the total of linnets had risen to 400. Another neglected and weed-covered site in Acton, visited in March of the same year, produced 50 chaffinches, 35 bramblings, 30 linnets, 20 tree-sparrows and 10 goldfinches. It became obvious that areas cleared for development, where there has been a lapse of time between the demolition and rebuilding, are well worth a visit outside the breeding season, ephemeral habitats though they may be.

In the nesting season greenfinches can be found breeding in St John's Wood and goldfinches were recorded there in June and July; it was not unusual for Christopher Holme to hear a male goldfinch singing in summer in a derelict garden in the early 1950s. The shy hawfinch may also nest and five birds were seen in Elm Tree Road, close to Lord's Cricket Ground, in June 1952. A few pairs of chaffinches may favour some of the larger gardens. In 1953 two pairs of blackcaps reared their young and single singing males have been recorded in a number of years. I have also heard jays, great spotted woodpeckers and spotted flycatchers and a pair of kestrels may manage to nest in some years. In Upper Norwood a pair of kestrels reared a young bird under the eaves of a four-storey house in spite of being harassed by feral pigeons so this attractive little falcon can often breed in the inner zones. The wren may still nest but its numbers seem to have gone down since the bombed sites were redeveloped. St John's Wood also represents one of the inner breeding strongholds of both the house martin and the swift. There is a colony of martins in Harley Road less than half a mile to the north of St John's Wood station on the Bakerloo line. This site was found in 1966 and six breeding pairs were observed in the following year. By 1970 there were some 15–20 pairs in this colony and also at a new location as well. The 1971 total was over 20 pairs. It was suggested by Stanley Cramp and John Gooders that 'the increase and spread of breeding house martins in the areas adjoining Central London in recent years is linked with the decrease in smoke concentration and a consequent increase in flying insects'. The inward spread is similar to that of the swift which has also been established in the St John's Wood area for some years and has now reached Maida Vale to the south-west. In the 1930's I used to see swifts hawking for flies every summer over Notting Hill in the west.

Any inner suburb may be visited by scarcer birds and St John's Wood is no exception with records of such species as white-fronted goose, waxwing, treecreeper, yellowhammer, fieldfare, cuckoo, sparrowhawk and peregrine. Mrs H. Rait Kerr observed several interesting species over Lord's Cricket Ground including peregrine, buzzard, curlew, golden plover, grey wagtail and wheatear; the last two species also used the Grandstand as a perch. I have seen woodpigeons, feral pigeons, house sparrows and a pied wagtail feeding on the ground during a Test Match against the Australians. One sparrow, of course,

SONG and MISTLE THRUSH, park and outer suburban birds. *Above,* song thrush at nest in rhododendron; *below,* mistle thrush nesting in ivy-clad hawthorn.

FERAL PIGEON, WOOD PIGEON and COLLARED DOVE. *Above,* London feral pigeon with plumage resembling that of wild rock dove ancestor; *centre,* wood pigeon about to drink; *below,* two collared doves at a bird table.

earned immortality and a place in the pavilion by being struck and killed by a cricket ball and on at least two occasions migrant wheatears have been seen at Lord's within a few paces of the wicket while play was in progress!

I began my bird-watching studies as a small boy in Kensington, particularly in Ladbroke Square which lies just to the north of Notting Hill Gate. It was the building of Kensington Palace which led to the growth of private houses in this neighbourhood which came to be known as the 'Old Court Suburb'. In 1837 a young speculator, John Whyte, had laid out here in rural Notting Hill a race-course known as 'the Hippodrome'. Its main entrance was close to the present Notting Hill station while the grandstand was built on the hill where St John's Church stands today. From an unedifying scene of racing, hooliganism and 'the piggeries and potteries' nearby, within only five years, the land was reverting to open country. Then in the middle of the nineteenth century there was a rise both in the population and in suburban building. On the site of the old race-course now rose the stuccoed and ambitious villas and terraces of the Ladbroke Estate, largely designed by Thomas Allom. Here were formed the leafy squares, avenues and crescents where the open spaces were extensive and exclusive. In the 1870s the building enterprises reached farther north along Ladbroke Grove towards the Harrow Road. Transformed in character by the construction of the Hammersmith and City Railway the Portobello and Quintin Estates, formerly with a social structure similar to that of the Ladbroke, soon became a lower middle class suburb.

Ladbroke Square consists of seven acres of tall trees, especially planes, poplars, oaks and horse chestnuts, shrubberies, flowerbeds and lawns. It is bounded on the north by the gardens of large houses built between 1849 and 1858 and on the south by a roadway. This green oasis which linked the grounds of Holland House with the Royal Parks has suffered little disturbance over the years, apart from a little tree felling, a barrage balloon and some near misses from bombs during the last war and a 'dig for victory' campaign in the First World War. From 1927–40 I kept records of the birds that I observed in Ladbroke Square. Altogether I listed 63 different species and these can be found in Appendix 1. Thirteen species bred over the period while six others were sometimes present in the summer. Eight species could be seen in the winter months and of the eighteen migrant species six consisted of warblers. Among the twenty birds that I regarded as vagrants were brambling, skylark, marsh and long-tailed tits, redwing, fieldfare and red-breasted flycatcher. Col. Richard Meinertzhagen, whose garden backed on to Ladbroke Square and who encouraged my schoolboy ornithological enthusiasms, also recorded cranes flying over in May 1924 and five waxwings on 22 January 1942. Some of the species that I saw in the square such as the green and great spotted woodpeckers, jay, stock dove and tawny owl almost certainly originated in the extensive and well-wooded grounds of Holland House. Miss Evelyn Brown, writing in the *London Naturalist*, described its bird-life: 'Anyone who has studied the bird life of an average south of England or even a Midland deciduous wood will know that they would see as many wild birds on a morning walk in Holland Park as they would in a similar country walk and at much closer range and with a much better chance of identifying them.' The jay first bred in Ladbroke Square in 1932 and I well remember seeing the platform of twigs in a hawthorn about fourteen feet above the ground. Since that year jays have also nested in the other squares and gardens nearby.

The character of a town and the lay-out of its streets has been called 'a compound of history'. It is extremely difficult to preserve urban identities and the conservation of a town's personality and character is rarely considered to be a desirable aim. One community that has survived can be found in North Oxford where Victorian development achieved a considerable sense of spaciousness. Stephen Gardiner, writing in *The Observer* in November 1972, said: 'The unity and strength of north Oxford as a worthwhile entity depends, very simply, on repetition – the repetition of the house and the garden. This leads naturally to the repetition of other important things – contrasts of red-brick and green foliage, of gaps between houses, of shadowy corners, recesses, garden sheds and so on. In particular, perhaps, it means the repetition of front doors and chimneys, creating a community background of an extremely pleasant kind.' In 1972 the area was under threat from plans to build higher density accommodation in Rawlinson Road but Oxford City Council finally put a preservation order on the endangered houses.

In 1946 I lived for nine months in a house in Polstead Road in the very heart of Victorian North Oxford; it was a tall semi-detached villa of three stories. At its back was a fair-sized garden which formed with others in Polstead and St Margaret's Roads quite a significant open space. This rectangular block of gardens was very typical of this part of Oxford with tall conifers, broad-leaved trees and many shrubs including *Ceanothus*, *Hibiscus*, *Philadelphus* and *Syringa*. The roads themselves were tree-lined and many of the trees, like the tall acacia outside the house, were well-developed and often reached to roof height. In this plot of gardens I recorded sixteen different breeding species.

The commonest of the nesting birds was the house sparrow with twenty pairs. The nests were built in roofs, under gables and occasionally in creepers on house walls. It was in the neighbourhood of Polstead and Rawlinson Roads that D. C. Seel carried out some of his researches into the breeding season, behaviour and food of the house sparrow. This was part of a much wider investigation in the Oxford area during which he found that the laying sparrows could be divided into two groups. The first which he called the 'early starters' was made up of females that were two or more years old while the second was composed of 'late starters' only one year old. Seel also found that there seemed to be some relationship between the laying of the first clutches by the early starters and the prevailing air temperature. The first year birds on average laid slightly smaller clutches than the older birds. The overall breeding season itself lasted from April to early August. It was interesting too to see that there was some variation in the kinds of food brought to the nest during the spring and summer. Flies were common in May, aphids in July and caterpillars between early May and June. In the Oxford suburbs the birds very often fed bread to the nestlings. The study also showed that adult sparrows increased the frequency of their visits to the nest proportionally with the size of the brood for broods of from one to three in size but for larger broods the frequency did not go up. The cock bird's share of the visits began to grow smaller in the later stages of the nestling period and conversely he began to show a great deal more display to the hen. In this display the male 'drew his head back over his shoulders, fluffed his body feathers, raised his tail, shivered his wings held out from and below his body, and called'.

The second commonest nesting species in my part of North Oxford was the starling with fourteen breeding pairs. Their nesting sites were similar to those of the house sparrows in rooftops and gable ends. Many of the loft nests were quite large but I never found one that compared in size to that found in Oxford by H. J. Harrison. This structure measured 3 feet high and 5 feet wide and all the material had been carried in by the birds through a vertical ventilation slit or loophole and so into the roof space.

After the house sparrow and the starling there was a drop in the numbers of the next most frequent breeding species – the swift. I found some four pairs in the two streets that bordered the northern and southern limits of my study area. The first birds to arrive back in the area appeared on 4 May 1946. The swift can often be found nesting in suitable Victorian villas and mansions in the inner ring of suburbs of many towns. On the whole it tends to avoid the central built-up zones of the larger ones but I have seen birds flying and hunting insects over some urban centres, just as one may see birds over Paris or Athens. Although swifts can be seen feeding over some of London's Royal Parks, they breed some distance away. Swifts' nests are not easy to locate since they are usually under the eaves of houses and the adult birds may not visit the sites very regularly even to build the nest or feed the young. Birds do, however, visit the nests in the evenings before retiring to roost and they can be seen and heard screaming round the roof-site and perhaps entering and leaving the nest holes. Some individuals, known as 'bangers', will also fly up to the nest holes of other birds and brush or bang against them with their wings before continuing their flight. The breeding birds may respond by looking out of the entrance holes and screaming at the 'bangers'. This activity which can also take place in good weather during the breeding season can be a useful guide to the nest sites of the swifts. The screaming parties that hurtle round the rooftops, and whose high-pitched cries it took me some years to record properly on tape, can also take place throughout the nesting season. I have found that they occur most regularly in spells of fine weather and when there is a reasonable concentration of birds in the district. They are less common early in the season and after the majority of swifts has left. I have many memories of parties of these crescent-winged birds flying headlong past my bedroom window in Polstead Road on warm summer evenings.

The swifts are able to find suitable nest-holes in older houses since cracks in the fabric often develop with age and many Victorian houses have big eaves and sometimes a space between the wall and the roof. The nearness of water is also an attraction for swifts and Stanley Cramp, reporting in his 1949 census of swifts, concluded that 'the swift is an urban bird mainly because it now needs buildings to provide nesting sites, but where these are present food seems to be the main factor affecting density, and areas with water tend to provide more food'. Both the River Thames and a canal were not far from Polstead Road.

North Oxford is famous for an intensive and long-term study of the swift which was carried out in the tower of the University Museum. For many years swifts had bred in the ventilators in the tower but in 1948 David and Elizabeth Lack replaced the ventilators with nest-boxes. In the following year these were provided with glass backs for easier observation. The life of the swift falls into phases. The first is a romantic one that takes place in the air and may keep a single individual bird on the wing for nine months or even longer. The second is a private and mysterious one which occurs at the nest usually in darkness but on which the Oxford studies have cast a new light.

The nestboxes in the museum tower enabled the Lacks to study both the spring return and the subsequent departure of this breeding summer visitor to Britain. It was interesting to find that the mean date of return in the spring varied by only nine days over six years. In almost every year once the first birds had come back the others continued to arrive on almost every day until the full complement was reached. This suggested that weather was not having any really great effect on the last stages of the swifts' journeys. It was found that the 'only serious gaps in the migratory return in spring have occurred during cold weather with northerly winds'. The breeding swifts usually pair with their mates of the previous season, if both have survived, but this association is not continued during the periods of migration or during the stay in the winter quarters. We know this because the adults of the pair normally return in the spring and depart in the autumn on different days. The re-formation of the pair is brought about by the tendency to return to the same nest site. C. M. Perrins later discovered that the University Tower swifts were not likely to breed successfully before they were four years old.

When a swift enters an occupied nest site it will be usually met with a characteristic threat display but if the bird in occupation is its mate this will rapidly subside. In 1955 I climbed the flights of swaying ladders inside the tower to fit a microphone close to one of the nest-boxes and I was able to record this incipient display in which the occupant rises on its feet, raises its wings and gives out a penetrating scream. Intruding swifts are almost sure to be engaged in combat and these battles can last from twenty minutes to as long as six hours! Some very excited encounters result when two birds that were not paired in the previous year meet at the nest for the first time.

The building of the nest often begins on the day that the later member of the pair finally arrives. The nest material itself is caught in the air and 'dead grass, hay, straw, dead and green leaves, flower petals, winged seeds, seed fluff, bud sheaths, cocoons, feathers and scraps of paper, including a bus ticket' were all found by the Lacks in Museum Tower nests. These very varied items are cemented to the nest with saliva and building work goes on throughout the period of incubation. There is some variation in the start of the actual laying due to weather conditions but the average date was 28 May. The eggs are normally incubated from the day on which the second egg is laid and the duties are performed by both parents. David Lack, in his engrossing book, *Swifts in a Tower*, described how one incubating bird used to rise up on the eggs whenever it heard an outburst of clapping in the nearby parks which greeted the regular fall of New Zealand wickets to a triumphant university eleven.

Food is brought into the nest by the swifts in the form of a tight ball of insects held together with saliva or of a more loosely compacted mass, and most of the food is gathered close to the nesting colony. If the weather is warm and dry the birds feed quite high up but on windy, wet days they can be seen foraging for insects low over areas of water. David Lack and D. F. Owen examined some eighty-odd foodballs brought to young swifts and they found that the commonest prey were *Homoptera*, which include the aphids, and *Diptera*, the two-winged flies, which include crane-flies, gnats and midges. In good weather insects from 5–10 millimetres in length were captured but in poor weather, when large insects were scarce, the prey tended to be smaller – from 2–5 millimetres. The chick is fed in the early part of its life on sections of foodball but, as it develops, it is eventually presented with the ball complete. The hunger call which I recorded in the Museum Tower is rather weak and plaintive.

Many swift nestlings leave the nest during the last ten days of July or the first fourteen days of August. At Oxford the mean date of departure over the years from 1947 to 1957 varied between 28 July and 5 August, with an average of 1 August. 1972 proved to be an exceptional year in North Oxford and C. M. Perrins reported five broods still present on 6 September while the last brood of two youngsters fledged on 21 and 22 September. The birds were in good condition and even slightly above average in weight. It was clear that laying had been accomplished about 23 July; in normal years this is the date at which the first young are leaving the nest. When a young bird flies from the nest it abandons it that season for good.

Four pairs of jackdaws nested in my small study area in North Oxford. These birds are not uncommon in some inner suburban rings where they may nest in roofs, chimneys and holes in trees. Church towers and castle ruins are favourite haunts as well. They are rather patchily distributed around London; I have seen them in Muswell Hill in small numbers and in the inner suburbs of Birmingham, Warwick, Wolverhampton, Liverpool and other towns. In some urban areas jackdaws are commoner in the winter months. The house martin and blackbird were equally well represented in my part of North Oxford with three pairs of each. The former built their mud cups under the eaves and against the outer walls of houses; in Oxford they could find assured supplies both of mud for nest construction and of insects for food. It seems that in some areas the density of house martins is often quite high in the inner suburbs and then it decreases towards the outskirts. W. B. Alexander found that at Oxford there were some 42 pairs of house martins per 1000 acres compared to a figure of 14–16 in the rural areas around the city. The same is true for those of London's inner suburbs where house martins occur. It is possible for mud to be obtained more easily from small ponds, puddles in dirt roads and even roof gutters than from the edges of reservoirs and rivers in the outer suburbs. I have watched house martins in Shepherd's Bush in West London collecting mud from a small lake in a busy municipal park.

Besides blackbirds both song and mistle thrushes bred in North Oxford in the proportions 3:2:1. Woodpigeons mustered three pairs but feral pigeons, although they sometimes visited the houses and gardens, did not breed. They are very common in many other inner suburbs as we shall see later. I also located two breeding pairs each of blue tit and chaffinch and there were single pairs of robin, goldfinch, great tit and hedgesparrow. Spotted flycatchers built a nest some twenty feet up in a creeper on the wall of the house where I lived. Altogether there were 16 breeding species represented by 63 pairs – a higher total than for Ladbroke Square and some other inner suburban

THE
UNIVERSITY OF WINNIPEG
PORTAGE & BALMORAL
WINNIPEG 2, MAN.   CANADA

areas. Nine other species were often present in summer but did not nest; these included the carrion crow which often breeds in the nearer suburbs where there are tall trees such as elms, poplars and planes. Rooks which frequented the grassy swards of Port Meadow often flew over the house and in that same year a pair was seen at a nest built on a chimney stack in Leckford Road. Greenfinches were common summer visitors and I saw a bullfinch pair on one occasion in May. A pair of coal tits was present as well but there was no evidence of nesting. Pied wagtails and swallows sometimes flew over the garden and a cuckoo came several times in April and May. During these two months and again in September a female sparrowhawk was a regular visitor chasing the house sparrows in the gardens. On 4 April, from my window, I saw her kill a sparrow and then carry it up to a branch of a fir where she plucked it over a period of three-quarters of an hour.

During my stay of nine months in North Oxford I also saw a number of migrants, vagrants and winter visitors. I did not record tawny owls but I heard them in other mature gardens in Oxford. If there are fairly large gardens and well-developed trees these owls will breed quite close to town centres and they can be heard hooting in squares and gardens outside the breeding season as well. This owl may sometimes appear more common than it really is because its voice carries so far. Certainly I have noted tawny owls in the inner suburbs of Rugby, Birmingham, Bristol, Edinburgh and other cities. A pair at Rednal was seen in daylight perching on a smoking chimney pot. Kestrels may also rear young on church towers, the ledges of buildings and the old nests of carrion crows, in holes in trees and in ventilator shafts. There were no collared doves living wild in Britain when I was at Polstead Road but it is now possible to find small numbers in the Victorian inner suburbs of, for example, Bristol and Birmingham. Robert Hudson found that in general the number of breeding collared doves near the centre of a town is inversely correlated to the size of its built-up area and birds are often absent from the centres of major British towns and cities.

As the nineteenth century progressed the suburban building continued and many houses were put up during the last forty years of that century. These new middle-class suburbs included Edgbaston near Birmingham, Camberwell and Hampstead near London. In his study of Camberwell H. J. Dyos showed that the class differences in that suburban area could be recognized by the species of tree planted in the streets – horse chestnuts and limes for the more affluent and acacias and laburnums for the middle income groups. Towards the end of the Victorian era some of these middle- and upper middle-class suburbs began to change their character. Many of the houses were taken over and turned into flats while in modern times others have undergone multiple occupation by immigrant groups.

A large part of Hampstead consists of avenues of large Victorian houses taller than those in St John's Wood and with smaller gardens. The region is later in date and so it lies farther to the north, away from the centre of London and south of Hampstead Heath. Here there is once again a small nucleus of adaptable species and the common resident birds include starling, house sparrow, great and blue tits, song thrush, blackbird, hedgesparrow, woodpigeon and feral pigeon. The finches, robins, wrens, mistle thrushes, crows and swifts are scarce and there are half a dozen house martin colonies. I have seen spotted flycatchers, an occasional great spotted woodpecker, pied wagtail, magpie and tawny owl. Jays are often observed in the gardens in Hampstead where they get up to many ingenious tricks. A pair used to come to the garden belonging to Mrs Denise Salfeld in order to feed from the nuts inside some spiral wire holders; 'the contents hung out of their reach but the male jay accidentally discovered that shaking the holder made several nuts drop out and then over a few weeks he perfected a technique'. This consisted quite simply of turning the bottom of the holder, eating half a dozen nuts and then carrying several off in his beak. Another jay in the same garden used to bury peanuts in a flowerbed. Ten days after one interment which was then completely covered in snow the bird was able to relocate his underground cache. Nomadic tits and finches drift through the Hampstead gardens in winter. In the autumn of 1957 there was an irruption of great and blue tits to Britain and some of these birds were seen opening milk bottles not only in Hampstead but at Beckenham and Balham as well.

Woodpigeons that live in these Victorian suburbs often build their nests in trees both in gardens and in the streets. One nest that I saw in a London plane was within four feet of the upper decks of passing buses! In the Belsize Park district of Hampstead, which was developed about 1860, the woodpigeons have taken to nesting on buildings as they have also done in Westminster and Kensington. According to R. E. F. Peal, 'At the side of the semi-detached houses, a rainwater pipe commonly leads from the gutter into the vertex of a right angle in the wall and nests are built by woodpigeons on these pipes, sheltered by the eaves and resting against the walls.' In one area of 62 houses in 1962 there were 11 nests on pipes and in the following year the number had risen to 15. In addition, there were also 5 nests in roadside trees in nearby Belsize Avenue. Some of the woodpigeons' nests on houses were later taken over by feral pigeons. Miss Terry Gompertz, who then lived a mile away, also saw woodpigeons nesting in similar sites. As a species the woodpigeon has spread and increased during the last hundred years and it has moved into a number of town and suburban areas.

The feral pigeon also seems to be increasing in many urban and suburban districts. It is, of course, a domestic strain of the wild rock dove which achieved its freedom to form free-living communities in many parts of the world; it is derived from semi-domestic stock, dovecote birds and racing breeds. Although feral pigeons are less common in, say, the region of St John's Wood with its large gardens, the houses and smaller open spaces of late Victorian Hampstead seem to suit them very well. They particularly like institutional buildings such as churches, museums and railway stations including those at Paddington, Waterloo and Victoria where they can often be seen feeding at night. In her illuminating paper in *Bird Study* in 1957 Miss Terry Gompertz analysed the reasons why a late Victorian inner suburb should prove such a suitable habitat for these birds. She wrote: 'In an area like Hampstead, however, the pigeon has comparatively few institutional buildings to exploit. It is chiefly dependent on the gradual wear and tear of large over-ornamented Victorian houses whose unhappy owners are forever coping with repairs. It is not an exaggeration to say that one of the chief favourable factors in the breeding ecology of the Hampstead pigeon is the shortage of buildings with ladders long enough to reach the roofs of the Victorian houses, and the great expense of erecting scaffolding. As things are, minor repairs to the top storeys are often left until some major job has to be undertaken. This delay may give one or two pairs of pigeons three or four years' undisturbed nesting.' Typical nesting and roosting sites can be seen in figure 3. Nearly all nests are in or on buildings but one pair of feral pigeons nested in the fork of a large black poplar in a small London garden and I have seen nests in France in trees as well.

Feral pigeons sit about for long periods on roofs, gable ends, window sills and gutters as well as pipes and ledges. Like their wild ancestors they choose, where they can, to breed in colonies and so they welcome unwired church towers and steeples, large lofts and attics and any open functionless architectural excrescences such as turrets and cupolas. Individual pairs can also be found nesting in air-brick spaces, ventilators, wooden eaves, lofts and on rain-pipe hoppers. In Hastings I filmed a deserted hotel in which every room was occupied by feral pigeons which flew in and out either through the open windows or those in which the panes had been broken by vandals. When I was directing a television film about the wildlife of London, Geoffrey Mulligan obtained some fine sequences of feral pigeons that were breeding on a rain-pipe hopper on the front of the Langham Hotel opposite Broadcasting House.

When a pair is breeding alone it seems that the nest site itself is guarded by the male against any intruding birds. However, attics with enough room for several pairs but only one small access hole may be colonized provided the occupying male is not so aggressive that he succeeds in keeping the other pairs out. When several different entrances are available to the colony then each pair may use only one

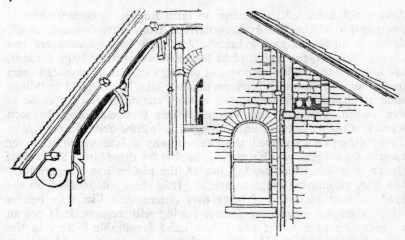

FIG. 3 Feral pigeons at Hampstead. *Left*, typical roost site; *right*, typical nest site. Reproduced from *Bird Study* by kind permission of Terry Gompertz.

of them. Birds will continue to use the same nesting site for as long as it remains undisturbed. When ventilators and window panes are finally repaired, holes filled in and air vents and spaces wired over the pigeons have to move on. By this time other properties may have deteriorated enough to offer more safe breeding quarters for the displaced birds.

Miss Gompertz pointed out that, although local authorities may try to control the numbers of pigeons in built-up areas, their plans are thwarted both by the tendency of the powers that be to 'hide their intentions behind an elaborate façade' and 'the casual good nature of ordinary people'. R. K. Murton has also described our ambivalent attitude to feral pigeons whereby thousands of people from Trafalgar Square west to the cities of the United States and east to those of Australia deliberately feed them at the same time as the local authorities do their utmost to remove them or reduce their numbers. Even the pigeons of St Mark's Square in Venice are now being caught and given their freedom in other Italian towns and cities. Feral pigeons have been accused of pecking down our historic buildings but when I put this question to Derek Goodwin who has made a special study of the world's doves and pigeons he thought that the people who said this had an ulterior motive. They might earn their living or part of it by catching pigeons or they might be officials who resented the pigeons because 'they provide a free and untaxed pleasure for so many people'. If mortar was being pecked for the lime and other minerals that the birds might need then they were only pecking at a building already in a state of decay. Goodwin feels that the damage and danger from disease from feral pigeons are far outweighed by the pleasure that they bring to young children and especially to old, poor and lonely people.

Anyone who has taken a close look at feral pigeons will have soon become aware of what seems a bewildering range of plumage patterns. As we have already seen, the feral pigeon is descended from the wild rock dove – a blue-grey bird with a white or whitish rump, two broad black bands across the grey wings, dull red feet and legs, and an iridescent green and lilac-purple patch on each side of the neck. The tail is bordered by a blackish terminal band. It is sometimes possible to see feral pigeons whose plumage matches quite closely that of the wild bird but they tend to have looser shapes, thicker beaks and larger ceres or 'wattles'. There are, in fact, many divergences from the ancestral rock dove pattern. Derek Goodwin has analysed the colour varieties of the feral pigeon as well as investigating how persistent they were and to what extent birds might be reverting to the original colour of the wild stock. On the whole feral pigeons are descended from the old-fashioned dovecote birds which were generally blue or blue-chequered in colour. Goodwin was able to distinguish seven colour varieties and these now follow with his tentative assessment of the proportions that they occupied in 1952 in the total London population.

COLOUR VARIETIES OF LONDON FERAL PIGEONS

1. BLUE	the original wild colour but with rump often greyish rather than white. Perhaps one tenth of total population.
2. BLUE-CHEQUER	similar to 1 but closed wing appears to be spotted with black. Some blue-chequers are darker than 1. About 50% of population.
3. VELVET	similar to 2 but the wing coverts are entirely black. About 5–8% of population.
4. BLACK	pure black birds are rare but slaty black more frequent. 5% of population.
5. MEALY, RED-CHEQUER and RED	similar respectively to blue, blue-chequered and velvet but with reddish brown markings on a sandy or brownish white ground. There is no tail bar and breasts and underparts are usually brownish. 5% of population.
6. GRIZZLE	a plumage in which the feather colours are mixed and streaked with white (intergrades exist between white grizzle – greyish-white with dark wing bars, iron grizzle – blackish-grey, and red.) About 5% of population.
7. PIED and WHITE	Any of previous types may show albinism especially on primaries, head, neck, rump and belly. About 10% of population.

Most of these colours can be divided again with smoky, silver-blue and pinkish tinges added. All the adult pigeons show the iridescence on the neck but this can differ both in tone and intensity according to the overall colouring. The iris of the feral pigeon is usually like that of the wild rock dove – a bright orange – but it is also possible to find irises of pinkish red, orange-yellow or dark brown. There is also a tendency for pied and red pigeons to be paired with mates of a similar colour but blues show no tendency to be mated with birds of the same pattern rather than to others with a lighter or darker plumage. Derek Goodwin suggested that two mechanisms either alone or working together might produce this selective kind of pairing. If young pigeons stayed near the nests in which they were reared, they would be more likely to mate with relations with a similar colouring and young birds might be imprinted on their parents. Certainly it seems very unusual for feral pigeons to forage much more than half a mile from their nest or roost site.

The diet of feral pigeons tends to vary with the habitat and birds will often gather in particular places where artificial feeding takes place or man-made foods are constantly available – park entrances, shopping parades, markets, railway stations, office blocks, grain stores and so on. Most of the birds' foods are obtained directly or indirectly from man. White bread, buns and cake make up an important part of the diet and the absence of vitamin B may lead to a form of paralysis and a condition known as polyneuritis. However, pigeons depend on those kinds of food for most of the year but birds in Hampstead also supplemented their diet with cheese, bacon, sausage, fish and scraps of cold meat. In Leeds feral pigeons took cereal grain, peas, peanuts, canary seed, millet and linseed which must have been given to the birds while domestic scraps included, according to R. K. Murton and N. J. Westwood, 'bacon rind, cheese, cooked meat, apple pips and peel, cooked peas, rice pudding, carrot fragments and grape pips'. Derek Goodwin added chocolate and potato chips and in the docklands of Manchester and Liverpool sorghum and maize were widely eaten. Birds also consume quantities of seeds and will visit parks, allotments, bits of waste land and even gardens to search for them. They have been known to take the seeds of shepherd's purse, treacle mustard, hedge mustard, knotgrass and black bindweed, as well as a number of other species. Although once dependent on the grain and horse droppings of Victorian stable-yards, the feral pigeon still benefits from the usually harmless and often friendly attitude of man.

No discussion of nineteenth-century suburban areas would be complete without some reference to the parks, commons and open spaces which survive among the houses of the inner zone. Feral pigeons from Hampstead visited the Heath for seeds and this green oasis supports the same core of breeding species and others which are still able to hold on despite the disturbance and the pressures from modern London. Nearly a hundred different species were observed in a recent year and of these more than a third actually bred. It is possible to find all three species of woodpecker, as well as nuthatch and treecreeper. Whitethroats, willow warblers and chiffchaffs nest regularly and in 1968 there were 21 singing male blackcaps. In recent years both wood and reed warblers have built nests, redpolls are often seen and the yellowhammer just maintains itself as a breeding species. The ponds have attracted great crested and little grebes, water rails, herons, mallard, gadwall, shoveler, goldeneye and shelduck. There are also migrants and other winter visitors to swell the annual total of species recorded. Like many other open spaces in the inner zone of towns Hampstead Heath suffers from very heavy use by visitors and their pets so that a real shrub layer, so important to many kinds of bird for food and nesting sites, can no longer survive. Cut off as it is by Victorian building the Heath still provides an important wildlife sanctuary and its birdlife can to some extent be linked with that of the built-up zones of Hampstead, St John's Wood and even Regent's Park.

This Royal Park is the largest of those in Central London or the inner suburbs and also has the widest range of habitats. It occupies an important place in the chain of open spaces and private gardens in north-west London. Its birds have been very well studied by Ian Wallace. Like so many other town parks it has grassy areas which are played over and trampled by countless feet, a bit of thin woodland, some shrubberies, a boating lake and an ornamental pond and garden. It is not unusual for over a hundred different species to be recorded in a year with about 30 of them nesting. I have described the birdlife of this park and the other Royal Parks in a book that I prepared for the Department of the Environment. Among the common species that nest there has recently been an increase in the numbers of great and blue tits, hedgesparrows, wrens and greenfinches but a decline in those of stock doves and woodpeckers. In 1972 great crested grebes and garden warblers bred and the heronry, founded in 1968, continued to flourish. Rare visitors have included the great grey shrike, hawfinch, little owl, crossbill and the black-eared wheatear that Christopher Holme and I saw in 1951. Regent's Park became one of the best-known spots in London for studying visible migration but this aspect of its bird life will be described in chapter 10. Black-headed and common gulls were regular in winter when I was watching birds in the park forty years ago, but herring gulls and lesser black-backed gulls are now appearing in small numbers by the lake. I have also seen redwings, linnets, skylarks, meadow pipits in the winter as well. The bird life of Regent's Park is to some extent influenced by its 22-acre lake with its six wooded islands. The park lies two and a half miles, as the crow flies, from St Paul's Cathedral which is very much on the inside fringe of the inner suburbs. Hampstead Heath can be found just over four miles from the same datum point and about the same distance from the Cathedral as Greenwich Park and Blackheath in the south-east.

From September 1964 to November 1966 P. J. Grant surveyed Greenwich Park and recorded a total of 91 different species. The park itself consists of about a hundred and eighty acres which lie close to an area whose development had largely taken place in the nineteenth century. Most of the park is open grassland but there are avenues of chestnuts and elms as well as three bird sanctuaries. The existing pond is not very large and, although it has been improved with the addition of aquatic vegetation and a floating island, its number of breeding and visiting water birds is rather low. The breeding population consists of some twenty-eight species which include willow warbler and blackcap; the breeding species in a recent year are given in appendix 3. The number of species is about the same as that in Regent's Park, Kensington Gardens and other town parks but lower than that for Hampstead Heath, where 39 species bred in 1971–2, and the outer Royal Parks. In Greenwich Park there was a density of 56 birds per 10 acres. This is about three times greater than in Regent's Park but this difference can be largely explained by the greater supply of nesting holes for house sparrows and starlings. However this figure is far below that of a hundred birds per ten acres for rural parklands.

Another interesting investigation into suburban parks of the inner zone was made in the 1960s by John Gooders who studied the birds of Clapham and Wandsworth Commons. Clapham Common, which I used to cycle across as a boy, was encompassed by large Victorian houses with fair-sized gardens but it has 'suffered considerable inroads of bricks and asphalt during this century'. It lies about four miles from St Paul's and covers about two hundred and twenty acres of flat land in the middle of the suburbs of Battersea, Balham and Clapham Junction, all largely developed by the 1870s. It has changed its character very little in the last forty years and consists very much of rolled grass swards with plenty of sports fields but only a few avenues and clumps of trees and practically no undergrowth – in fact, a typical park of the inner suburbs. Wandsworth Common is situated about five miles from St Paul's and is a little smaller. On the whole it is quieter and less heavily visited than Clapham Common and is practically enclosed by old houses with large gardens, the grounds of schools and a hospital as well as nurseries and cemeteries. Wandsworth's open spaces are rather like those of Clapham but it also has some rough boggy ground, a few bushes and rather more trees especially birches. Both commons have ponds with islands which provide nesting sites for several aquatic species of bird.

The total number of breeding species and birds present in the summer on both commons was 22. The mute swan, tufted duck and spotted flycatcher nested only on Clapham Common and the swift, great tit and chaffinch on Wandsworth. Mallard bred in both places as well as moorhens, coots, woodpigeons, carrion crows, jays and blue tits. Wandsworth held over twice as many song and mistle thrushes and eight times as many hedgesparrows as Clapham, reflecting the differences in the amount of tree or scrub growth. Starlings and house sparrows were common at Clapham where, according to John Gooders, 'the duck-feeding habit is much more strongly developed among the more numerous human visitors'. A list of the breeding species can be seen in appendix 2.

When we come to look at the winter populations of the two commons we find a considerable likeness with some twenty-four or twenty-five species. Diving ducks are however more frequent at Clapham where a total of a thousand black-headed gulls is also not unknown. I have seen common gulls regularly in winter on Clapham Common as well as a few herring and lesser black-backed gulls. Pied wagtails also occur in both places and I used to wonder if some of those that I saw before the last war were using the roost described by David Seth-Smith. The birds assembled on some roofs in Balham and then about a hundred and fifty of them roosted in some hollies on a busy main road; 'a bus stop was just opposite the trees into which the birds were crowding, and a powerful electric street lamp lighted them up as they perched on the outermost twigs preparatory to seeking snug roosting sites'.

Some six miles from St Paul's Cathedral is Bishop's Park in Fulham which was regularly visited by P. J. Strangeman. It lies along the River Thames near Putney Bridge where late Victorian developments spread along the Surrey bank of the river and twentieth-century housing sprang up on its northern boundary. The park is a 30-acre recreation ground, seven times smaller than the two commons which I have just described, with a churchyard, the grounds of Fulham Palace and some allotments. Eighteen species of bird were known to have nested between 1958 and 1964 – a smaller total than for Wandsworth and Clapham Commons. However it was possible to hear as many as thirty-five hedgesparrows in song and their territories were fairly evenly spread through the park. The list of breeding species can be found in appendix 2. The winter population consisted of about fifteen different species.

What can one deduce from these investigations into the bird life of the parks of the inner suburbs? It is clear that only a restricted number of species can exist in built-up areas and the greater proportion of these originated in woodlands or woodland ecotones. There are eleven species of bird that have bred fairly regularly in all five of the inner suburban parks that we have examined in this chapter. They are mallard, woodpigeon, carrion crow, jay, blue tit, mistle thrush, song thrush, blackbird, hedgesparrow, starling and house sparrow. Moorhen, tawny owl, great tit and greenfinch nested in four of the five parks and wren, robin, spotted flycatcher and chaffinch in three. In two only of the parks was it possible to add as nesting species tufted duck, mute swan, coot, stock dove, pied wagtail, goldfinch and bullfinch. Most parks of the inner suburban zones of British towns can muster some sixteen or seventeen breeding species while the more favoured ones, with large stretches of water, woodland and shrubberies may be able to boast twenty-five or so. In 1972, thirty-one were reported in Hyde Park and Kensington Gardens; this was the highest total since records began. It may be of interest to record in passing that the annual total of breeding species for the outer Royal Parks of Richmond and Bushey is about fifty for each of them. The parks may also provide records of rare vagrants. In 1972 there were observations of willow tit, scaup, goldeneye, guillemot, sparrowhawk and a nightingale in the inner London parks.

Few of the Victorian inner suburbs have preserved their unity untouched. Properties have fallen empty and then been demolished to make way for blocks of flats and concrete tenements. Occasionally in the pre-planning stage, as we have seen, an enlightened architect will make provision for some of the larger trees that survive from the mansion gardens or terrace plots to be included in the new design. Carrion crow, woodpigeon and even jay may nest in these tall relics of the Victorian age. Recently there has been a reaction against giant blocks because of 'the Anglo-Saxon sentiment for greenery and a tradition of single family living'. A typical example of the new ideas is that of the Lillington Gardens Estate in Pimlico with a density of two hundred bed-spaces to the acre. Here two-fifths of all the houses are at ground level with gardens or patios, while the remainder are joined by roof-streets three or four storeys up. In the design every front door is supposed to lead into a street, lane or alley. This is an attempt to compromise between the stereotyped cardboard council estate and the uncoordinated growth of middle-class suburbia. It is also intended to integrate the new estate into the nineteenth-century streets nearby by making its scale match the height of the old stucco terraces while its dark red brickwork is also supposed to blend in with the surrounding buildings. Some of the trees are as tall as the blocks and it will be interesting to see whether the estate can support species other than a few foraging feral pigeons, starlings, sparrows and perhaps an odd blackbird or blue tit. Shrubs and cover make all the difference to a bird population essentially woodland in origin.

At the end of this chapter it might be useful to summarise the status of the most typical of the breeding birds of inner suburbia. The species are classified in sections from the least promising to the most promising habitat.

STREET, HOUSE and SMALL GARDEN	*Regular* – feral pigeon, woodpigeon, blackbird, starling, house sparrow. *Irregular* – swift, jackdaw, hedgesparrow.
HOUSE WITH LARGE GARDEN	*Regular* – great tit, blue tit, mistle thrush, song thrush, robin, wren. *Irregular* – carrion crow, jay, great spotted woodpecker, spotted flycatcher, greenfinch, chaffinch, goldfinch.
SMALL PARK (with FORMAL POND)	*Irregular* – mallard, tawny owl, pied wagtail.
LARGE PARK (with LAKE)	*Irregular* – mute swan, tufted duck, coot, moorhen.

CHAPTER 3

The Outer Ring i. Estates and Factories

As we have already seen in the first chapter, the 'stereotype' of suburbia is the middle-class residential suburb. With its housing estates and industrial sites, where very little grows that can in any way be called natural vegetation, this outer ring of development can still show a remarkable richness in its bird life. It is very much a story of the more adaptable species finding success in their life alongside man while those unable to tolerate man or with too specialized habitats just disappeared as the tide of housing engulfed their breeding sites. It is the birds that were able to occupy the residential and industrial estates that mush-roomed throughout England and Wales in the inter-war years that form the subject of this chapter. Among the rows of houses and gardens, the roads and factory blocks, the new parks and surviving open spaces the community of breeding birds was formed very largely from species with a woodland origin. There will also be some reference to the New Towns of the post-1939–45 War period and to the council estates that have been built to 'in-fill' those open spaces left after the original building schemes had been completed. The remaining open habitats of the outer ring – the parklands, allotments, cemeteries, churchyards, waste ground and so on will be discussed in the next chapter.

The character of many middle-class suburbs is easily revealed by a rather formal lay-out of roads, usually at right angles to each other, and by the rows of uniformly built and often similar semi-detached houses. In the lower middle-class areas provision is sometimes made for terraces of houses with smaller gardens and with garage spaces available only for the houses built at the terrace ends. It is, however, the semi-detached house which since 1918 is 'more than a symbol of the suburb, it is in fact the suburb'. Where upper middle-class estates were built the houses might be detached or semi-detached but they were enhanced by larger gardens, winding avenues and roads, pleasant vistas and considerable variety in the houses themselves and in the landscaping. Here among the pleasant acres of Metro-land or Hands-worth Wood it is possible to find the large cars, the boats parked in the garden, the golden labrador retrievers and there are no factories or industry to spoil the almost rural calm.

The great rush of development of these suburban estates took place between 1925 and 1935. These new agglomerations of houses had to be built on land that had already experienced a totally different use. In many instances farmland, market gardens, orchards and golf courses were taken over by the developers. What effect does 'suburbanization' - an ugly word! - have on the bird life? In June 1937 E. C. Rowberry gave a lecture to the London Natural History Society on the way these new types of housing development changed the avifauna. His study was made in an area of about three-quarters of a square mile of fields, orchards and hedgerows near Osterley Park in south-west Middlesex. Here he found between 1927 and 1928 some thirty-two species of birds and these he divided into three categories - 'common', 'more than two pairs' and 'also bred'. In the first group were the following eleven species: song thrush, blackbird, robin, great and blue tits, hedge-sparrow, wren, whitethroat, starling, chaffinch and house sparrow. In the second group Rowberry placed nine species: swift, house martin, woodpigeon, skylark, willow warbler, garden warbler, lesser white-throat, greenfinch and linnet. The other birds that he found breeding in very small numbers were tawny owl, cuckoo, turtle dove, great spotted woodpecker, mistle thrush, spotted flycatcher, pied wagtail, carrion crow, jay, goldfinch, bullfinch and tree sparrow.

Rowberry repeated his census two years later in 1930 by which time a great part of the land had been developed and some of the orchards had also been cleared for building. Eight breeding species had been lost; these were tawny owl, house martin, turtle dove, spotted fly-catcher, pied wagtail, lesser whitethroat, goldfinch and tree sparrow. Five other species that were still nesting were showing signs of a decrease - great spotted woodpecker, skylark, willow warbler, garden warbler and whitethroat. It was clear that some birds were failing to adapt to the changing environment while others including swifts, starlings, great and blue tits and house sparrows, were nesting in growing numbers. Six years later - in 1936 - Rowberry made his last census of the birds in the new outer suburb. Most of the land was now covered with houses and all that remained of the original open space was a small area of playing fields and hedgerows. By this time only twenty-two species of bird were nesting - a third had been lost but the total biomass had been increased by 120 pairs of breeding starlings. The great spotted woodpecker, mistle thrush, willow and garden warblers and the bullfinch were lost as nesting birds but lesser white-throats and tawny owls had come back and the magpie had appeared for the first time. According to *The Birds of the London Area*, which reported E. C. Rowberry's studies, 'the carrion crow, jay, linnet, whitethroat, lesser whitethroat and cuckoo survived only in a six-acre wild garden and orchard' which shows clearly the value of even a small area of scrub and wild land inside a built-up area.

About eight miles north-east of this estate lie two other similar suburban regions which were also developed at about the same time. These were built on land that was once devoted to farming and golf-courses where the breeding birds had included such interesting species as partridge, sparrowhawk, corncrake, cuckoo, wryneck, yellowhammer and a number of different warblers. The larger of the two regions is close to Neasden and its 330 acres hold some 3600 semi-detached or terraced houses. Here some sixteen different species normally breed – the same figure that Rowberry obtained if one excludes the birds of the wild garden and orchard. A mile or so to the north is a smaller area of 49 acres also carrying an estate of inter-war houses and here Leo Batten found thirteen species breeding.

The suburban part of Neasden has been my special study for more than twenty-three years and I have given some indication of the birds that I have found at Dollis Hill in a chapter in *Woodland Birds*. In this chapter I want to describe in detail the ornithology of this very typical outer suburb and to compare it with Leo Batten's research north of the Brent Reservoir and with the observations that have been made in other suburbs in the country. Dollis Hill was developed by the firm of Costain's between 1928 and 1935 in a manner typical of many such builders in Britain. Most of the houses were built in pairs with shared drives or, more rarely, individual drive-ins. The front gardens were not large but those at the back varied in length from perhaps sixty to a hundred feet or more. Today the highest layer of shrub or small tree growth at maturity is about twenty feet high but in many of the gardens a blackcurrant bush or a hydrangea may be the tallest growing plant. A few gardens may contain taller trees such as ash, willow, sycamore or Lombardy poplar or even an old oak or elm left over from the open country before the estate was laid out. A much higher proportion have plum, apple and pear trees – and in 1973 some of these are past their best – or small ornamental ones such as flowering cherries, laburnums and hawthorns. My own back garden, right in the middle of the Dollis Hill estate, is 180 feet long and covers about one-tenth of an acre. When I first moved into the house in 1951 it boasted four apple trees, a pear and a Victoria plum. Today only the pear and one apple are still flourishing but my replacements include two willows, a sycamore, an ash, a species of *Prunus* and two elders. There is also a *Philadelphus* which provides a nesting site for blackbirds and a winter roost for blackbirds and house sparrows. There is also a shrub layer formed from raspberry canes, brambles, a thicket of lilac suckers, *Cotoneasters*, and bushes of *Cydonia japonica, Forsythia* and *Kerria*. There are also stretches of mown and uncut grass and some flower-beds. I like to think of my suburban garden as a kind of woodland ecotone.

In the period of my study I have observed 77 different species flying over it or actually in it. The most regular nesting birds have been

GREAT TIT, a hole-nesting bird that breeds in all but the most highly developed parts of towns.

WREN and HEDGESPARROW, two shyer suburban birds. *Above,* male wren in song on chainlink fence; *below,* hedgesparrow, an unobtrusive bird very much associated with privet hedges.

woodpigeon, great and blue tits, blackbird, robin, hedgesparrow, starling and house sparrow. The song thrush has also bred in some years and there are single nesting records of chaffinch, goldfinch and tree sparrow – in short, eight regular, one irregular and three unusual species. In some of the other houses and gardens on the estate I have found mallard, swift, carrion crow, mistle thrush and greenfinch breeding but the shy species such as tawny owl, jay, wren and bullfinch are confined to the parklands, allotments or gardens of one or two older houses. The percentage of total pairs, or the dominance, for my area of housing can be seen in figure 4; it is set alongside Leo Batten's chart for his census plot of thirty-year-old houses to the north of my 1928–35 estate, which 'fell about mid-way between the extremes of poor quality crowded estates with small gardens which are found in the eastern end of the area and the luxurious large detached or semi-detached houses with huge, well-wooded gardens in the south-western section'. There were many indigenous and exotic species of tree and shrub of which the commonest were Monterey cypress, willows, beech, mountain ash, cherry, lilac, laburnum, laurel, apple, pear, silver birch, oak elm and privet. There are considerable similarities between this area and that of Dollis Hill where, in addition, the roads of the estate were ornamented with horse chestnut, lime, Norway maple, London plane, necklace and white poplar, robinia, whitebeam, tree-of-heaven and seven kinds of thorn. Many of the trees had been originally bought by the local residents coming into the new houses but some of them were later replaced by the local authority because they were too large or because, as one alderman announced, they could supply 'much nicer' trees.

Leo Batten found his census area rather poor in bird species although the total density of nearly six hundred pairs per square kilometre, together with the breeding house sparrows, would have produced a figure comparable with that for the richest broad-leaved woods in Britain. In Ealing D. Ferguson recorded some 641 territories per square kilometre; this figure did not include sparrows and the higher figure was primarily due to a large number of nesting starlings. Both of these densities are higher than I found in my study area which, besides the tract of houses, also included a lot of grassland in the local park, allotments and some factory areas where there were few breeding sites. Nevertheless, the regular breeding species in the outer suburbs are typically woodland birds and some of them find this region better woodland than real woodland since they will nest there in greater densities than in their original forest homes. Yet this is a comparatively recent development since suburbs themselves are a fairly recent phenomenon.

Both Leo Batten and I found that the commonest species was the **house sparrow.** D. Summers-Smith, the authority on this successful

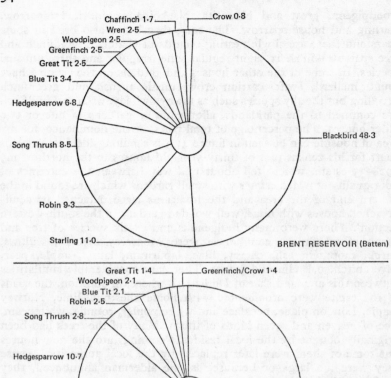

FIG. 4 Dominance (percentage of total pairs) for two inter-war housing estates (house sparrows excluded). The diagram for the estate near the Brent Reservoir is reproduced from the *London Naturalist* by kind permission of L. A. Batten.

bird, reported that 'house sparrow densities are higher in suburban than rural areas; hence the spread of suburbs is likely to benefit the sparrow'. It is a difficult bird to census accurately but I have found that by watching song posts and roof holes over many years it is possible to arrive at a fairly close estimate of the population. From 1951–65 there were some nine hundred pairs breeding every year at a fractionally lower density than that found by Stanley Cramp in Bloomsbury and by W. G. Teagle in Lambeth, both nearer to London's heart. They were, however, breeding at a density which was more than three times greater than that for suburban Stockton-on-Tees. In my suburb there has been a decline and the total stands now at somewhere between six hundred and seven hundred pairs. Stanley Cramp and A. D. Tomlins reported a decrease in central London, which was not satisfactorily explained, but I believe that, at Dollis Hill, better maintenance of roofs, eaves and gutters is largely responsible: there is supporting evidence from a similar drop in the number of breeding starlings.

Most house sparrow nests are built in roofs, ventilators and pipes, but others may be in creepers on walls, in holes in tree trunks and sometimes in quite open situations like the tops of rain-pipes where they curve towards the house wall from the gutter above. The nests in my loft are often built on the floor with open cups or they may be suspended from the underside of a tile with a classical domed form; they are made from dried grass, particularly couch and common meadow grass. Feathers for the nest lining are sometimes carried from up to a quarter of a mile away. Domed nests are also built in many years in thorns in the local park and I recently counted four such structures in a tree on one of the estate roads. I have recorded breeding in every month of the year as well as song and communal display chases. The birds are always present and provide a great deal of the character of a suburban garden. On 21 January in 1958, between 8 a.m. and 4.15 p.m., there were never less than fourteen sparrows in my garden and for more than twenty minutes in the afternoon there were over two hundred. When they also have a winter roost in the garden, sparrows are present for 24 hours of the day. Birds will regularly rip up my yellow crocuses, celandines and polyanthus, but in the summer considerable quantities of green and black fly are taken and I have often watched male birds gathering this aphid harvest from my rose bushes. They are regular bird-table birds and can remove the nuts from tit feeders without much difficulty. D. C. Seel, who watched a pair of house sparrows at an observation nestbox in suburban Pinner in Middlesex, found that the male's share in feeding the young increased during the nestling period from a minor to a major role and I have often watched a group made up solely of cocks looking for insect food in summer. I have sometimes found dead nestlings on the ground and in May 1972 a male flew out from the nesthole in the roof and dropped a dead chick from about eighteen feet in the air right at my feet. The house sparrow is well able to take advantage of the food, nest sites and material that man unwittingly or deliberately provides but it reserves for itself a certain reticence and prudence in behaviour that

makes it difficult for us to approach it, and in this way its survival is
assured.

One of the best ways to sample the bird life of the outer suburbs
fairly quickly is to walk round the streets just before dawn in the spring
and early summer. This is the method that I employ to count the
numbers of singing males and then to plot their territories. I start the
count when the dawn chorus is at its height and keep it going for not
much more than twenty-five minutes. My annual census begins at the
time when territories are being occupied and, as it is repeated regularly,
I am soon able to separate males holding territories from unpaired
birds. I have introduced a number of people to this suburban dawn
chorus including Derek Jones and Dilys Breese of the BBC's natural
history radio series, *The Living World*, and all have been surprised by
the volume and variety of this early morning chorus in suburbia.
Street lighting and higher temperatures also affect suburban birds and
may induce them to sing at night. I have often heard phrases of song
from robins and hedgesparrows deep in the night. In 1967 I listened to
a robin singing in the middle of a winter night close to a sodium lamp
near Stanmore in Middlesex. Blackbirds seem liable to give their
alarm calls at any time in the dark.

The **blackbird** is also an important contributor to the choruses of
suburbia. Its adaptability and catholic choice of food and nesting sites
are well illustrated by the way in which it changed from being a shy
woodland bird to one of the most successful of all suburban birds. At
Dollis Hill and near the Brent Reservoir it is, after the house sparrow,
the dominant breeding species. Each year somewhere between one
hundred and seventy-five and two hundred and twelve pairs nest
within half a mile of my home. These birds nest earlier than those in
woodlands but their clutches are generally smaller. Leo Batten found
that the mean clutch size is 3·78 compared to 3·91 in woodland; he
also discovered that each blackbird pair fledges 2·57 young in rural habitats but 3·28 in suburban ones. The yearly mortality among the adult
birds is higher in the London suburbs but the survival success is greater
in winter and lower in summer than in the country. A comparison of
the weights of our local blackbirds in cold winters with those in rural
districts has been made by the weighing of birds caught at a roost in
Brent and at another at Northward Hill in Kent. The birds from north-
west London averaged 125 grams each, while those from Kent managed
on average only 92 grams. It is thought that the mortality in the nesting
season may be due to predation by cats and the effects of traffic. On the
other hand more nestlings and more juveniles are produced in the
outer suburbs than in country districts. Two broods are regular at
Dollis Hill, three are not uncommon and in 1958 a pair that had built
on an unfinished sparrows' nest on a pipe under the eaves of my
neighbour's house raised four broods in the same nest. At one point the

hard-worked male was simultaneously feeding the fledged young of the third brood and the newly hatched chicks of the fourth. The male blackbirds in north-west London also come into song earlier than those in the country and I have heard full song between December and August.

The next commonest nesting species is the noisy thrusting **starling** with a density three times higher around my home than to the north of the Brent Reservoir. It is also much higher than for any rural and woodland areas that I have visited. All of the nests on the estate have been in houses but as we have already seen there has been something of a decline in numbers due to better repair of house roofs and gables. All the hole-nesting starlings in the trees are in the local park. From 1952–72 a pair nested each year in my own loft by entering through a small gap under the lead covering on a bay window; the birds had to struggle for up to eight seconds at a time to get through but in 1965 the hole was enlarged for their comfort. Other typical nest sites are under loose tiles, at the corners of roof ridges, at the bases of chimney stacks where the lead or mortar has come away and under detached planks on wooden gable ends. Perhaps one of the commonest sights in suburbia is that of a starling, perched on a television aerial with wings a-flutter, uttering his random and incredible combination of whistles, clicks, rattles and imitations of other animals or mechanical devices. There is quite a high mortality among fledglings from cats but I have watched adults encouraging their newly fledged young to fly up from lawns and gardens to the safety of the rooftops. According to Dr J. C. Coulson more hens than cocks breed in their first year resulting in a greater mortality among females; cats take quite a high toll of the birds searching for food on the ground.

One of my favourite birds is the rather shy **hedgesparrow** and this lives and breeds at a greater density at Dollis Hill than in British and Irish beechwoods and pedunculate oakwoods. In the suburbs it is very much a bird of the privet hedges and here it admirably conceals its shapely little nest. I have also found nests in shrubs such as thorns, lilacs and almonds. The regular trimming of hedges may cause some disturbance to the birds but the hedgesparrow can accept this activity provided the nest is not left completely exposed. There has been some tendency for house occupiers on suburban estates to grub out hedges as they find their cutting an increasing nuisance and the species has shown signs of a decline where this has been on a wide scale. The hedgesparrow is rather a shy and retiring species, creeping about the lawns and flowerbeds and around the base of the bird table but the cocks often sing from some prominent perch like a rooftop, aerial or tree. The **wren** is rather more a bird of parks, allotments and large gardens. E. A. Armstrong was of the opinion that 'it is a welcome resident in very many gardens, but only where bricks and mortar do not predominate over greenery. In populous areas where each house has its pocket-handkerchief garden wrens do not find congenial quarters'.

In the early part of this century the **song thrush**, according to Charles Dixon, was 'the commonest thrush' in outer London, but today it is outnumbered by the blackbird by anything from six to fifteen to one. It is rather a conservative bird and is not able to use the range of nesting sites that the blackbird can. The song thrush is also less hardy and does not avail itself of the many foods eaten by the blackbird which was described by Desmond Morris as 'dietetically adventurous'. From 1951–9 the song thrush was a rare visitor to my garden but then in 1960 a bird took up a territory and sang. Since that year a pair has nested annually in my garden or close to it. Blackbirds are dominant over song thrushes and regularly chase and harry them. I found song thrushes in my suburb at about the same density as in English pedunculate oakwoods but lower than that to be found in another suburb a mile or so to the north.

I suppose that it is the **robin** which perhaps epitomises gardens and gardening more than any other bird. I have been able to trace a slow and unspectacular increase since 1951 with a few territories in some of the smaller gardens being taken up firstly in the winter and then in the summer. The more varied the garden the more attractive will the robin find it. The ideal habitat is formed from fruit trees for song posts, shrubs for cover, rough grassland and some bare earth which is regularly turned over while creepers, earth banks, nest-boxes and man's rejected tins and pots can provide safe nesting sites. In the spring of 1973 my pair of robins built their nest in a hanging peg bag just below the kitchen window. Others favour open sheds and car ports in neighbouring gardens.

Both the **great** and **blue tits** are not as common as they are in woodland but they form an interesting and small part of the bird communities of the outer suburbs. The blue tit is generally rather more frequent than its bigger relative but both species, in the absence of mature or old timber on the estates, are very dependent on nest-boxes. There is a great deal of competition between the two species and in individual clashes victory can go either way. In suburban areas blue tits will nest in drainpipes, letter boxes and street lamps. Douglas Carr once watched a pair of blue tits carrying moss to a bus stop indicator fixed to a ten-foot post. The sign was made out of a piece of sheet metal folded vertically in the middle to form two sides with the words BUS STOP and the bus numbers on each. The folding of the metal strip left a gap about half an inch wide at the fold and about three inches wide at the other end of the post. This gap was plugged at the top and bottom by two more strips of metal with a semi-circular hole at the broader end of the bottom, and it was into this hole that the nest material was taken. According to London Transport this is quite a widespread habit. An interesting observation by A. Blackett has cast some light on the adaptability of blue tits since, an hour before daylight, he was able to watch two birds in a sycamore feeding 'by the light of an adjacent street lamp'.

The **woodpigeon** can be found on the inter-war estates because many of the trees planted in streets and gardens when the area was developed have reached a sufficient height to offer reasonably safe nesting sites. In both the areas that Leo Batten and I studied the woodpigeon represented some two to three per cent of the total number of breeding pairs. Between 1951 and 1961 the population at Dollis Hill nearly trebled, but with some local shooting and the felling of larger trees in the roads the number has since declined. I have found woodpigeon nests in robinias, elms, London planes, ash trees, horse chestnuts, sycamores, trees-of-heaven, poplars and several species of *Prunus*. The birds sometimes build their nests in such dense tree foliage that access to the site is difficult and the eggs may be knocked off the platform of twigs. I have not found any nests on buildings. Actual breeding may begin in March and I have seen unfledged young in October. In 1973 I watched a pair building a nest in a street tree in the last week of September. Song can often be heard in every month of the year but it tends to be most frequent from mid-February to mid-September.

Feral pigeons may also nest in the outer suburbs, especially around industrial sites and shopping centres. If they can enter private lofts through loose or missing planks on wooden gable ends they may establish small colonies in the houses as well. They range up to half a mile or more in their search for food and I have sometimes counted more than a hundred spread through the residential estate although fewer than half a dozen pairs actually breed within it; the others nest on the factories, parades and workshops on its borders. Birds will come regularly to well-known feeding spots and can be quite a nuisance on my bird table. Private houses with east- or south-facing rooftops may be used regularly for sun-bathing, preening and just 'lounging about'. House sparrows, which also pursue woodpigeons and starlings, often formate on a flying feral pigeon. The small pursuer tucks itself in just behind one of the pigeon's wings and, keeping perfect station, remains in the same position, following with absolute precision every bank, wheel and climb that the larger bird undertakes, which according to Derek Goodwin 'is flying well above its normal travelling speed'. The pursuit is headlong and dramatic to watch and may last for half a minute or more. The pigeon may alight and the pursuer then land a few feet away. If the pigeon then resumes its flight the sparrow may be off once more but I have seen the smaller bird break off the chase in mid-air. Just the sight of the larger bird flying across the area often seems to be enough to stimulate the sparrow to give chase.

In my area of outer suburbs the **collared dove** is a mere vagrant but this exotic newcomer may breed in some suburban areas with large gardens; the numbers seem to fall off where the gardens are small or medium-sized. The largest breeding populations are in suburban areas and J. A. Hicks found that the number of nesting doves near a town centre is inversely correlated to the size of its built-up area so that, with such exceptions as Edinburgh, Liverpool and Hull, the birds are absent from the centres of major British towns and cities. He found, for example, in the neighbourhood of Bexhill that whereas there were 40 pairs per square mile in an urban habitat the figure rose to 64 among the small suburban gardens and 88 among the larger ones. The birds normally breed from March to September and October but in mild weather the season might start in January and be extended to November. Among the species of tree that collared doves have used for nesting are spruce, pine, silver fir, yew and ivy as well as various thorns and fruit trees, lime, poplar, birch and horse chestnut. These charming little birds occur in the country, where they may be numerous enough to be regarded locally as a pest, in the suburbs of many towns including Birmingham, Sheffield, Leeds and Manchester, but they are rather thinly spread around the London area.

There now remains a small handful of species that might reasonably be expected to nest on some of the pre-1939 War estates. **Mallard** sometimes succeed in raising young in the less well-tended gardens but they are then faced with the problem of getting the young birds to the safety of a pond or lake. On several occasions my daughter and I have shepherded a duck and her brood more than half a mile across three minor roads, a very busy thoroughfare and finally the arterial North Circular Road to the waters of the Brent Reservoir. The duck's average speed of march is as high as two miles an hour and this speed must put a considerable strain on the physical reserves of the recently hatched ducklings. I often see mallard flighting over the estate between the small lake in the local park and the bigger waters of the reservoir while aerial chases in spring are very common. In winter I may see up to fifty birds by the park lake. Where tall planes, elms, poplars and oaks survive on the estates from earlier times **carrion crows** may build their stick nests from which they sally forth over the roads and gardens taking a toll of the eggs and nestling birds of other species. **Kestrels** sometimes breed in old crows' nests and hollow trees; these predatory birds take a lot of sparrows and starlings. Similarly a few pairs of **tawny owls** may also hold on but I have found that grey squirrels and the loss of elms through Dutch elm disease have brought about some local reductions in numbers.

Jays prefer parklands and older gardens but they are adaptable birds

ROBIN, SPOTTED FLYCATCHER and WREN, three suburban species nesting in walls. *Above left*, robin; *right*, spotted flycatcher – a summer visitor; *below*, wren.

PIED WAGTAIL and BLACK REDSTART, two species sometimes breeding on gasworks, power stations and industrial sites. *Above,* pied wagtail at nest in a garage; *below,* black redstart at nest in a factory at Lowestoft.

and may even nest in small thorns and other trees in suburban back gardens. The **magpie** has been spreading through many suburban belts and has begun to penetrate further into the hearts of towns. In 1971 a pair bred successfully in a central London park and birds now occur widely in the environs of such cities as Dublin, Manchester, Edinburgh, Glasgow and Aberdeen.

The commonest of the **finches** is generally the greenfinch, building in fruit trees and tall shrubs and hedges and even, as I have found on occasion, in street trees. This robust bird is a great lover of peanuts and will come regularly to gardens where they are supplied. The goldfinch may also breed and is in some ways very much a suburban bird; in 1972 a pair built a neat little nest of grass and moss, lined with thistle down, about sixteen feet up in an ash tree in my garden. The chaffinch is also a suburban bird but only a few pairs hold territories in my area and there is only one nesting record for my garden. Hawfinches have been known to breed in the outer suburbs and a pair reared young in North Harrow in 1956, but the species is not easy to census. It prefers gardens with good cover and in this respect is rather like the bullfinch. Certainly where there are large gardens and houses in the outer suburbs the finches are better represented and on many of the inter-war estates they tend to be marginal species.

Pied wagtails and **spotted flycatchers** are not unusual and even **grey wagtails** have been seen hunting insects along gutters in the outer suburbs. **Swifts** are not common since there is a shortage of building sites in the newer houses but **house martin** colonies can be found where water is not too far away. The birds may build on houses quite soon after they are finished but they are subjected to a certain amount of persecution from tidy-minded house occupiers who object to the droppings. Martins do not nest at Dollis Hill but there are colonies not far away on the northern bank of the Brent Reservoir where Leo Batten described it as a 'common summer resident breeding in many streets'. A survey made by L. E. Bouldin of house martin colonies in East Lancashire showed that the colonies in suburban areas were slightly larger than those in urban areas – 3·3 nests compared with 2·8 – but smaller than in rural districts where the average number was as high as 5·9. A quarter of the nests were on detached or terraced houses and about twelve per cent on semi-detached. The **sand martin** is not perhaps a very typical bird of the outer suburban ring of residential estates although it may nest in embankments as we shall see in the next chapter. Nevertheless sand martins were able to rear young in a drainage hole in a brick wall by a residential road on the outskirts of Marlborough. The hole was only two feet above the pavement but in spite of passing pedestrians and traffic the martins brought four young to the fledging stage. The nearest known colony was at least seven miles away.

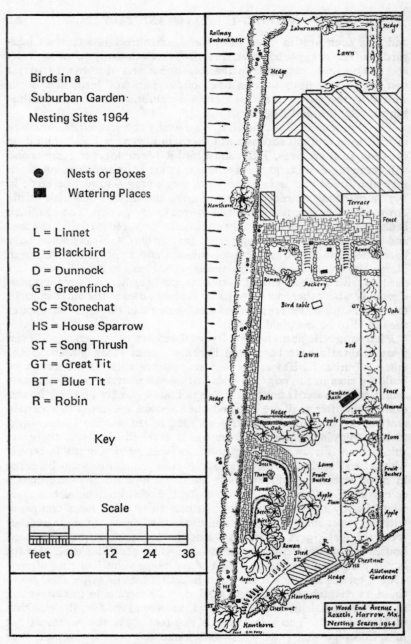

FIG. 5 Birds in a suburban garden in Harrow, Middlesex. Reproduced from *Bird Notes* by kind permission of the R.S.P.B.

So far I have been describing the bird life of the typical 1925–35 estates but many of these developments embraced or were contiguous to rather older houses whose gardens contained more mature timber as well as shrubberies and large expanses of lawn and flowerbed. From these important sanctuaries and from others formed by the grounds of hospitals, cemeteries and parks certain bird species may invade the estates especially outside the breeding season. These are often tawny owls, jays, magpies, mistle thrushes, great spotted woodpeckers, spotted flycatchers, bullfinches, coal tits and goldcrests. If the islands of gardens and open spaces are large then it may also be possible to find green woodpeckers, treecreepers, nuthatches, collared doves and that increasingly common little finch the redpoll. Blackcaps and willow warblers have bred in the grounds of a hospital at Dollis Hill, now demolished, and the chiffchaff, which has never bred at Dollis Hill, has nested in scrub by the Brent Reservoir. But the last species cannot be regarded as truly 'suburban'.

In the winter months there is often a change in numbers among some of the resident birds and at the same time the winter visitors begin to put in an appearance. Some of the breeding species may disperse throughout the estate. Great and blue tits will come into small gardens and visit bird tables, and thrushes, finches, robins and even wrens will be seen in gardens where they are quite unknown in the summer months. One February day in 1958 I watched twenty blue tits in my own garden and this was at the time when survivors of the autumn irruption of 1957 were still being reported in many suburban areas. It was interesting to note that there were no attacks on milk bottles, paper or putty around my home unlike Hampstead, Balham and a number of other districts where these different aspects of tit behaviour were observed. Many blue and great tits went into houses and attacked, in descending order of frequency, wallpaper, books, newspapers, lampshades, notices and labels while others went for calendars, letters, printed forms, blotting paper, toilet rolls and tissue paper, curtains, towels, bedspreads, telephone wires and candles. One blue tit had a dustbath in a powder bowl standing on a dressing table. This was not, by the way, a rehearsal by Alfred Hitchcock for his film *The Birds*. Outside the houses attacks were also made on paint, whitewash, mortar, milk bottles and especially putty. One explanation for all this seems simply to be that a large number of tits in a new habitat just carried out the kind of exploratory searching that they would do in autumn in a more familiar environment such as a wood. Starlings have also been seen eating putty in Somerset when birds pecked at the newly glazed windows on a building site. In the winter months some of the resident birds gather in those estate gardens where the cover is good and food at hand. On a January day I have found that in any five-minute period from dawn to dusk 'there were never less than 16 individuals of four species in my garden; at one time the number rose to 39 individuals of eight species'. Blackbirds often gather at favourite feeding grounds and small parties of finches drop in to visit the bird table from time to time. I have had as many as six greenfinches on the table at the same time and not necessarily in severe or snowy conditions. In recent years siskins have begun to visit gardens and one bird stayed three months in my own garden. As a result of an appeal from Robert Spencer and Geoffrey Gush some seventy-three letters came to them reporting this growing habit; of these 41 related to suburban gardens and so indicated clearly the way in which siskins were penetrating built-up areas.

The most obvious of the winter visitors to the estates are the gulls which can be regularly seen sweeping back and forth over the gardens and streets, dropping down to pick up scraps and then carrying them off to a more sheltered spot. Other birds sit about on the chimney stacks and roof ridges. The commonest species is the black-headed and I sometimes see as many as seventy birds foraging near my house. These expert scavengers spend the short winter days feeding in the suburbs and then, as the afternoons wear on, they begin to gather and set course for the reservoirs or estuaries where they spend the night. In the winter of 1952–3 common gulls also began to appear in the autumn but these were rather shy at first and always obtained their food indirectly by harrying and chasing the black-headed gulls which had already retrieved morsels and were forced to give them up. The screaming pursuits made the smaller birds drop the food which was caught before it fell to the ground. Now, however, the common gulls are sufficiently bold to gather their own food but they have not as a result dropped the skua-like harassment of the black-headed gulls. The arrival of common gulls in suburban areas in England added a new habitat to a bird whose original environments had been those of grassland and freshwater. I usually see a few herring gulls each winter and perhaps lesser black-backs as well which I also observe on autumn migration. The great black-backed gull is a rather scarce visitor each winter.

In those winters when the weather is especially severe there may be rarer birds present in the suburbs and these, together with the migrants that pass through or over the estates, will be the subject of chapter 10. In addition to these two categories there are also vagrants that appear for no apparent reason in the outer suburbs – birds that have wandered or got lost, wind drifted birds and so on. Of course, if you live in an area for some time you are likely to come across these curiosities. I see herons and mute swans flying over at various times of the year perhaps between visits to various less well-frequented waters. Among the vagrants that have appeared at Dollis Hill are bittern, Canada goose, buzzard, sparrowhawk, pheasant, little owl, kingfisher, great and lesser spotted woodpeckers while near the Brent Reservoir in recent years there have also been a small petrel, hoopoe, and waxwings in 1947. I have not seen waxwings near my home but in 1965 they were observed in the suburbs of Coventry and Birmingham and in the following year there were reports from Handsworth Wood and Selly Oak. In invasion years it is always a good idea to keep an eye open for these lovely birds wherever there are berried trees and bushes as well as orchards.

So many foreign birds are now kept as cage birds that it is to be expected that some of them will escape. In the twenty-three years in which I have lived in Brook Road at Dollis Hill I have seen 15 escaped budgerigars, a lovebird, an African grey parrot, a rose-winged parakeet, an African black-headed weaver and the remains of a yellow-headed Amazon parrot. There must be many similar lists available for other suburban areas of Britain.

We have already seen that both the distribution and density of our suburban birds depend on secure nesting sites and guaranteed supplies of food. Most of the species are also of woodland origin and in their ancestral forests they would have been preyed upon by foxes, stoats, adders, hawks, owls, crows, magpies, jays, jackdaws and perhaps squirrels. In suburbia the predation is of a different kind but there are still predatory birds and mammals, and man, to some extent, also takes a hand. Where hens are kept in gardens or the houses are close to allotments and waste land, the brown rat may get a foothold. Although the numbers of this rodent are strictly controlled, some rats may take the eggs and young of various birds, and young mallard suffer especially badly. Almost certainly the cat is the most important enemy of birds but its numbers and so its overall effect vary over the years. In 1951 I estimated that there was one cat to every five households, in 1961 one to every twelve and in 1971 one to every eight. It is interesting to trace the change in fashion and budgerigars tended to supersede cats as domestic pets in the late 1950's and early 1960's. We have already seen that cats can influence the number of female starlings. In my district I have not been able to plot any changes in the bird population that are matched by the fluctuating community of cats. The victims of my local feline hunters are the adults of feral pigeon, woodpigeon, blue tit, song thrush, mistle thrush, blackbird, robin, starling, chaffinch and house sparrow as well as the young of mallard, woodpigeon, blackbird, song thrush, robin, starling and house sparrow. Cats, of course, vary a great deal as individual hunters. Some are well fed but still remain efficient and ruthless killers, others make aggressive sounds but take no action and others just cannot be bothered. It would seem that the cat fills the ecological niche that is occupied in the countryside by our native carnivores and adders. Where it has succeeded in getting a foothold in some of the older gardens, parks and allotments the grey squirrel can make dangerous forays into the suburban estates, taking both the eggs and young of many different species. If its numbers grow high it can have an appreciable effect on bird populations. No grey squirrels appeared on our estate before 1965 and, although their headquarters remains in the local park, dreys have been built in private gardens as well and animals have been known to hibernate in roofs which form secure refuges for them. A certain number of squirrels die on the roads each year. Two squirrels only have ever come into my garden; the first was hand tame and sat on my shoulder (not a local one!) and the second was rather shy and closely mobbed by blackbirds, house sparrows and a robin. I think that although my trees are varied they are not really tall enough to satisfy the squirrel's needs.

The most important bird predators are tawny owls and carrion crows. In the London suburb of Morden Geoffrey Beven found that 45% of the food taken by tawny owls consisted of birds; this figure could be compared with one of 93% for a central London park and only 10% for a rural oakwood where small mammals were very common. These suburban owls were apparently taking house sparrows, thrushes and starlings as well as such scarcer species as chaffinches and robins. My tawny owls have had to subsist largely on birds but as they are now no longer breeding their effects as predators are greatly reduced. However this has been to some extent counter-balanced by the pair of kestrels that nested in 1972, rearing one young, and in 1973 when the chicks were stolen by collectors. Kestrels will snap up birds from the size of tits to that of blackbirds and starlings and I have seen house sparrows taken from rooftops, street pavements and bird tables. In March 1972 a kestrel, flying like a sparrowhawk, passed low through my garden and nearly picked off my resident male blackbird. Carrion crows take a heavy toll of eggs and young and much of the hunting is carried out in the early morning. My crows have evolved a technique in which they fly round and round a clump of bushes or small trees until the nerve of any sitting or brooding bird is broken and she flies off her nest with perhaps a loud series of alarm calls. The crows, which have been hunting together, then sidle down into the upper foliage until they find the nest. Jays and magpies also take a toll of eggs and nestlings.

Even in a suburban land of plenty there is a great deal of competition among birds for the available food supplies. Parasitism among birds is not uncommon and many species will chase and rob other birds of their food. We have already seen that common gulls will force their smaller relatives to yield up their takings. The following table is a summary of my observations in an outer London suburb of birds chasing, attacking and robbing other species of food. On the left-hand side are the attackers and on the right-hand side the victims. Some birds, it will be seen, can qualify for both lists.

FOOD PARASITISM AMONG BIRDS AT DOLLIS HILL,
NORTH-WEST LONDON, 1951–73

Parasite	Victim
Mallard	Feral pigeon, woodpigeon, blackbird, house sparrow, black-headed gull
Herring gull	Black-headed gull, common gull
Common gull	Black-headed gull
Black-headed gull	Mallard, feral pigeon, woodpigeon, starling
Woodpigeon	Feral pigeon, blackbird, starling, house sparrow
Great tit	Blue tit, house sparrow
Blue tit	Great tit, robin, hedgesparrow, house sparrow
Fieldfare	Blackbird, starling
Blackbird	Song thrush, great tit, hedgesparrow, house sparrow
Robin	Great tit, hedgesparrow, siskin, house sparrow
Starling	Blackbird, song thrush, hedgesparrow, house sparrow
Greenfinch	Blue tit, house sparrow
House sparrow	Blackbird, hedgesparrow, greenfinch, chaffinch

Quite a number of the encounters that made that list possible were observed on my bird table and no consideration of the ornithology of the outer suburbs would be complete without an examination of the way in which man has influenced the bird life. Some of his activities are a direct intervention in favour of the birds while others may prove to their disadvantage. In a general sense all birds that can find food, roosting and nesting places in our gardens and around our buildings benefit from man's suburban way of life. The adaptable birds become tamer but reserve prudence for themselves. Our houses offer safe nesting sites as well as places for resting, sun-bathing and singing. I now have well over a thousand observations each of blackbirds, starlings and house sparrows using television aerials for song posts while other birds I have watched on them singing or giving territorial calls include woodpigeon, blue tit, mistle thrush, song thrush, willow warbler, hedgesparrow, greenfinch, goldfinch and tawny owl. Man also provides a lot of waste material which birds can use in the construction of their nests such as newspaper, cellophane wrappings, sweet papers, bits of newspaper, wood shavings, rags and bits of cloth. All of these items have appeared at one time or another in the nests of starlings, mistle thrushes, song thrushes, blackbirds and house sparrows. Pieces of string and twine, wool and plastic bindings are also taken and in some places wire is employed by pigeons as a basic nest material. Chicken runs are a valuable source of nest linings and I have found feathers from them in the nests of starling, house sparrow and tree sparrow. I have seen a female hedgesparrow collecting up the white hairs blowing about on my lawn while I was still grooming my dog and a blue tit once spent ten minutes pulling out hairs from my dog's blanket which had been hung out for brushing and airing. One of the blue tit nests in a garden nestbox was lined with burnt felt taken from the remains of a bonfire in a neighbour's garden.

Birds also derive benefit from man's activities in the garden since the soil is turned over and kept exposed revealing a rich insect and invertebrate fauna to feed such birds as song and mistle thrushes, starlings, robins and hedgesparrows. If the gardens are poorly tended then weeds can flourish, especially such species as chickweed, broad-leaved plantain, groundsel, dandelion, sowthistle, creeping thistle, couch grass, meadow grass and shepherd's purse. Goldfinches, greenfinches, house sparrows, and perhaps bullfinches and even linnets may come to these supplies of seed. Goldfinches in particular have increased in gardens and they began to penetrate the suburbs around Birmingham in the early 1950s. Feral pigeons and hedgesparrows are also visitors to the less well-tended areas when seeds become available. Insects may be quite common in blocks of gardens where there are trees, flowers, lawns and perhaps *Brassica* crops. Starlings look for leatherjackets and wireworms and I have also seen them rising up from the rooftops to heights of sixty to a hundred and fifty feet to catch flies and ants on the wing. House sparrows also go flycatching in this way and they take many different kinds of fly, swarming ants, aphids, adult moths such as the yellow underwing and butterflies such as the large, small and green-veined white and the small tortoiseshell. In those gardens where the grass length is kept down then the turf provides a most important feeding zone for thrushes, starlings, carrion crows, pigeons, pied wagtails, hedgesparrows, house sparrows and mallard and gulls. My pear tree is subject to periodic attacks from starlings which in some dry seasons will strip the tree of its fruit leaving the cores attached to the branches. These predatory birds also raid blackcurrants, raspberries, loganberries, plums, apples and elderberries. Blackbirds and some of the migrant warblers often feed on blackberries and woodpigeons and jays can play havoc with crops grown in suburban back gardens. Many berries can be found on garden shrubs and most of my snowberries are taken whole by blackbirds; other shrubs such as roses, various *Cotoneaster* species, barberries, firethorns, flowering currants, spindle trees, wayfaring trees, guelder roses and honeysuckles carry fruits which are attractive to birds. It is also perhaps worth remembering that the seeds of garden herbaceous plants, including sunflowers, evening primroses, antirrhinums, pansies and others are often favoured by birds. A systematic planting scheme is one positive way to improve the value of a suburban garden as a bird sanctuary.

During the last two decades or so there has been a steady rise in the deliberate feeding of birds. The greater part of the food given to them consists of bread, particularly white bread which may be harmful to them as it is doughy and may swell in the crop. I have kept an account over the years of the birds of the outer suburban ring that have definitely eaten bread and not just pecked at it. In all there are 23 species and this is quite a high total. They are mallard, herring gull, common gull, black-headed gull, lesser black-backed gull, feral pigeon, woodpigeon, carrion crow, jay, great tit, blue tit, coal tit, song thrush, blackbird, robin, hedgesparrow, starling, skylark, greenfinch, chaffinch, siskin, house sparrow and tree sparrow. Birds are very much attracted by nuts and fat and the R.S.P.B. list other foods recommended by different writers on feeding garden birds – bones for their marrow, cheese, porridge, oats, coarse oatmeal, puppy food, hemp and canary seed, sunflower seed, ant pupae, bacon rind cut into small pieces, dried fruit such as currants and sultanas, apples and baked potatoes. Desiccated coconut is not suitable but half a coconut hung up in a tree with the meat facing the ground is an asset in a bird garden. Some proprietary food mixtures are available and one of them has induced at least fifteen different species to come to my bird table. A British Trust for Ornithology garden bird feeding survey was started in the winter of 1970 and it has shown that over sixty species will take food artificially given to them at feeding stations. The 'top ten' in this list are blackbird, starling, house sparrow, blue tit, robin, greenfinch, hedgesparrow, great tit, song thrush and chaffinch. From about 1957 great spotted woodpeckers began to visit bird tables in gardens in the West Midlands and overwintering blackcaps, chiffchaffs and even garden warblers have been known to feed at tables. A male blackcap that visited a bird table in a Nuneaton garden fed on cakecrumbs and suet. We saw in the last chapter how well jays can cope with nut containers. A brambling that came to a suburban garden at Addiscombe in Surrey used to hang from a container to get at the food. Tony Soper has drawn up a very valuable guide to the use of bird tables in particular and bird gardening in general.

In recent years powerful campaigns have been mounted to underline the dangers that can threaten the wildlife of Britain and these have received publicity in the press, and on radio and television. However, practical methods of conservation are available not only to the owners of large domains but even to those with only very small gardens. An editorial in a special issue of *Bird Notes* – the journal of the R.S.P.B. – which was published in 1964 claimed that, 'However large or small their garden may be, it is certain that there are many people who are in a position to offer to a variety of birds most if not all of five essentials – security, food, water, cover and nesting facilities.' To enable my garden in suburbia to meet these needs I have planted fruit-bearing trees and shrubs to provide both security and food as well as cover and nesting sites, kept a dog to discourage cats and squirrels, dug a pond to give water for drinking and bathing, put up nestboxes and left small holes in the eaves of the house and preserved some wild places untouched.

In the same issue of *Bird Notes* T. L. Bartlett described his suburban garden in Harrow in Middlesex where in 34 years he observed 67 species in or over it while 15 actually bred within its 150-foot length, including linnet and stonechat. Figure 5 shows the nesting sites in that Harrow garden. My suburban garden is closer to the centre of London but it will be remembered that I recorded 77 species over 23 years of which 12 actually built nests. If the 'feeders' of birds can become 'bird gardeners' and 'bird conservationists' then the birds will benefit enormously. Figure 6 shows a layout planned by the Royal Society for the Protection of Birds for a small suburban garden. Of course if you install a pond and stock it with fish then a heron or kingfisher may drop in to try its luck. In any case the sight of birds coming to drink and bathing in sight of the kitchen or lounge window is always a pleasing one. Robins and blackbirds will also come and hunt for flat-worms, tadpoles and other aquatic life.

Bird tables, wire mesh containers, seed hoppers and suspended coconuts and peanuts will attract a variety of birds which can bring pleasure from their antics while feeding, their threat displays to each other and their close proximity to the house. There is one very interest-ing by-product from using seed mixtures on a bird table. When uneaten seeds fall or are blown off the table they often germinate and so pro-duce exotic aliens which bloom on the flowerbeds to the surprise and sometimes the delight of the garden's owner. David McClintock listed a number of these bird seed plants, including red clover, ribwort plantain, fat hen, thorowax and fennel, all of which have appeared in my own garden. According to McClintock a search in Germany by Karl Müller in 1950 revealed 229 bird-seed plants. Apart from these casuals elders and hawthorns have sprung up around my home as the result of being bird sown and these have increased the natural food sources for birds in the garden.

As long ago as March 1954 the Reverend P. H. T. Hartley made a plea for the back garden ornithologist who is able to observe the same birds at all hours of the day and throughout the seasons. He believed that 'the back-garden birdwatcher, watching the story of his "common" birds unfold from month to month has at once the delight of intimacy and the satisfaction of that placing of each observation in a setting of other observations which is the essence of research'. Although I have been delighted to visit bird haunts in Africa, the Camargue, Spain, eastern Europe and other rewarding regions, it has always been with great pleasure that I have returned to the bird community of my own garden where the individuals are special to me and may carry their own pet names, bestowed not in an anthropomorphic way but with affection and detachment.

So far I have been describing the positive ways in which man has helped the bird life of outer suburbia. Now I have to consider the

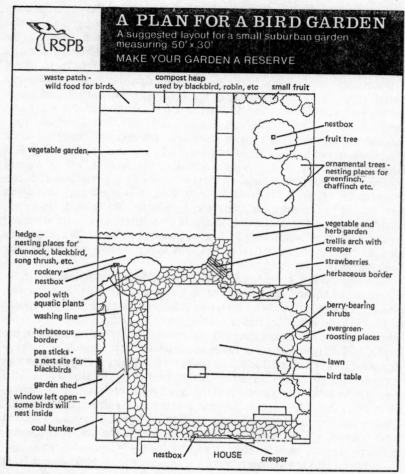

FIG. 6 A plan for a bird garden. Reproduced by kind permission of the R.S.P.B.

adverse effects of man in this environment although in relation to the benefits that I have mentioned they tend to be small. Woodpigeons are systematically shot in some suburbs but on the whole the direct actions against birds are fewer than those that occur in the open country. Boys sometimes use air pistols and catapults but in most of the estates these are so dangerous to humans that they are soon discouraged by action taken against them. There is some indication that air guns are being carried more openly and perhaps used in suburban areas in the north of England and Scotland. Birds nesting in private gardens are not likely to have their nests plundered or eggs taken by boys in the way that some woodland and hedgerow nesting birds may suffer. In my own neighbourhood I have found an increasing regard for the welfare of birds. Depredations by birds may lead to fruit, peas, brassicas and other crops being given protection through free-blowing metal strips, rotating propellers, scarecrows, nets, muslin and black cotton but, apart from the odd bird that finds its way under a net and cannot get out, the birds are not seriously affected by these precautionary measures. I cannot trace any positive effects from toxic chemicals in my local gardens but I would recommend the R.S.P.B.'s little guide, *Pesticides and the Gardener*, for anyone using control measures in suburban gardens. Better care of property has reduced the number of roofs available for nest sites, and the heavy and often ugly pruning of street trees may restrict possible sites as well. However, woodpigeons and sometimes blackbirds and thrushes may be attracted by the pollarded condition of London planes and limes. We have seen already that the removal of privet and other hedges can affect the hedgesparrow's numbers.

I have very few records of birds being killed after flying into telephone wires and cables strung across roads and gardens. For the first twelve years of my study of an outer suburban estate I had no records of birds being killed by traffic on the road. In 1962 I wrote that 'this must surely be due to the range of vision available to a flying bird in the Dollis Hill area, where most roads are wide and few front gardens have much high cover, as well as to the town bird habit of rising up above an approaching car and often being carried over it by the slipstream. It is the bird crossing the narrow country road with high hedges which so often dives down low above the road surface and is struck by a vehicle'. From 1963 the incidence of road casualties began to mount, affecting feral pigeons, which were increasing as a species, blackbirds and house sparrows. It may be of interest to record that I discovered dead hedgehogs, which had always been on the estate, only from 1963 onwards. It was clear, as subsequent surveys showed, that the volume of traffic along two or three of the through roads was growing, that there were more heavy lorries using back doubles and that the overall speed of traffic in a 30 m.p.h. restricted zone was rising. I have also seen more cats that had been killed by traffic in the last two years than in the preceding twenty.

It was inevitable that a large part of this chapter would be devoted to the *residential* estates on the outer suburban belt. However, often contemporary with and close to these housing estates arose factories and industrial sites, gas works and power stations to provide both power and employment for the new suburban masses. On the whole factory areas are not particularly promising bird habitats unless they also include shrubberies, rough ground, flowerbeds, grass swards, trees and so on. The breeding communities of the factories near me that stretch along the North Circular Road consist of feral pigeons, house sparrows, starlings, a few blackbirds and one pair of pied wagtails. The feral pigeon manages to roost and build its nest on ledges, inside roofs and in ventilators and from these sites the bird goes foraging in the gutters, gardens and shopping centres close by. There is sometimes rather a shortage of nesting materials on industrial sites and feral pigeons have been known to build their nests of rusty galvanized wire. One of these weighed as much as 2 lb 7 oz. Collared doves have also been known to use soft wire for the structure of their nests. There is an interesting record of a pair of grey wagtails feeding their young at a factory site at Carshalton near the River Wandle while a pair of black redstarts nested at Beddington Cement Works in the late 1940s.

House sparrows are common and find many breeding sites among the factories and warehouses. Their remarkable adaptability is demonstrated by the way in which birds have been known to feed throughout the night at the transmission plant of the Ford Motor Company at Halewood in Lancashire. The factory is brilliantly lit and the sparrows can be seen almost anywhere but they tend to gather where the workers take their regular tea-breaks. I have seen sparrows in the hangars at London Airport, in a restaurant in the London Zoo, on the stages of the BBC's television film studios at Ealing, in the nave of a London church and in a coach of the Bakerloo line of the Underground. Some of the house sparrows that live in industrial habitats appear to suffer from 'industrial discoloration' and their feathers are darkened by some deposit on their surface. The white patches on sparrows that live around various factories are more likely to be of genetic origin than caused by chemical bleaching. Every year I see at least one sparrow in my garden with one or more white feathers in the wing or tail. One hen was so evenly marked that my family used to call her 'Snowfinch'.

Starlings are also able to cope with the noise and disturbance on many industrial sites where they successfully raise young year after year. They have been less able to adapt to the smog which has been produced in many industrial regions. One February morning in 1959 several hundred were found dead in the streets of Sleaford after a night of smog. After an examination of a random selection of corpses the Department of Animal Pathology at Cambridge found that the deaths were largely due to asphyxia resulting from severe smog. Starlings that flew around in fog and were unable to reach their roosts in Bishop's Stortford in January 1958 and on Merseyside in January 1959 were subsequently found to have extensive pulmonary damage. Birds are often disorientated by fog in which the levels of air pollution may be rising.

Students of the Open University have recently completed a study of air pollution in Britain; with the aid of a simple sampling kit the students measured the amount of sulphur dioxide in the atmosphere as an index of pollution and 1500 viable responses were obtained. In the non-smokeless zones there were above average readings in areas of high-density housing, in medium-density housing mixed with industry and in industrial areas with some residential accommodation. As one might have expected the readings were much lower in the open country, in rural communities, in the centres of small towns and in medium-density residential communities without any industry. The students also found that if the weather deteriorated into conditions of overcast and drizzle the recorded sulphur dioxide levels went up. Making zones 'smokeless' did not always have an effect but the sulphur dioxide level was reduced in medium-density residential areas with a little industry. In high-density regions the 'smokeless' ratios were much above the 'non-smokeless'; it was thought that this might be related to the interesting fact that solid smokeless fuels contain some twenty per cent more sulphur than coal while there is also a lot of sulphur in the heavy fuel oils necessary for commercial central heating. Black spots that were found by the Open University students included Dudley, Stockport, Bradford, Rotherham, Nottingham, York, Middlesbrough, Sunderland, Goole, Aberdeen, Hitchin, Grays and Loughton in Essex. All these localities had levels of sulphur dioxide higher than, for example, the official United States quality criterion at which plant injury occurs and leaf drop takes place. Sulphur dioxide penetrates the tissues of plants through the stomata and the cells are destroyed. It would seem that some suburban areas are too polluted to support certain insect-eating birds even where mature or ageing timber can be found. Smoke abatement elsewhere has led to an improvement in insect faunas and the variety of birds dependent upon it. Over the past twenty years British urban concentrations of smoke and sulphur dioxide have dropped by about two-thirds and a quarter respectively but it is estimated that over two million tons of smoke and one million tons of dust are still spread every year over Britain from chimneys and factory outlets. Besides sulphur dioxide the compounds of fluorine and chlorine can also have adverse effects on the plant life. Atmospheric pollution may have been responsible for the disappearance of the nuthatch from some suburban areas but the reduction of smoke in the London area has led to an increase in what John Parslow called 'aerial plankton' available to house martins and swifts which now breed close to the heart of the city. Insect-eating warblers have also increased in the Royal Parks as breeding species. It is interesting to see to what extent some birds will tolerate various kinds of pollution and Max Nicholson has described how a rookery near Newton Abbot survived years of being smothered by white dust from a nearby cement works.

In many parts of the outer suburbs there are gasworks and power stations which form part of the industrial complexes. Here one may also find a community of birds similar to the one that I have described for the factory sites – feral pigeon, starling, house sparrow, pied wagtail and perhaps blackbird. Carrion crows and woodpigeons may rest on the structures and other species may roost in them. Kestrels often nest on gasworks and electricity power stations and their pylons and raise their young on the metal framework of gasholders and on very tall chimneys. In south-eastern England the environs of gasworks and power stations may also attract the black redstart, an exotic bird of the southern Palaearctic which spread north after the last Ice Age and became adapted to a life close to man. Its strange song – a rapid warble followed by a characteristic rattling note – can be heard from the roofs of many buildings in Europe and it has awakened me in dusty villages in Castile, in a back street in Paris, in Alpine villages and among the hills of Greece. The black redstart was first proved to breed in Britain in 1923 and three years later it began to nest annually in the London area. Three pairs bred from 1926–41 over a set of roller doors in the old Palace of Engineering at Wembley. A rise in the population during the 1940s was brought about as a result of the blitz which left many bombed sites behind it and these proved to be very suitable habitats for black redstarts. The birds used ledges for nesting and searched for ants, flies and other insect food among the stones and over the open deserts of rubble. It was at first thought that, as the bombed sites were built over again, the population of black redstarts was going down but B. S. Meadows has shown, after a survey in the London area, that the principal breeding sites had become 'concentrated along parts of the River Thames and River Lea where heavy industry occurs. Outlying heavy industrial areas such as Croydon and the industrial sprawl from Paddington North to White City and Park Royal are also important sites'. The species favours these industrial complexes and clearly dislikes residential suburbia. A survey of birds breeding near London from 1964–69 showed that twenty pairs could be found at power stations, eighteen pairs at gasworks, eleven pairs at other industrial sites including timberyards, railway sidings and riverside warehouses, nine pairs on areas cleared for building and seven pairs on remaining bombed sites. Favourite haunts have been Croydon and West Ham Power Stations and Beckton and Tottenham Gasworks. At Tottenham, where *Chironomid* midges from a polluted stream provide a valuable source of insect food, black redstarts, as well as pied wagtails and swallows, flycatch close to the walls of an electricity station where they are less likely to be attacked by the kestrels which nest on the same site. At Walsall Gasworks a pair of kestrels nested in the retort house. A pair of wheatears spent the summer at Little-brook Power Station and grey wagtails were seen feeding as well. Little ringed plovers and other waders sometimes occur on the ash lagoons at power stations and a great grey shrike was seen at Barking Power Station in December 1970. An interesting development is the introduction of nature trails in the grounds of two Central Electricity Generating Board power stations at Didcot and West Burton.

Before ending this chapter I would like to mention two features of the outer suburbs which deserve attention. The first is what has come to be known as 'the garden suburb' and the second are the new housing developments inside the outer ring of suburbs. Some garden suburbs, like that at Hampstead, are now encompassed by estates built since the First World War but the bird community remains similar to that of the upper middle-class suburbs – richer than that of the surrounding estates but less varied than that in the green belt or on the outer fringes of development. Even the garden warbler has been known to overwinter in Hampstead Garden Suburb, and redpolls and crossbills have been reported as well. Welwyn and Letchworth were conceived as single units set in the countryside and, although they may possess certain features which can also be found inside well-planned 'garden suburbs', they are more town in character than suburban. Incidentally, the bird life of the Letchworth area has been described by A. R. Jenkins. The New Towns, which must owe something to the philosophy and ideas of Ebenezer Howard and are designed to satisfy the demand for individual houses with gardens, are independent and thus not strictly suburbs. If they have suburban features then obviously these must resemble planned suburbs. There seem to be some tendencies towards a residential segregation in the New Towns based on class which complicate the social structure of, say a place like Crawley. The New Towns are often designed by architects trying to bridge the gap between what is desirable in environmental planning and what is economically possible. Avenues of small trees or single trees planted on patches of grass may be all that there is to remind the citizen of the twentieth century of his rural past. Where there is a lack of variety in planning the bird life will be limited too and can perhaps be compared with that in the very early stages of the 1930 estates. Small gardens, too few trees and open spaces, little or no water and a lack of shrubberies are inimical to all but the very hardiest and most adaptable of bird species. There can be very few nest sites and these are essential for a varied bird community. Harlow was designed within a countryside framework and Milton Keynes is to have, so we are told, plenty of trees. It will take some time to judge the results. A suburb or a New Town where houses and factories are set in a varied and sympathetic plan, where trees, shrubs and grass screen and soften the visual impact of many dwelling units, where building materials are chosen with imagination and understanding, and where flowers bloom and birds sing is surely a more satisfying environment for man than regimented rows of boxes in rectangular frames where right angle succeeds right angle and few living things can provide any kind of relief.

Another disturbing feature of suburban life for the conservationist is the growing tendency, as population pressures increase, for the small amounts of open space already squeezed into the outer suburban ring to be 'in-filled' with new working-class planned estates of houses, blocks of flats and schools. The greatest loss is usually that of allotments or 'leisure gardens' as some councils prefer to call them. In 1961 about ten per cent of the area within half a mile of my house was occupied by allotments which provided welcome green oases within the desert of brick and pebble-dash. By 1969 the percentage had fallen to four per cent and three years later to two per cent. In 1974 the figure had sunk to less than one quarter of one per cent. In their place are three schools, blocks of flats and box-like houses with gardens just big enough to hold a rotary clothes drier. The only trees now are new singles planted on the tiny patches of grass and the roads are extended to give parking space for cars. Vandalism often results in damage to the few shrubs or trees that are put in. These planned working-class estates provide much-needed housing but it seems a pity that the quality of their surroundings is often dull and unimaginative.

Other kinds of development on the old allotments include low-rise flats and here fine old thorn hedges have been replaced by functional wooden fences with concrete uprights. The ground is now largely covered with asphalt, concrete and ornamental cobbles. There are a few surviving trees – oaks and horse chestnuts but some of these damaged by the building operations are now dying – and a number of birches, sycamores and other trees have been planted to 'landscape' the small stretches of grass. In the six years since these flats were built no bird has nested within the perimeter fence of the estate. In 1972 I said of this new development: 'A few sparrows and feral pigeons sometimes potter about the roads or rest for brief spells on the roofs. Crows only rarely perch on them, preferring the trees outside from which to keep an eye on the flats. The only birds of interest are those that pass over on migration and for which these flats are just one more part of the growing desert of bricks and mortar beneath them.' Much of this is also true of the larger complexes of tower blocks, clusters of flats and houses in the newer estates. Chalkhill Estate in north-west London, which lies a mile farther out than Dollis Hill, houses some 5000 people in blocks of flats and smaller units at a density of some hundred and thirty-seven to the acre, nearly three times the figure for the inner suburbs of London. There are no gardens here, just heavily trodden lawns and a few trees of which the smaller ones are showing signs of damage from human mishandling. Leo Batten found that the breeding community of birds was restricted to seven species – woodpigeon, blackbird, blue tit, house sparrow, starling, carrion crow and feral pigeon, and most of these were dependent on the few mature trees left standing.

There is a great personal satisfaction in coming to know any small area intimately. In this way it is possible to recognize rises and falls in bird populations, to compare the bird community inside the district with others outside and to discover new species and new colonists. The future of my part of suburban London is changing and this is in the dynamic nature of environments and ecosystems. But I fear that the suburbs of tomorrow will have little or no place for birds unless planning authorities come to recognise the contributions that conservationists can make. It is well known that birds show preferences for certain habitats not only because they offer food and breeding sites but because of what the late Dr David Lack called 'the psychological factor'. As this factor changes for me, so I am sure that I shall find my own part of suburbia less and less appealing.

CHAPTER 4

The Outer Ring ii. *The Open Spaces*

THE ring of outer suburbs around any town or city is generally a patch-work of planned housing estates, factory sites, allotments, parks and playing fields, recreation grounds, cemeteries, churchyards, rubbish dumps and waste ground. The sprawling belts of development are criss-crossed by roads, railways and sometimes rivers and canals. Parts of this complex are sometimes in a state of instability, for example, where older, villa-type houses with large wooded gardens are being replaced by high-density housing estates, where allotment space is being 'in-filled' for houses, schools and reservoirs, where factories are being erected on unused or neglected land and where gardens and trees are being lost to the bulldozers so that main and arterial roads can be widened and improved to form ringways and motorway-type links. Within the outer ring there are often reservoirs and lakes, small pieces of surviving farmland and sometimes golf-courses but I am reserving the birds of these habitats for a later discussion.

As development swallows the remaining open spaces there is an inevitable decline both in the density and the variety of the nesting birds. Leo Batten in his study of the area around the Brent Reservoir found that whereas 71 different species were able to breed when the region was only 10% urbanised, at 30% the total had dropped to 64, at 50% to 53 and, when the building up of the region had reached 65%, only 43 different kinds were recorded. He predicted that when the urbanisation of the district reached 100% there would be only 20 species left; this is about the figure for my estate at Dollis Hill. It is the variety of habitats that produces the greatest number of different breeding species and so the survival of open spaces in our outer suburbs is of vital importance in the conservation of our wildlife.

A glance at the map of the suburban rings around our towns and cities will soon reveal the presence of municipal parks and other often quite small open spaces. Some of the parks are large like Sutton Park near Sutton Coldfield, Woollaton Park near Nottingham, Heaton Park on the outskirts of Manchester, Bute Park in Cardiff and Phoenix Park in Dublin. Generally the parks are rather smaller but are often of great interest like Handsworth Park in Birmingham, Calderstones Park in Liverpool, Roundhay Park in Leeds and Holyrood Park in Edinburgh.

Most of the parks are municipally maintained and typically they consist of areas of grass kept short by periodic cutting with gang-mowers as well as some avenues or groves of tall trees, asphalt paths, flowerbeds, a few shrubberies, tennis courts and perhaps some playing fields and a pond or small lake.

One outer suburban park that I have studied is made up of some seventy acres of land on a south-facing slope. It was established about seventy years ago and is completely surrounded by twentieth-century development. It contains a lot of grassland part of which is used for football pitches in the winter, and this is intersected by long avenues of London planes, while a number of fine oaks and elms from the original house grounds and countryside grow either singly or in clumps on the grass swards. There are also Italian poplars, willows, horse chestnuts, sycamores, cherries, almonds and hawthorns. The shrubberies have always been very few and, at the time of writing, as they have been easily penetrated by children, they are systematically being removed. The most extensive piece of rather thin cover was composed of laburnums, cherries, *Laurestinus* and tamarisks growing up through a thicker layer of *Berberis, Cydonia japonica* and flowering cherry. In this park there are also an open-air swimming pool, a very small lake, a bowling green, a putting area, some hard tennis courts, a house and a walled garden. The typical nesting species number nineteen; they are mallard, woodpigeon, tawny owl, carrion crow, jay, great and blue tits, wren, mistle thrush, song thrush, blackbird, robin, spotted fly-catcher, hedgesparrow, starling, greenfinch, goldfinch, chaffinch and house sparrow. In 1972 the only breeding species in the surrounding suburban area that did not breed in the park but nested on the allot-ments, factory sites and residential estate were six in number; of these, three were only first or second records of nesting (kestrel, whitethroat and willow warbler) while the pied wagtail and tree sparrow were limited to two pairs each on factory and allotment sites and the only numerically significant nesting species missing from the park was the feral pigeon which used it solely for feeding purposes. A pair of stock doves bred in the park until 1954 and may have done so in 1956 and 1957. In 1973 a pair of kestrels nested for the first time but the young birds were stolen from their elm-tree hole by professional collectors. For some years after the last war much of the southern part of the parkland was under cultivation and skylarks bred there every year until the land was rehabilitated.

The various habitats in this park were distinctive and each was im-portant for birds. Feral pigeons can be found near the small lake where they are often fed and, when not foraging, they use an ash tree and a horse chestnut for resting and preening. Their numbers have risen steadily over the years with artificial feeding. The lake is also very popular with mallard which nest in holes in some of the surrounding

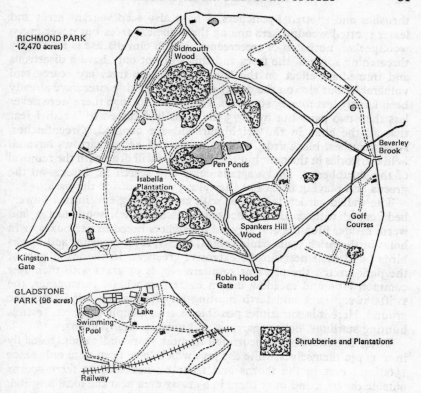

RICHMOND PARK
·(2,470 acres)

Sidmouth
Wood

Beverley
Brook

Pen Ponds

Isabella
Plantation

Golf
Courses

Spankers Hill
Wood

Kingston
Gate

Robin Hood
Gate

GLADSTONE
PARK (96 acres)

Lake

Swimming
Pool

Shrubberies and Plantations

Railway

FIG. 7 Contrast in shrubberies and plantations in two outer suburban parks.
(Not to scale.)

trees. In 1951 the winter maximum for these ducks was only twenty but
ten years later it had risen to 71. Since that year there has been a slow
decline despite a lot of feeding by human visitors and this drop in
numbers is due, I believe, to growing disturbance on a reservoir some
three-quarters of a mile away to which these birds flight both during
the day and night. In spring the mallard explore many places for
breeding sites and I have seen up to twenty-one birds at a time sitting
about in the trees. The open-air swimming pool, which is closed to the
public in winter, provides a peaceful retreat for the mallard and during
one February there was a fine drake pintail there as well.

Two pairs of chaffinches and goldfinches have their territories
among the cherries, almonds and thorns. Several pairs of starlings nest
in the elms, oaks and planes as well as carrion crows, woodpigeons,
great and blue tits, mallard, house sparrows, and occasionally mistle

thrushes and spotted flycatchers. I have also seen vagrant great and lesser spotted woodpeckers among these ancient trees but never green woodpecker, nuthatch or treecreeper. Dutch elm disease is now sadly threatening some of the trees and this will not only have a disastrous and immediate effect on the landscape, where trees are scarce and vulnerable, but also on the tawny owl whose nesting sites have already been largely lost to grey squirrels. From 1951 to 1970 there were never less than two pairs but by 1973 the birds had ceased to breed. I fear that all the elms in the neighbourhood are doomed. Greenfinches, song thrushes, blackbirds, robins, wrens and hedgesparrows have all held territories in the park but their densities will drop with the removal of the shrubberies. Pied wagtails come and search for insects on the greens and playing fields but they always nest outside the park.

The walled garden is laid out with crazy paving and formal flower-beds edged with small box hedges; it is sheltered, south-facing and warm inside. Blue tits and spotted flycatchers breed in nestboxes or in holes in the brick walls while robins, wrens, song thrushes and black-birds build their nests in the extensive creepers. In the lower part of the park stretch the pleasant southern slopes of grass with their few common blue and meadow brown butterflies where, in summer, the swifts sweep back and forth hunting for the insects rising from the ground. Here it is sometimes possible to see a magpie and even kestrels hunting starlings, house sparrows and unwary feral pigeons.

There is quite a heavy acorn fall in most years and woodpigeons fly in to gorge themselves while the jays which have been here only since 1960 and nest in the thorns and taller bushes used to ferry acorns outside the park and bury them in a grassy area near the local hospital. In the winter the grasslands in the park are visited by flocks of starlings, feral pigeons, woodpigeons, carrion crows and, in some recent winters, parties of redwings which roosted in two of the old oaks. Lapwings are occasional visitors and one or two meadow pipits may turn up in winter as well. It is a common sight to see black-headed and common gulls looking for worms on the grass and, in wet conditions, 'paddling' with their feet to induce them to come up to the surface. In February there are often quite large assemblies of common gulls and the biggest that I ever recorded was one of 300 birds in 1958. Herring and lesser black-backed gulls are much less frequent. Woodpigeons roost in the park and are subjected to spasmodic and irregular shoots; they feed in spring on the swelling tree buds. Migrants often appear in the park and swallows and house martins can be watched flying over every year but these visible movements will be more fully discussed in chapter 10.

Brookvale Park in Erdington, Birmingham, is rather similar in some ways to the park that I have just described with well-kept gardens, shrubberies, and both bowling and putting greens. B. W. Jones found that the breeding population had the same basic core of nesting species but its somewhat larger pools provided nest sites for the moorhen and temporary sanctuary for more exotic birds like the great crested grebe, teal, scaup, tufted duck, pochard, goldeneye and smew. The bigger the park lake the greater the numbers and variety of waterfowl that can be observed there. Green and great spotted woodpeckers, goldfinches and coal tits were only visitors to Brookvale but rooks, jackdaws and magpies were resident. Scavenging birds do particularly well in parks and certainly crows, jackdaws, jays, starlings, great tits, blue tits, blackbirds, robins, chaffinches and house sparrows have been seen in London parks exploring the contents of litter baskets. In some of the larger parks in England the hawfinch and the woodcock may nest and since the 1950s goldfinches and bullfinches have been establishing themselves in many parks where there are fairly dense and undisturbed shrubberies. Some of the warblers too may succeed in nesting in small numbers.

London's enormous outer ring of suburbs embraces the Royal Parks of Richmond and Bushey, while other open spaces such as Kew Gardens, Osterley Park and Beckenham Place Park provide important bird habitats and sanctuaries. I have already outlined the bird life of London's Royal Parks in another book and I propose only to indicate the variety of birds that can be found in the parks of outer London. It is possible to find a list of the nesting birds for the larger of these open spaces in appendix 4. Fuller details can be found for most of these areas, where they are Royal Parks, in the reports of the Committee on Bird Sanctuaries in the Royal Parks (England and Wales), published from 1928 onwards and now issued annually free with copies of my book for the Department of the Environment. It is clear from looking at these reports that there is a very wide range of breeding species. The Report for 1971–72 showed that in the latter year there were 39 nesting species in Kew Gardens, 47 in Osterley Park, 48 in Hampton Court and Bushey Parks, and 53 in Richmond Park. The actual total of different kinds observed in that year reached nearly 70 at Kew and hovered below or around the century mark in the three other parks. Of the breeding birds that could be seen in some, if not all, of the parks with more rural habitats, the most interesting included such aquatic species as great crested and little grebes, mallard, tufted duck, moorhen and coot, waterside species such as reed bunting and sedge warbler, park and farmland species such as green woodpecker, jackdaw, pheasant and partridge, woodland species such as great and lesser spotted woodpeckers, jay, coal tit, nuthatch, treecreeper, and finally predatory species such as kestrel, tawny and little owls. Such a variety can only be explained by the range of different habitats to be found in the larger tracts of ground and open space and it can be reproduced in other parks within the outer suburban ring of British towns. Each park may contain a river or large lakes and pools, woodlands, heaths,

grasslands and scrub, and real countryside may indeed not be far away.
Most pieces of parkland are smaller and less varied, of course.
Beckenham Place Park consists of some two hundred acres of land on
the southern outskirts of London not far from Bromley. Here, in 1964,
28 species of bird were found nesting and these included such woodland birds as the nuthatch, treecreeper, redstart, blackcap, garden
warbler, willow warbler and spotted flycatcher; it seemed likely that
kestrel, little owl, tawny owl and great spotted woodpecker had nested
as well. In that year a total of 62 species was actually observed. The
grounds of hospitals often include wide expanses of grass, groves of
trees and shrubberies which resemble parkland in their character. One
hospital that I have known in the outer suburbs has lawns and flowerbeds but also a broad belt of poplars, horse chestnuts, sycamores and
other trees and shrubberies of holly, elder, willow and young elm.
Twenty species have bred here and nearly sixty have occurred over the
years. Within three miles of my home in the outer suburbs there are
seven other hospitals and in their grounds is often a core of suburban
breeding species enhanced by rare nesting birds in some years – birds
such as blackcaps, coal tits and so on.

A particularly interesting habitat in outer suburbia is that formed by
plots of allotments where patches of cultivated earth are set among
strips of grass and weeds rather like the squares on a chess-board.
Cover for birds often exists in nearby hedgerows, bramble brakes and
small planted fruit trees. There is often a small belt of forest trees
growing alongside the allotments and perhaps separating them from
roads, houses and factory buildings; these rows of trees often mark the
old field lines. Water is usually available perhaps from a pond or
stream or more probably from tanks fed by stand-pipes for local
irrigation. There is nothing in nature quite like this habitat which
forms an ecotone, or tension belt, between the environments of farmland and suburban house and garden; it may well contain elements
from both bird communities. The nearer the allotments are to the
town the stronger the suburban element, and the farther away the
greater that of farmland. I have already given an indication of how
much allotment land has been lost in my own suburban area during the
last decade. In 1961 there were four large groups of allotments and three
small ones within half a mile of my house; by 1974 only one of the
small ones still remained representing one fortieth of the 1961 acreage.
While most of the plots were under cultivation the bird community
was a fairly stable one of typically suburban birds enhanced in places
by the presence of trees and cover near at hand. When they began to
deteriorate, after the allotment holders had been given notice, their
value as an environment for some birds rose considerably for a time.

The allotments which I have watched for more than twenty years lie
either on the sunny, southern slopes of a hill or on the summit of a

250-foot cone of land on the London clay. The area of the summit allotments has been reduced in the last five years by half, while in 1974 the remaining half is also being developed. It is interesting to record that at the time of maximum glaciation in the British Isles more than one hundred thousand years ago the ice sheet reached just about as far south as these allotment plots. It left behind over the Eocene clay a greyish friable soil which was easily worked and very different from the London clay below it which is sticky and unworkable in winter and rock hard in summer. There are pebbles of flint up to three inches in length in the glacial deposit. Strawberries have been widely grown on it as well as peas, beans, onions, beetroot, lettuce, cabbage, celery, carrots, Brussels sprouts and such flowers as sweetpeas, dahlias, chrysanthemums, hollyhocks, gladioli and so on. There are a few small isolated fruit trees and a small group of apple trees on one plot only. The allotments cover 6·3 acres and are bordered on one side by a chain-link fence along a road, on the second by a thorn hedgerow and some small trees, a brick wall and a row of garages from the area of flats built earlier on adjoining allotment plots, on the third by some elms, beeches, cherries and sycamores growing on a piece of rough ground and on the fourth side by a belt of mixed trees the other side of a wooden fence.

This strip of trees is a remnant of what was once one of the most important habitats in the area – a small piece of woodland formed by sycamores, elms, ashes, limes, horse chestnuts and ancient pedunculate oaks growing in close canopy. Underneath was a shrub layer of hawthorn, privet, elder and willow, while the ground zone was rich in cow parsley, bluebells, nettles, ivy and pink purslane. Next to it was an old orchard and some chicken runs all forming the most important wildlife sanctuary in the district. Until most of the woodland and all the orchard and the chicken runs were removed for low-rise flats this suburban plot held crows, jays, woodpigeons, great and blue tits, wrens, song thrushes, blackbirds, robins, hedgesparrows, starlings, greenfinches, goldfinches, house and tree sparrows all of which nested every year while tawny owls bred in many years as well. Willow warblers nested in 1957 and may have done so in the preceding two years and blackcaps bred in 1958 and possibly also in 1952, 1955 and 1956, when single pairs were present. In 1969 – a year after the site was largely cleared – chaffinches nested for the first time in my own garden 250 yards away. In winter many nomadic parties of tits used to come to the woodland strip. As a habitat the allotments benefited from the closeness of the trees and there was a constant interchange of birds between the two environments. As it is now known that the allotments will shortly be converted into an underground reservoir crowned with lightweight houses, there has been some vandalism among the trees whose trunks have been burned or hacked and I have been trying to persuade the

Brent Council which has shown considerable interest in and sympathy for conservation matters to preserve the last trees before it is too late.

On the fringe of the allotments are several old oaks and these provide the breeding headquarters for two pairs of tree sparrows. This tiny colony is the nearest to central London from the north-west but it cannot possibly survive the development that is about to take place. Already the growing disturbance has led a pair to nest in one of my tit boxes in the spring of 1973 but, although four eggs were laid, the adults eventually, to my deep regret, deserted. Had they managed to breed I might just have saved half this precious little colony. The footholds that tree sparrows have in partly built-up areas are often precarious and colonies may consist of only a few pairs. Yet in Scandinavia, Russia and the Far East they are very much birds of towns and buildings and live side by side with the house sparrow. A small pond nearby used by the tree sparrows for drinking has recently been drained. It had survived from the pre-estate farm. Common newts spawned in it and mallard used to nest by it and went on visiting it until the spring of 1973.

The community of breeding birds on the allotments themselves was a fairly simple one. In fact the dominant breeding birds in descending order were blackbird, hedgesparrow, song thrush, robin, wren, greenfinch, chaffinch and mallard. The fruit trees and bramble bushes satisfied some of the shrub nesters while thrushes and blackbirds built also on the ledges of fences and among the creepers on some of the sheds.

On the southern limits of my study area is a region which was once entirely composed of allotment plots. About one third of it is now occupied by rows of small box-like houses. In March 1973 the remaining two-thirds were cleared to make way for a large comprehensive school as well as some playing fields and open space. At my request this area was scoured by the bulldozers and excavators before the breeding season to avoid the wholesale destruction of the eggs and young birds of a community that had grown in density since the allotments fell into disuse. Into oblivion were swept several tall poplars, thickets of sallow and hawthorn, blackthorn and bramble as well as thick hedges and a few small oaks. I listed the plants that grew here before the clearance and they included some interesting species for a suburban area – hedge mustard, bladder campion, greater stitchwort, cow parsley, hogweed, cut-leaved geranium, hop trefoil, meadow pea, field rose, comfrey, burdock, viper's bugloss, common hemp nettle, wild teasel, hardheads, bristly ox-tongue, black bryony, cock's foot, Yorkshire fog, common marestail and two single plants of compact rush. With lack of cultivation, goldenrod, Michaelmas daisy, garden arabis and celery had spread widely over the area. This was the only locality in my study area for the large skipper butterfly, while meadow browns were abundant.

A few hedgehogs and woodmice lived there and there was also a small colony of domestic rabbits.

As plots were increasingly left to themselves the density of breeding birds went up, especially of blackbirds, song thrushes, wrens, robins, hedgesparrows, greenfinches and goldfinches. In May 1955 there had been two singing whitethroats but they did not find mates. Seventeen years later, in the summer of 1972, a pair did nest and I also watched a pair of willow warblers and a second singing male which departed towards the end of May. The willow warblers successfully reared young in a bramble brake – the first breeding record in the area since 1957. Jays and carrion crows have been regular visitors in summer and in recent years a magpie has been present as well. These neglected allotments were richer in the variety of breeding species and in the density of nesting birds than the summit allotments where the plots were regularly worked. In fact, they more closely resembled some allotments a mile to the north, which were censused by J. H. Wood in 1968 and 1969, but which, like my summit plots, also carried dense hawthorn thickets and hedges, fences, a few elms and oaks along the boundaries and plenty of sheds and lockers for tools. This census plot to the north was described by Leo Batten as 'a mosaic of small holdings with a considerable variety of crops including potatoes, turnips, strawberries, runner beans, tomatoes and other vegetables'. This was quite a rich habitat for birds and, being farther away from the town than my allotments, had a community structure more like that of farmland. In all there were 21 breeding species on the 29 acres of allotments – this was a much higher total than I could muster for my two groups of plots. The census gave the percentages of total pairs – what is called the dominance – as follows; blackbird 23·6, greenfinch 14·1, hedgesparrow 12·2, linnet 11·4, song thrush 6·3, goldfinch 5·1, wren 4·5, robin 4·3, skylark 4·0, blue tit 3·1, whitethroat 2·8, chaffinch 2·0, great tit 2·0, bullfinch 1·2, while the remaining small group was made up of spotted flycatchers, reed buntings, tree sparrows, lesser whitethroats, sedge warblers, magpies and kestrels. House sparrows could not be censused and so were not included in the percentages. The dominant positions of linnet, skylark and whitethroat all reflect the more 'rural' nature of these plots and the presence of reed buntings and sedge warblers the existence of water not too far away.

In the migration seasons my allotments have been important as feeding areas and, from the elevated position of one group, valuable for carrying out visible migration watches. They provided resting places too for many night migrants which I have seen shortly after dawn dropping down from the sky into the tree canopies and into the bramble clumps, especially blackbirds, song thrushes, redwings and warblers. In the autumn months, besides the migrants, flocks of up to a hundred house sparrows came to feed on the plots; they searched chiefly for the seeds of grasses, chickweeds and docks. Small numbers of tree sparrows joined the resident birds and both species used to assemble in a thick thorn hedge for resting, preening and as a point of vantage. Linnets were present each winter in small numbers while visits from both the bullfinch and the redpoll were increasing with each season. Flocks of from thirty to forty greenfinches and goldfinches were often present from late summer to spring. In the autumn of 1973 the greenfinch flock on the neglected summit allotments rose to sixty in size. The chaffinch is always a very scarce bird in the winter months but is one of the commonest autumn migrants passing overhead. The four kinds of finch favour different foods and Ian Newton has described that of the greenfinch as chiefly the seeds of chickweed, dandelion, groundsel, goat's beard, charlock and persicaria all of which grew on the plots that I studied. The goldfinch with a thinner bill probes into the heads of such composite plants as thistles, dandelions, groundsels, teasels and burdocks all of which again grew on my southern allotment plots. The bullfinch with a larger beak cannot insert it into the seeding heads and so it bites off pieces from the side of the seedhead and these are turned in the bill to remove the seeds. 'The bullfinch', according to Dr Newton, 'is thus limited to feeding from those *Compositae* which have small, soft seed-heads, such as sowthistles (*Sonchus*) and groundsels (*Senecio*), and does not normally tackle the larger thistles (*Cardus, Cirsium, Onopordon*).' The linnet has a short broad bill and specializes in the seeds of farmland weeds especially brassicas, fat hen, mugwort and persicaria. On my allotments the redpoll seemed to favour willow-herbs and mugwort but the tansy, also mentioned by Dr Newton as a favourite food, did not grow there. Chaffinches forage very much on farmland looking for cereal grains and they will also take the seeds of common weeds but the bird is a rarity on many suburban allotments.

Other regular winter visitors to the allotments were woodpigeons and jays which caused some alarm among the human tenants but did not result in any direct action against them. Feral pigeons could be seen searching for weed seeds while great and blue tits used to hunt through the small trees, brambles and bean poles for aphids. Small flocks of starlings worked their way over the plots, a few meadow pipits overwintered each year but the pied wagtail was rather scarce. Kestrels were irregular visitors and never hunted over these allotments very seriously. In the autumn of 1973 grass choked many of the plots and I have never seen so many common field grasshoppers. Although finches were still able to feed on various seeds on plants growing above the grass stems, song thrushes, blackbirds, robins and wrens largely disappeared. A few blackbirds came for the blackberries but they did not settle on the ground any more. At all times of the year allotments play an important part in the life of many birds and their replacement by buildings and sports fields can only lead to an impoverishment in the density and variety of the bird life.

Scattered throughout the outer ring of suburbs are many small pieces of land that can best be described as waste. They could be a cleared bombed site, a bit of land fenced off and awaiting an unknown future, derelict industrial sites, old spoil tips, quarries, marl holes, disused dockland areas, rubbish tips, unused railway tracks and abandoned lines, or even a cemetery never put to its original purpose and allowed to become overgrown. This kind of habitat can range from a bare, unpromising desert of rubble and stones with a few stunted plants to a rich 25-foot high piece of scrub and woodland. In the outer suburbs wasteland may be quite ephemeral whereas in the neighbourhood of industrial towns it may be quite persistent.

In its initial stages a piece of wasteland consists of bare ground derived perhaps from the original earth after the passage of a bulldozer or from the detritus of brickworks, coal mines, quarries, clay pits and dumped rubble. Man has scratched away and delved into many parts of the land leaving cavities and scars which can remain almost immutable. In some places the richness of the soil or the steepness of exposed and artificial slopes is such that the undisturbed growth of plants and scrub has created miniature wildlife sanctuaries. In the slate-bearing regions of North Wales and among the coalfields of the south huge ugly tips of rock, shale and spoil mar the countryside and many suburban districts. At some of them mosses, lichens and a few ferns struggle on and give them a less artificial look. Perhaps a few pipits can be heard, a starling may have a nest on the side of a digging or in a pile of stones or slates while in the north of the Principality a few choughs build their nests in the old quarries. In others there may be pied wagtails, stock doves and perhaps kestrels. Old lead and copper workings can show a high toxicity to plant life but if there are spoil heaps of non-economic materials brought to the surface as well these may be colonized by plants. William Condry has found that at a copper mine near Dolgellau there 'grows an abundance of thrift and vernal sandwort'. The tips from limestone workings and cement factories are often rich in scrub and may carry a representative community of the birds of developing woodland. Some of the disused non-toxic heaps are being planted with trees while others have grown their own green coat of birch or thorn. The Coal Board deliberately afforests some of the old tips and heaps and allows forestry interests to look after others that they own.

In the beginning a piece of non-toxic wasteland is steadily colonized by plants. The first-comers are those with wind-borne fruits – what Richard Fitter and J. E. Lousley called the 'advance guard of parachute troops' – rosebay, Oxford ragwort, Canadian fleabane, common and sticky groundsels. Other wind-carried plants include coltsfoot, mug-

wort, creeping thistle and sow thistle. Coltsfoot has long scaly underground stems which creep below the fine top surface of rubble while
another important colonist – bracken – sends its roots deep down into
cracks and crevices in the coarser rubble below. Other plants may be
introduced on the shoes of pedestrians and the wheels of cars, from
alfresco meals, from nearby gardens and the excreta of birds. These
plants of the waste ground were a feature of the bombed sites after the
last war and were well described by Richard Fitter in *London's Natural
History*.

As the plants take hold and begin to produce seed so the seed-eating
birds begin to arrive and we saw in the last chapter how attractive these
areas can be for birds. As the flora becomes properly established so the
number of insects and other invertebrates begins to rise. One piece of
cleared ground with a developing plant life was shown to hold 13
different kinds of butterfly, 31 kinds of the larger moths, 12 different
sawflies, 21 spiders as well as other small animals including snails and
slugs. Such a piece of land must have an attraction for birds. A small
strip of wasteland close to the BBC Television Centre provided the
subject of a twenty-minute film that I directed for television. It was
about thirty yards square and was completely surrounded by a high
chain-link fence. Weeds grew in profusion and there were many kinds
of invertebrate life. Starlings, house sparrows, feral pigeons, woodpigeons and greenfinches came regularly to this tiny bit of enclosed
land completely surrounded by towering blocks of flats. In 1952, on a
similar piece of ground at Woodford Green in Essex, I watched a
pair of red-backed shrikes feeding a fledgling.

In the last few years some sixty acres of wasteland have appeared in
the neglected and derelict Surrey Docks which have become overgrown with weeds, bushes and small trees, revealing a natural plant
succession. Here in 1970 three or four pairs of linnets bred – an
example of a seed-eating bird – as well as some seven or eight pairs of
yellow wagtails – essentially insect-eating birds. The latter species can
survive on grassy waste ground and in 1937 two pairs of these attractive
wagtails nested on such land by the edge of the Latymer Upper School
playing fields in West London: I used to watch them between the
overs! The dockland area also held three pairs of skylarks – birds which
eat about equal amounts of plant and insect food. A cock whitethroat
was heard in song but perhaps the most surprising visitors was a pair
of red-legged partridges that were first observed in June 1971 and then
again in late August of that year but this time with eight small young.
In October and November a covey of twelve birds was seen. In 1973
lapwings, ringed plover, little ringed plover, reed bunting, yellow
wagtail, skylark, red-legged partridge, sedge warbler, whitethroat,
meadow pipit, goldfinch and linnet were all reported nesting. The
commoner species such as blackbird, hedgesparrow, pied wagtail,

starling, greenfinch and house sparrow appeared as well with occasional redpolls and meadow pipits. This site is, of course in Inner London and close to the river, but its avifauna shows very clearly how birds will take advantage of patches of undisturbed wasteland when they become available. In 1968 yellow wagtails also nested on a three-acre piece of derelict land not far away from the Surrey Docks which, according to L. W. Cornelius, was 'strewn with rubble and covered with typical bombed site vegetation (common melilot, mugwort and rosebay the dominant species)'. On suburban wasteland the variety of birds may be quite high and rubbish tips, water-filled gravel pits and sewage farms may be productive places as we shall see later in this chapter and in the book.

Some of the most extensive urban and suburban areas of derelict land are to be found in the industrial regions of the Midlands and the north of Britain. In the 'Six Towns' of Stoke-on-Trent rows of terraced houses can be found grouped around old coal mines, clay pits and pottery factories. Once-thriving industries have left behind them whole areas of wasteland whose character gives an unmistakable look to the whole environment. Spoil tips dominate the skyline and disused marl pits reflect in their dull waters the drifting smoke of the Potteries. With their fringe areas these grim tracts of land form a considerable region of derelict space – bigger, in fact, than that in any other County Borough in the country. In 1969 there were 1648 acres of this waste ground with the prospect of more arising from the running down of local mineral operations. Only Dudley, Walsall and West Bromwich approached Stoke in their total amounts of derelict space. The City of Stoke-on-Trent's programme for the reclamation of this land is one of the most advanced in the country with plans for landscaped 'forest parks' at Hanley, a sports arena in an old marl hole, a new horizon of levelled and afforested tips and the preservation of 'walk-about' and 'kick-about' zones for recreation. The old railway tracks will be planted with attractive berry-bearing shrubs and any thorn hedges will be kept to ensure green corridors to link various parts of the complex together. Full provision was also to be made for picnic sites, car parks, a riding centre and ski-slope, camp sites and playgrounds. In some areas semi-mature and large trees would be introduced to give an 'initial visual impact'.

This imaginative scheme of landscape renewal was the brainchild of forward conservation planning and both the Staffordshire Trust for Nature Conservation and Land Use Consultants, under the Chairmanship of Max Nicholson, the former Director-General of the Nature Conservancy, are involved. At the time of writing the bird life is not especially varied and is made up of elements from an agricultural and a low scrub community. In autumn I have watched some very large flocks of linnets on the tips as well as greenfinches and goldfinches. The new schemes are designed to rebuild from a study of the surrounding countryside the pre-industrial pattern of semi-natural vegetation and to establish on the raw clay and shale soils new areas of woodland, scrub and grassland. The Staffordshire Trust which has suggested suitable trees and other plants for establishment is also supplying the seeds of common local flowers to assist the natural colonization of eroding or slipping banks and slopes. This is a long-term scheme and the objective is to clear all derelict land within the next few years. It will be interesting to trace its success as a practical exercise in reclamation and conservation and to watch the growth of bird communities within these areas.

Just as there can be a succession of plant life in a wood, so provided the soil is not too 'hungry', there can also be one on waste ground from the first weed colonists to a scrub stage of developing shrubs and trees. Bushes can be mixed with tree seedlings but the scrub is usually fairly open in places and may hold both a varied flora and fauna. Scrub itself is an ecotone between forest and prairie but 'before forest can conquer the grassland surrounding it, shrubs are needed as the pioneer invaders'. Scrub is a familiar sight in many places but its development is less common in urban and some suburban areas. It best establishes itself on undisturbed ground that can be found on some factory sites, on bits of marginal land, by the sides of reservoirs and railways, near allotments and by the edge of existing woodlands.

A remarkable example of this kind of scrub can be found on some twenty-four acres of land in the Borough of Brent. The ground was intended to be a cemetery and was initially equipped with a chapel, a shelter and work accommodation for the staff, but after 1965 it was no longer needed. It retained some mature oak and elm trees, some patches of gorse and a small rather polluted stream from the open countryside before the plot was fenced. On the boundaries lay houses, roads and some playing fields. Regenerating elm is now colonizing a field inside the fencing while hawthorn, blackthorn and oak scrub is rising to a height of 25 feet. The mammal and insect life is very varied; there are foxes, moles, grey squirrels, short-tailed voles, pigmy shrews, hedgehogs and weasels among the mammals while the range of butterflies includes the Essex skipper in its first recorded Middlesex station.

In a detailed study of this old cemetery plot Leo Batten found some 210 pairs of birds holding territories in the 24 acres it covered. He reported that 'This is one of the highest densities recorded in any British woodland type, whether native trees or exotic.' Suburban woodlands do hold high densities of birds but the almost unique character of this particular one is attributed to the wide diversity of habitats and the presence of nearby gardens as an additional source of food. Twenty-six species of bird bred regularly and an average assessment over three years showed the following number of territories;

blackbird 37, robin 27, hedgesparrow 23, song thrush 17, blue tit 16, wren 14, great tit 12, greenfinch 10, willow warbler 7, bullfinch 5, blackcap 4, whitethroat 3, willow tit, carrion crow, lesser whitethroat, goldfinch, chaffinch, all 2 each, and 1 each for mallard, kestrel, magpie, jay, coal tit, garden warbler, chiffchaff, yellowhammer and reed bunting. In addition, cuckoo, pheasant, spotted flycatcher, mistle thrush and redpoll held territories in only one of the three years. A pair of grasshopper warblers nested in 1964 and a pair of whinchats in 1960. Turtle dove, skylark, swallow, house martin, tree pipit and linnet were observed but not thought to be holding territories. This is very much a scrub and woodland avifauna but its richness, just seven miles from the centre of a big city, is remarkable. It proves beyond question the enormous value to wildlife of an undisturbed area of woodland, even a small one, inside an outer ring of suburbs. This remarkable habitat, once threatened by housing developments, is now preserved as an educational field centre protected inside a ring of allotments, a plants nursery, gardens and an adventure playground. If municipal authorities could be persuaded that the conservation of such an area was worthwhile then suburban birds and other wildlife would have protection and security. Surrounding and more typically suburban habitats would benefit from the spill-over from the sanctuary's reserves of species and numbers. Where small pieces of woodland and scrub are close to new housing estates they are likely to suffer from wanton vandalism and from the treading down of the shrub layer and ground zone. Only proper fencing which can also deter the dumping of rubbish can give any sort of protection.

Each year in Britain we use and discard 750 million paper bags, 375 million aerosols and perhaps 1000 million cans as well as vast quantities of plastic waste. Local authorities have to collect and dispose of nearly 20 million tons of domestic refuse every year. The cleansing departments of our municipal authorities are faced with a growing problem in the disposal of household and industrial waste. There are usually four courses available to them – open dumping, controlled tipping (land fill), composting and incineration. The open dumping system has been widely employed in recent years, disfiguring the landscape and giving rise to obnoxious smells. Controlled tipping is quite widely practised; the percentage of rubbish disposed of in this way by one Midland town rose from only 20% in 1936 to 80% in 1955. In many outer suburban areas, including parts of London, the refuse is deposited on areas of wasteland, particularly old diggings and quarries, marshy ground, pools, reservoir edges and similar sites. Typical sites that I have seen include an old stone quarry on the outskirts of Swanage, wet ground in the Gordano Valley in Somerset and the fringes of the Brent Reservoir in north-west London. The dumps rise in height and may be finally sealed with earth perhaps to be developed with houses or sown and converted into playing fields and recreation grounds. Despite the apparently unprepossessing character of this waste ground habitat, there is often a most interesting bird life to be found especially on the larger tips.

It is a fascinating and remarkable experience to visit a large rubbish tip during, say, an October morning. Lorries are departing and others are arriving to discharge their loads of rubbish in a white flurry of screaming black-headed and common gulls. Overhead herring gulls and black-backed gulls circle and glide, waiting until the lorry departs before dropping down with thrashing wings to scuffle and fight among their smaller relatives. Here in this jungle world of the rubbish dump it is 'devil-take-the-hindmost'. Not far away a black flock of crows and visiting rooks is sweeping back and forth over the mounds of refuse wreathed in white drifts of slowly rising smoke. Noisy and aggressive starlings are picking over the rejectamenta of a city, rising up in alarm as a great black-backed gull swoops low over them and then dropping down once more to take up their anxious feverish quest. The air carries a peculiarly sharp fetor of unclean dustbins and of acrid subterranean fires. You have to pick your way over rusting bicycle frames and bits of twisted metal, around grey-green sagging mattresses, disembowelled chairs and settees and ancient brown-stained stoves and refrigerators. It is just possible, above the sharp cacophony of caws and screams and the roar of engines, to hear the thin torrent of a late skylark's song coming from the sky above, and a sudden burst of liquid notes betrays a charm of goldfinches dipping in flashes of gold over the mounds of stinking, smouldering rubbish. From near your feet come the sudden strident rasps of a house cricket basking in the artificial warmth of his strange compost heap which gives him life in an alien land. There is a late wasps' nest in the steep bank of boxes, paper, bottles, tins and tyres, nurtured by the same warmth and revealed by a double trail of worker wasps flying back and forth on their hard-working forays. A large rat squeezes its way out from under a crushed and rusty biscuit tin, dragging its tail over the muddy filth and watched by a kestrel hanging with winnowing wings above the dump. Now oily black pools and deep ruts make the going hard while Corporation employees give ribald encouragement. It is a strange world indeed but on an October day there may be more birds present, both in number and variety, than in any other habitat for miles around.

The actual habitats on a rubbish tip can vary quite a lot and these were investigated by A. Gibbs from a three-year survey into the bird life of the dumps which lay inside London's outer suburban ring or on the edge of the countryside. In the former group were Charlton and Hendon in Middlesex, Fairlop and Ripple Level in Essex, and Walton in Surrey. The latter group of rather more rural tips included Holwell Hyde and Lodge Hollow in Hertfordshire, Leatherhead in Surrey and

Pratt's Bottom in Kent. Rubbish tips were found during the survey to range in size from just a pile of cans in the corner of a field to a square mile or more in extent. Gibbs divided the areas of the dumps and tips into seven different habitats which he listed as follows:

1. *Original ground*	Pools, marshy land, scrub, rough pasture, gravel and other diggings.
2. *Refuse colonized by plants*	Layers of old tipped materials such as ashes, soot and earth compacted and overgrown with plants.
3. *Open 'spoil'*	Bare stretches of ground without plants but useful as resting places for birds.
4. *Buildings*	Permanent structures to house incinerators, processing machinery and sheds.
5. *Fresh domestic and industrial rubbish*	Recently delivered and perhaps burning material, largely composed of cardboard boxes, paper, tins, bottles and stale food.
6. *Processed rubbish*	Piles of 'macerated' domestic rubbish, ash, peelings, glass, plastic broken into small pieces.
7. *Water*	Areas of shallow puddles and waterlogged ruts.

The survey showed that the most regular bird visitors were various gulls and crows, house sparrows, starlings, feral pigeons, kestrels and pied wagtails. The chief attraction for the birds is the food, of course, and this is retrieved very largely from the fresh and 'processed' rubbish and only pied wagtails and kestrels did not feed directly on food in the rubbish. The new deliveries of refuse were eagerly awaited and examined by the gulls but the greatest feeding activity took place on the mounds of processed material where 'many hundreds of Starlings, Sparrows, *Corvidae*, Feral Pigeons and gulls may be seen packed tightly into a small area, frantically scratching and pecking about like Domestic Hens'.

Where areas of the tip become overgrown with bushes then a scrub bird community may form. Yellow wagtails have nested at several dumps where there is grassy vegetation, and they have also been known to breed at slag heaps in the Potteries and pit mounds at Bilston. Whinchats have also been reported nesting at sites not covered by the survey. Grey wagtails have reared young at Fairlop and oyster-catchers have bred by the rubbish dump at Rainham Marsh in Essex. The tips are really better known for their foraging birds and of these the gulls must be the most conspicuous and easily observed. Counts were made at the various tips and these showed that the black-headed gull was the most numerous in winter, ranging in numbers from about five hundred birds at Charlton to 4000 at Holwell Hyde. Herring gulls were common in autumn and winter with two or three hundred at most tips and up to a thousand at Fairlop. Common gulls were reported at all the tips with numbers ranging from around fifty at Hendon to five hundred at Holwell Hyde. The largest number of lesser black-backed gulls was seen between July and October with a maximum of about a thousand at the Fairlop dump. Great black-backed gulls were less common but a hundred or so often remained at Holwell Hyde for much of the winter and there were up to two hundred at Walton one December. The gulls searched for food in all parts of the tips and were even seen to fly inside the drifting smoke in their quest for scraps.

It is only in the last sixty years or so that the gulls' habit of spending the winter inland has become widespread. A British Trust for Ornithology investigation in 1952–53 found some 333,000 gulls wintering inland; eleven years later the total had shot up to 500,000. The birds were very largely concentrated in three regions – the reservoirs and tips around London, the Midlands and East Anglia, and a belt across industrial Lancashire and Yorkshire. This marked rise in numbers has been attributed to a population explosion among the gulls of the Baltic countries and other parts of Europe and to a rise in controlled tipping in those areas where there are also reservoirs to give the birds safe and undisturbed roosting places. The actual numbers of gulls at any of the rubbish tips seems also to depend on the amount of disturbance they have to face there.

Carrion crows, rooks and jackdaws also visit tips but they rather depend on the proximity of other feeding areas. Rooks, for example, will fly up to three miles or more from rural areas in the north to reach the Hendon dump. House sparrows are common visitors and after 207 of these birds had been collected from the Oxford rubbish tip it was found that they were unusually and uniformly dark. The washing and drying of their skins resulted in a considerable lightening in all the specimens and revealed natural pigments that had been obscured. The conclusion was that the whole sparrow population at the Oxford tip was discoloured in this way – a warning to those who might have thought that this was an example of melanism in a local population. Pied wagtails feed around the fresh refuse and near the puddles, while the commonest finches are chaffinches with varying numbers of linnets, goldfinches, greenfinches, bramblings and tree sparrows. Skylarks and meadow pipits were found on tips with open, weed-covered areas while scarcer visitors often included tits, woodpigeons, wheatears, whinchats, stonechats, bullfinches and lesser spotted woodpeckers. Jays and magpies were seen at some of the more rural dumps, and coots and moorhens were observed at Charlton feeding on the tip away from their usual pool. A common sandpiper and a swan were recorded by a pool on the Hendon site and I have watched a hooded crow in the same place but it is a scarce bird there. This is a different situation from that at the turn of the century when Charles Dixon reported that 'The traveller by rail on any of the north-bound trains from the Metropolis is sure to see the Hooded Crow here and there in the fields.' Short-eared owls,

BLACKBIRD, the typical nesting bird of suburban gardens. *Above*, male in breeding plumage; *below*, female with young in nest.

ROBIN and BLUE TIT, two mainly insect-eating species of suburbia. *Above,* robin in song; *below,* blue tit.

merlins and sparrowhawks have been seen on the grassland and rubbish dumps near Southampton Docks and an interesting stranger at the Meads tip near Bishop's Stortford was a fulmar flying among the gulls. In February 1963 there were 24 whooper swans on the Drogheda town rubbish dump in Eire. Of course, car breakers' yards and the premises of scrap-iron merchants may sometimes be used as nesting sites and ports of call for migrant birds.

The most remarkable rubbish dump that I have ever visited was at Entressen in La Crau in southern France in 1973. Here the refuse from the city of Marseilles is banked up in twenty-foot high mountains over hundreds of acres of land. This was a controlled tip but a large section of it was still open and fierce winds had carried plastic and paper bags, cardboard boxes and fabric hundreds of yards from the dump, festooning trees, bushes, fences and even rooftops with ghostly white banners. A high chain-link fence had been broken down and was no longer able to trap the blowing refuse. In many ways the bird life was not so surprising and not so different from that on a British dump. Vast numbers of jackdaws, feral pigeons, magpies and house sparrows were searching for food scraps on the tip while herring gulls, but this time of the Mediterranean race, flew overhead in big flocks. What made it more interesting, however, were the black kites beating in their characteristically buoyant way above the strange ugly landscape. Twelve of them were sitting hunched and disconsolate in a dead tree just like the hooded vultures I watched in a tree by the village rubbish dump at Seronera on the Serengeti Plains. Nightingales sang close by, a great spotted cuckoo rasped out his calls and crickets chirped around my feet as I stood in the centre of this man-made shambles.

Within three miles of my home in north-west London there are eight cemeteries, a crematorium and a large number of churchyards of varying size and richness in their shrub and tree growth. Like the grounds of some hospitals these spaces can all provide valuable and undisturbed retreats for suburban birds. It has been estimated that there are perhaps about 18,000 churchyards in England, providing 20,000 acres of wildlife sanctuary sometimes in the middle of apparently unpromising environments. Some species such as the jackdaw, swift, feral pigeon, house sparrow and barn owl may actually nest in the towers and steeples while rooks, jays, woodpigeons and tawny owls may breed in the broad-leaved trees in the churchyards. One of the features of many churchyards are the conifers that can be found growing in them. The commonest are examples of the native yew but Kenneth Williamson has also indicated the presence of more exotic conifers that were planted in the middle of the nineteenth century, including the Sawara and Hinoki cypresses from Japan, the Chinese Arborvitae, Mediterranean cypresses, Wellingtonias and Monkey-puzzles. Where conifers occur in churchyards the coal tit, goldcrest and collared dove may nest while the treecreepers excavate roosting places in the soft bark of the Wellingtonias. There may perhaps be redpolls and sometimes, after a Continental invasion, a few crossbills but the community is very much a scrub or woodland one.

Kenneth Williamson's study of the bird life in the churchyard at Tring in Hertfordshire has provided an interesting insight into the value of this kind of habitat. Here there are wild flowers in plenty and the lichens showed a very wide range of species. George Barker found, by the way, that in the London area 65% of lichens occur in churchyards and cemeteries and that they 'can be relatively accurately dated and their rates of growth measured. This has some bearing on recording the effects of air pollution'. In a churchyard the combination of buildings and walls, grass, trees, shrubs and a few wild spots, enriched perhaps with nettles, forms a congenial environment for animals and plants which may be under pressure in the rest of the neighbourhood. There were 23 breeding species of bird at Tring and of these the dominant one was the greenfinch representing about sixteen per cent of the total; this is a bird that has adapted quite well to the suburban environment. Blackbird and house sparrow were close behind with 11% each, followed by blue tit and hedgesparrow at 8% each, song thrush, robin and starling at 6%, great tit and wren at 4%, bullfinch and chaffinch at 3%, feral pigeon and blackcap at 2% and then at 1% each – woodpigeon, collared dove, swallow, house martin, carrion crow, jackdaw, coal tit, goldcrest and linnet. It would be interesting to know more about the association between yews and coal tits and goldcrests. I know of at least three instances where in one area the only breeding pairs of goldcrests are in churchyards or large gardens where these trees are present. It seems likely too that more than three hundred and fifty churchyards have yew trees more than two and a half centuries old. At Tring there were also records of swift, treecreeper, pied wagtail, sedge warbler and lesser whitethroat with the last two obviously migrants which passed on. Churchyards have been described by Williamson as 'nature reserves in miniature' and they perhaps need to be managed so that the best parts may be preserved and 'tidying up' operations controlled to avoid the destruction of the wilder parts. Too much spraying and thinning out of the shrub layer would seriously affect the insect life and the scrub birds. Perhaps this kind of management would best come from the local County Naturalists' Trusts.

Tring was a rich and valuable reservoir of birds but other churchyards may support additional bird species. I have seen both kestrels and barn owls in church towers while the trees in some places have been the homes of stock doves, great spotted and green woodpeckers, jays, nuthatches, mistle thrushes, redstarts and spotted flycatchers. Some shrub layers have held long-tailed and marsh tits while I have also watched pheasants and willow warblers among the gravestones. In winter the yews and other berry-bearing trees are often stripped by the local thrushes and blackbirds while redwings and fieldfares may come in from outside for the berry harvest. Elders will attract starlings and parties of finches will search out any thistles or other seeding plants. Churchyards are usually different in character from their immediate surroundings and should be looked upon as the centre of a wider environment.

Cemeteries usually represent a much bigger tract of land. Some of the newer ones are just plain open spaces of grass with symmetrically arranged headstones, small ornamental trees, roses and flowerbeds. Here the short well-mown turf can offer a useful feeding ground for thrushes, starlings, crows, pigeons, pied wagtails and house sparrows which may breed in nearby houses, gardens or parks. A few gulls may come in winter to search the lawns for worms and other small animals. There is usually a lack of breeding sites, territories are few and the distant sound of taped music perhaps replaces the songs of birds. In those parts of suburbia where there are still older, larger cemeteries, perhaps in a state of increasing neglect, the story will be different. Victorian cemeteries like those at Nunhead, Highgate and Kensal Green are especially vulnerable to the ravages of time, but with their groves of limes and horse chestnuts, their shrubs of laurel and privet and their ivy-covered monuments they are now important wildlife reserves. With graves sometimes prised open and desecrated and the tombstones damaged by vandals, these old burial places are obviously running down. Eventually they will be cleared since their cost of up-keep is high and carefully managed municipal cemeteries generally are much more appealing.

Burial grounds certainly may be important to wildlife and foxes have been reported breeding at East Finchley, Hendon Park, Highgate, Wallington, Crystal Palace and Beckenham in the London suburbs. Similarly they provide sanctuaries for birds. I have visited some of the old-established cemeteries and have recorded mallard, carrion crow, jay, starling, mistle thrush, song thrush, blackbird, robin, wren, hedgesparrow, pied wagtail, spotted flycatcher, great tit, blue tit, coal tit, greenfinch, goldfinch, redpoll, bullfinch, house sparrow, goldcrest and tawny owl; this is almost a typical list of outer suburban birds. Redpolls have been known to nest by Golders Green Crematorium and in 1949 barn owls bred in Elmers End Cemetery, both in the outer suburbs of London. In 1948 young red-backed shrikes – at a time when the species was still breeding in a number of English and Welsh counties – were seen entering a large wire refuse basket in Putney Vale Cemetery to look for insects among the wreaths and dead flowers. Another pair of shrikes bred in Lavender Hill Cemetery near Enfield in 1954. It is always possible for quite uncommon birds to find a haven in these places and since 1937 Brompton Cemetery, which is, of course, in inner London, has held nesting great tits, house sparrows, song thrushes, robins, spotted flycatchers, goldfinches, mallard, and the scarcer species such as jays and black redstarts. Migrants often use cemeteries for rest and food and the hoopoe which I saw in May, 1973, stayed several days in Roundwood Park in Brent but also sought retreat in the nearby cemetery where it was not disturbed.

The extensive areas of railway sidings, yards and tracks in the outer suburbs are often comparatively empty of birds but, where coaches and other rolling stock are cleaned, house sparrows, feral pigeons, carrion crows, starlings and gulls are the most frequent visitors, foraging for scraps from the trains as well as food left by the railway workers. Near town centres the embankments are often concreted or bricked but cavities and cracks in them may be exploited as nesting sites by starlings, house sparrows and sometimes pied wagtails. As long ago as 1912 sand martins bred in the artificial holes formed from drain-pipes in a railway embankment at Clapham Junction; we have already seen how sand martins used a similar site in a suburban road in Marlborough. Another group of drain-pipes was used by martins until 1944 near Earlsfield Station in south London. Pied wagtails once built a nest under a rail at Colliers Wood Station and in April 1971 a black redstart was in song at Stratford Station on the Liverpool Street main line. Cables are often suspended along the revetments by the side of railway tracks and I have seen nests of both song thrush and blackbird built either behind them or balanced on the top. Bridges across the lines are one of the strongholds of feral pigeons and these birds will also use rail bridges over roads, often to the discomfort of pedestrians passing underneath.

The earth banks and slopes of many railway lines are richly colonized by plants. The nearest rail track to my home in the outer suburbs carries on its banks trees such as sycamores, regenerating elms, birches and robinias, shrubs such as broom and bladder senna and carpets of Japanese polygonum, everlasting pea, yellow toadflax, yarrow, mugwort, hoary cress, horse radish, coltsfoot, Michaelmas daisy, creeping thistle, clovers of several species and sometimes plants of cypress spurge and mullein. The wind-borne seeds of Oxford ragwort – one of the best-known of trackside plants – were speeded on their travels by the windy gusts from passing trains. On one bank near Neasden there are colonies of the field grasshopper, common and holly-blue butterflies, small skippers, small coppers, white and meadow-brown butterflies. I have travelled up and down this line many times and on the whole have found it not especially exciting from the birds that I have recorded along it. The banks are generally cut twice a year, but London Transport have agreed to my request to leave one rather rich butterfly bank alone during the summer. When the other banks are mown, often for the first time in June, the process leaves a tall 'stubble' which is too high and thick for the regular grass-feeding birds. In autumn there are sometimes greenfinches, linnets and goldfinches on the seedheads and in winter house sparrows will visit the birches. Blackbirds may nest in or use some of the bushes as song posts and a kestrel may come along to hover above the banks in its search for small mammals.

Not all railway embankments are as dull as the one that I have just described. In other areas, where disturbance both from man's activities and from passing trains is less, other species may be found. Tree pipits and corn buntings often sing on the telegraph wires and stonechats may breed in very small numbers. In 1866 James Edmund Harting wrote of the whinchat that, 'A favourite situation for their nests is the banks of the railway between Kenton and Harrow, where they build in numbers.' There has been a decline in numbers recently and this attractive bird has undoubtedly suffered from the early cutting of the vegetation along the banks. In the late nineteenth century Richard Jefferies used to watch red-backed shrikes using wires as perches close to Clapham Junction Station in south London, but this species too has undergone a severe reduction in numbers. Where berry-bearing shrubs such as cotoneasters and pyracanthas have been planted along the tracks, birds such as thrushes and, more rarely, waxwings may keep coming back, especially in cold weather, until the bushes have been stripped of their fruits. In my experience regularly used railway lines with a great deal of fast-moving traffic and mown banks are much less interesting than they used to be.

On the other hand the modernisation of Britain's railway system has brought about the closure of many miles of track and sidings while other tracts of land used by the railways have also fallen into disuse. According to a release in 1966 from the Council for the Preservation of Rural England the Estate Department of the Railways Board was free to dispose of some 2500 miles of old track with another 2000 scheduled for later closure. Some sections of track that could be easily absorbed into nearby agricultural land were bought by landowners and farmers, while more difficult stretches with cuttings and embankments still remain. Here scrub formed from willow, hawthorn and blackthorn often springs up with low brakes of bramble and, as one might expect, scrub birds such as blackbird, robin, wren and hedgesparrow are common. There are also hedgerow birds such as corn bunting, yellow-hammer, greenfinch, bullfinch, chaffinch, linnet, long-tailed tit, willow warbler, whitethroat, magpie and in southern England, perhaps nightingale, lesser whitethroat and turtle dove as well. In a study of the whinchats breeding along a disused railway in Ayrshire D. B. Gray found that the embankments were used 'only for nest sites, very little food being collected on them'. These old tracks provide a great deal of interest for the bird watcher as well as a recreational resource for human walkers and riders. For these reasons they are worth preserving and managing.

So far we have been looking at the single features that make up the complex ring of what we have called the outer suburbs. An indication of the great variety of open space in a comparatively small area was given by D. R. Mirams who investigated a strip of open land less than one and a half miles wide, which lay east of West Bromwich and was ringed round by an extensive belt of industrial and housing estates. In this area of 'arable and pasture land, woodland, a reed-fringed lake, a stream (badly polluted), water meadows and canals' a total of 63 different bird species was recorded. Among the residents were reed buntings, tree sparrows, nuthatches, great spotted woodpeckers, tawny and little owls, kestrels and partridges. Coot and lapwings, swallows and yellow wagtails bred in some numbers and whinchats nested one year. It was Charles Dixon who reported how in the London area the whinchat could be found breeding in meadows where 'the dread notice-board proclaims an "eligible building-site" . . . and will doubtless do so until these self-same meadows are converted into the hollow pretences of suburban gardens.' The presence of water improves the avifauna and illustrates the value of varied habitats close to each other.

Before ending this chapter and our review of the varied and interesting environments in the outer suburbs, I would like to mention the small town whose centre is compact and not particularly large but which is now encompassed by a suburban ring. This is generally formed from a belt of post 1939–45 War houses in development plots built into a virgin countryside straight out from the town. Stratford-upon-Avon is a good example of this kind of development. There is no inner ring of suburbs because the town, originally perhaps an old market, fishing or industrial foundation, has remained practically unchanged for many years. One example that I know well, and there are quite a few to be found, is that of Peterhead in Aberdeenshire where a council estate was laid out in 1960 on the southern edge of the town. The succession of birds bore some resemblance to that described in the last chapter. A farmstead and its land were replaced by streets of mainly semi-detached houses and small gardens. Shortly after the estate was completed rooks could be seen sitting about on the roofs and they still come today but in smaller numbers. Herring gulls started to visit the gardens, skylarks were still singing above some of the houses and a corn bunting established a regular song post on a television aerial. The gardens were at first bare of vegetation but lawns, hedges and flowerbeds were soon laid out. No real shrubs developed in most gardens but a few fuchsias, willows and honeysuckles provided some shelter. It was not until 1972 – some twelve years later – that a pair of blackbirds was able to breed, using a sprawling honeysuckle on a shed as a nesting site. Even by that year the density of breeding birds was far below that of a rather poor sycamore wood not far away. However, by the winter of 1973–4 a few robins were holding winter territories only and there were black-birds, common, black-headed and herring gulls, rooks and a few song thrushes, wrens and blue tits foraging in the estate. At the other extreme some more southerly and less exposed towns have new suburbs on their borders which benefit from a quicker and richer shrub growth as well as from their proximity to rich farmland nearby. In this way some of these small towns have what might almost be called 'garden suburbs'. This pleasant state of affairs lasts only until a new outer ring develops beyond the first and a new suburban sprawl begins.

CHAPTER 5

The Edge of the Countryside

IN the last three chapters we have traced the birds of suburbia from the inner ring of development outwards to the very edge of the countryside. This peripheral region is shown on a One-Inch Ordnance Survey Map by increasing areas of green indicating forest and woodland, of white to show farmlands and airfields, of blue to mark the rivers, reservoirs, flooded pits and lakes, and of black stippling to illustrate the parklands. It is a mixed land of farms, orchards and market gardens, commons and downland, golf courses and electricity pylons, motorways and airfields and green belt countryside. Most of the landscape is an agricultural one and of the region lying between fifteen and twenty miles from St Paul's Cathedral at least seven eighths is devoted to farming and horticulture. Here the more affluent commuters live, travelling in by car or train each day into central London but enjoying the rural pleasures of their homes at the weekends. Some of those who live in this rustic simplicity also work in the numerous villages that are enbosomed in this green zone which lies beyond the outer limits of suburbia but into which the licking tongues of development spread their lines of brick and concrete. For this reason it is not possible to ignore the subject of this chapter or to dismiss it as irrelevant in a book about suburban birds.

By far the greater part of Britain is cultivated farmland but the amount is decreasing as housing, industry and new systems of communication continue to bite into it. In the 1950s farmland was being converted to urban uses at the rate of some 36,500 acres a year, while in 1964 Sir Dudley Stamp put the overall annual loss at between 50,000 and 70,000 acres. As most farms contain some grassland, arable ground, wood and perhaps hedgerow, they provide important habitats for birds. In highland Britain the hedges are largely replaced by stone walls and these often provide nest sites for wagtails, redstarts and other birds. About one third of Britain is devoted to arable land and one fifth to grassland, made up of either semi-natural meadows, or leys which are ploughed and resown with mixtures of clover and grass seed. The farms that are undoubtedly richest in birds are mixed farms with the widest range of habitats within their boundaries, especially tall, straggling hedges, some forest trees, scrub and rough copses, orchards, streams, marshy ground and ponds. 'The best farms', according to Kenneth Williamson, 'are those showing the greatest fragmentation of the habitat'. Such farms can hold between forty and fifty different breeding species but the average for farmland discovered by the Common Birds Census carried out by the British Trust for Ornithology was rather lower; a farm in Worcestershire yielded 22 species, another in Hertfordshire 33, and a third in Westmorland 35. I recorded 39 species on a 172 acre farm in Warwickshire and this figure seems roughly the same as that for agricultural land around London.

In the central English lowlands the blackbird is the dominant farmland species, followed by the hedgesparrow, skylark, robin, chaffinch, whitethroat, yellowhammer, blue tit, song thrush, linnet, wren, great tit, tree sparrow and greenfinch. The Common Birds Census found that both partridges and skylarks occurred at twice the density on arable land than they did on grass. Wren, robin, willow warbler, chiffchaff and chaffinch were commonest on grassland farms. On poorer grasslands whinchats, yellow wagtails and, if wet ground is available, snipe and redshank may breed as well. The yellow wagtail has also been known to nest in fields of growing oats and beans.

Over eighty per cent of the bird community of farmland is composed of birds of woodland origin. In the Lowland Zone of Britain the steppe species such as partridge, lapwing, skylark and wagtail seldom make up more than sixteen per cent of the whole community or less than seven per cent. Predatory birds and swifts, swallows and house martins form a very small part of the total. Gamebirds and turtle doves seem to do well on the grasslands of eastern England, stock doves, little owls and redstarts in the west, and skylarks, lapwings, snipe and curlew in the north. Williamson also found out that the farmland communities in the north and west were in a much more fluid state than those in the Lowland Zone which enjoyed more stable climatic conditions. As a breeding habitat for birds farms are, I suppose, intermediate between true woodland and the suburbs, but nesting success is higher in suburban sites than on farms. Hedgerows provide an important part of the mosaic of farmland habitats and a well-cared for hedge is poorer in birds than a neglected or overgrown one. The creation of hedges after the enclosures must have brought about a sharp increase in the numbers of yellowhammers, whitethroats, lesser whitethroats, willow warblers, hedgesparrows, greenfinches, goldfinches, linnets, long-tailed tits, magpies and other scrub-loving species. Unfortunately hedgerows are being eroded away at a very fast rate, particularly in areas such as East Anglia. It seems that this process can only be accelerated by the wider growing of cereals, the greater use of machines and the rearing of stock in houses and sheds. Rooks are closely associated with tall hedgerow trees and will lose many nesting sites, some of considerable antiquity, through the effects of Dutch elm disease.

In winter the pasture lands are often visited by lapwings, skylarks and meadow pipits, redwings and fieldfares, rooks and jackdaws, crows, starlings and gulls. For ten years Stuart Crooks and Paul Moxey studied the wintering lapwings on a farm in north-west Middlesex. The first birds arrived in early October and their final departure took place in early March. The birds generally preferred ploughed fields but there was a haphazard shift from ploughed to pasture land and back again at various times during the winter. Finches often come in flocks to rough farmlands, particularly chaffinches, greenfinches, goldfinches and linnets. Outside the breeding season the chaffinch is very much a bird of stubble and root fields, as well as stackyards where it meets its other relations. In December 1970 one observer estimated that there were between 1500 and 2000 greenfinches in a sorrel-covered cabbage field at Chorley Wood in Hertfordshire and with them were also between 2500 and 3000 linnets. Finches will also congregate with sparrows around manure heaps and in farmyards. Woodpigeons often flock in hundreds to feed on the cabbages and Brussels sprouts and they are now also very much associated with the cereal and clover ley type of farming. Feral pigeons often flight out into the fields to feed, and collared doves are showing signs of a spread in rural areas although they are very much birds of suburbia; these doves of eastern origin are not uncommon at granaries, maltings, chicken farms and game stations where grain is not too difficult to find. In February 1970 I tape recorded a remarkable chorus of collared doves and house sparrows at a granary near Manea in the Fens; there were scores of doves in and around the buildings. Jays are great stealers of peas as well as occasional raiders of potatoes and corn. Kestrels, barn owls, little owls and tawny owls can often be seen hunting over farmland for small rodents and other prey. The birds of farmland are a very interesting community and in the fringe lands around our towns and cities their activities may be very apparent to human observers.

The more rural parts of Britain owe much of their spring delight to the pink and white fruit blossom that spreads in great drifts across the landscape. In the ten years after 1939 orchards took up about 270,000 acres of England and Wales, 9500 acres of Northern Ireland and 1300 acres of Scotland. An orchard is a habitat of a special kind and, if there are also old and mature trees, it may be quite rich in bird life. The newer and more carefully maintained orchards are much poorer. One orchard of eleven acres that I studied had a community of 68 birds of 24 different species and these included breeding magpies, redstarts, treecreepers, green and great spotted woodpeckers and little owls. I have also seen hawfinches and pied flycatchers in orchards while some of the wryneck's last British haunts have been in this habitat. It is possible that many orchards are in rather an unstable condition as a result of man's interference through the use of fungicides and the tilling of the soil. The value of orchards as habitats depends on the age of the trees, the method of husbandry, the types of spraying and how much of the invertebrate life remains. Their only value may be as food resources from buds and fruit if there are no breeding sites and the insect community has been destroyed.

In spring I have seen numbers of birds attacking the buds and blossoms of trees, bushes and flowers. House sparrows will rip up yellow crocuses, primulas, polyanthus and forsythia, revealing a degree of wanton destructiveness and clear preference for yellow that marks the springtime whiling away of their considerable reserves of leisure. They also will attack, according to J. D. Summers-Smith, who is the authority on the house sparrow 'buds from practically every known type of fruit tree and bush'. Bullfinches sometimes search out forsythia and lilac bushes but they favour particularly the buds of fruit trees and this is of much greater economic significance. Dr Ian Newton has found that the bullfinch 'now removes the buds of fruit trees on such a scale as to constitute one of the greatest problems with which the fruit-growing industry has to contend. The damage is indisputable'. The blossom buds are picked off at their bases and the birds remove the embryonic centres that would become the fruit. Dr Newton found that the buds of plums and pear trees are the most vulnerable to bullfinches with gooseberries, currants, apples and cherries in descending order of importance. Certain varieties of fruit bud are liked more than others and so more readily taken – for example, 'William' and 'Conference' pears more than 'Comice' and 'Hardy', 'Morello' cherries more than sweet ones and dessert apples more than cookers. The buds of cultivated trees are also chosen in preference to those of the wild species. The bullfinch can take off fruit tree buds at the rate of 30 or more to the minute and sustain an intake rate of 25 to the minute when attacking those of pear trees. The feeding is carried out very systematically with birds landing near the tip of a branch and removing every bud in turn as they work their way towards the bole of the tree. The trees which lie on the edge of the orchard and nearest to woodland or scrub are attacked first and then the bullfinches move steadily deeper into the orchard. A party of a dozen or more bullfinches can wreak havoc in an orchard in a few days. However, some research has suggested that half the buds could be removed from a pear tree without there being any effect on the size of the final crop of fruit on that tree.

In the last thirty years the bullfinch has spread from its initial home in the woodlands and scrub into both farmland and some parts of suburbia; its arrival in these new habitats has had a serious effect on many orchards. Fruit growers have tried to reduce the damage in gardens by wiring or enclosing their bushes and small trees but this is not a practical step in orchards. The birds soon become used to scaring devices and, if chemical deterrent sprays are used, the birds peel off the affected outer layers on the buds. Baited wire boxes have been quite successfully employed and the captured birds then humanely disposed of. As a result of his six-year study of bullfinches near Oxford Dr Newton was able to suggest another form of control. He found that the seeds of ash trees figure high in the winter food of these finches and good crops of seed usually occur in England every second year. The fruit grower is consequently only in real danger when the ash seed crop is a poor one. By trapping the birds in the autumn the natural supply of seed is preserved and the date when the bullfinches will make their move towards the orchards is thus delayed and the damage lessened. This method of control is now in general use, based on an ecologist's detailed studies. A few other species such as tits, goldfinches, greenfinches and house sparrows may attack fruit buds and in April 1965 a thousand redpolls were seen taking buds in a pear orchard near Canterbury in Kent.

Numbers of different birds will also take ripe fruit. Blackbirds, blue tits, song thrushes and house sparrows have all eaten ripe fruit on the tree. In an interesting survey of damage done by birds to ripe apples and pears in orchards in southern England in 1961 E. N. Wright and T. Brough examined 188,000 fruits and found that the percentage damage of the fruit was Cox 2·6, Lord Lambourne 6·6 and Conference 3·1, with a mean percentage damage of 4·1. Crossbills during their periodic invasions have been known to attack apples for their pips while hawfinches specialize in cherry stones and the seeds of damson and blackthorn. Anyone who has fruit trees will probably know how, after the fruit has fallen, wasps, red admirals, flies and many birds will come to the feast, including blackbirds, song thrushes, mistle thrushes, fieldfares, redwings, starlings, woodpigeons and feral pigeons. Once some 200–250 bramblings were watched feeding in an orchard at Eynsford in Kent but these birds were more attracted by the weed seeds than the fruit.

Undoubtedly, many of the rural areas outside towns with suitable soils may be devoted to market gardening. If this land primarily raises commercial vegetable crops then the bird community resembles that of farmland. If, however, it is covered with small fruit bushes, shrubs, vegetables and flowers, the bird life is more like that of suburban gardens and allotments. At one time market gardens were widespread around London. In 1754 they covered a wide tract of land along the River Thames between Chelsea and Brentford. By the end of that century there were 10,000 acres in Middlesex alone that were intensively cultivated and producing cabbages, cauliflower, celery, onions, peas, radishes and other crops. By 1850 the most important areas in that county stretched from the river west to Chiswick and Brentford and north towards Hackney and Enfield. This kind of land use can still be found in regions to the north-east, south-east and west of the metropolis. Market gardens can also be found in the vicinity of many towns; those in Northamptonshire, for example, are sometimes on land long since restored to agricultural use after the extraction of ironstone.

The birds of market gardens will be influenced to some extent by the presence of nearby scrub or woodland and farmland from which they can come to raid the crops and to which they can return for shelter and breeding sites. Intensively grown strawberries near Tiptree in Essex have been attacked by blackbirds, song thrushes, turtle doves and house sparrows but the the greatest amount of damage was caused by linnets which came in a steady trickle to pick off the external seeds particularly from such varieties as 'Talisman' and 'Cambridge Favourite'. Dr R. K. Murton found that flocks of linnets, sometimes up to five hundred birds, also went for the seedheads of Savoy, candy-tuft and forget-me-nots. Jays will feed on some horticultural pests but they also like peas and soft fruit. I once watched a magpie digging up newly planted shallots which it carried away and buried elsewhere. Woodpigeons are extremely greedy feeders and single crops of shot birds have revealed as many as 163 peas and 3 ounces of spinach. Stock doves sometimes appear in market gardens where, like wood-pigeons, they will eat beans, peas and the leaves of a number of different vegetables. As a species they seem to have been rather vulnerable to agricultural pesticides and their decline in the 1960s may have resulted from the application particularly of organo-chlorine seed-dressings. Finches play rather a mixed role. In the breeding season the chaffinch takes insects and their larvae but during the rest of the year some cereals and plenty of weed seeds. Greenfinches have been known to dig up planted seeds but they also feed on those of many different weeds. The goldfinch is a delightful and harmless bird to have around while the hawfinch which sometimes consumes green peas is too rare to be a significant pest in market gardens. We have already seen the kind of havoc that bullfinches can wreak in an orchard but they can also have an effect in market gardens and nurseries by attacking the buds of lilac, clematis, Weigela and forsythia and the fruit of blackberries. Starlings often forage over strips of grass in their search for the soil fauna but these adaptable birds may also turn their attentions away from animal food to fruit and the pickings around poultry farms. As we have seen, blackbirds like strawberries but they are also pleased to include in their diet raspberries, currants, cherries, figs and even tomatoes. Both mistle and song thrushes have a liking for the same kinds of fruit and even robins and lesser spotted wood-peckers will eat currants and raspberries. Among the warblers the blackcap and garden warbler are both addicts of fruit in the summer while willow warblers, whitethroats and lesser whitethroats have also been reported taking currants and similar fruits. The West Midland

Bird Report for 1953 announced that the yellow wagtail was now 'a common breeder on the Vegetable Research Station at Wellesbourne where the change of land from agriculture to horticulture has coincided with large increase'. Pheasants may feed on both peas and tomatoes and even the moorhen has been known to add berries and fruit to an already catholic diet. To keep these enemies of market gardeners at bay various devices have been experimented with over the years – scare-crows, dead birds, noise-making machines, blowing strips of metal, explosions and sound reproducing equipment to broadcast the distress calls of birds to dissuade them from staying too long.

Some of the areas on the edge of the countryside may be occupied by greenhouses. In the Lea Valley to the north of London and in the rose, tomato and flower-growing regions of fenland they may cover quite large areas. Smaller aggregations of greenhouses can be found in the vicinity of many towns and cities. In recent years these glass and metal structures have proved rather attractive to pied wagtails which have chosen to roost and nest in some of them. There are at least twelve sites where pied wagtails have bred in greenhouses and their roosting habits will be discussed more fully in chapter 9. Thrushes, robins, wrens and house sparrows may also nest inside greenhouses if they can have regular and proper access to their interiors.

Undoubtedly one of the great attractions of the outer suburban fringes are the many pieces of woodland that still survive in almost a rural setting. Over the years huge areas of timber have been felled in the neighbourhood of towns but undisturbed woodlands, with a wide variety of native and introduced trees, can be very rich in bird life. Here can be found many of the seventy-eight or so species which are associated with woods and their marginal habitats. Each piece of woodland is a miniature ecosystem with a community of plants, birds, mammals, insects, reptiles all living in association with each other and linked by a complex web of interdependent strands. It is a highly intricate world under the influence of the soil which has arisen from the rocks below, the climate and the various activities of man. Britain's countryside is very much a patchwork quilt of small woods, hedges and hedgerow trees, fields, commons and grass and the birds to be found in it were largely displaced from the disappearing woodlands. Two thousand years ago as much as sixty per cent of Britain was under trees but today agriculture is the dominant activity over eighty per cent of the land. The more adaptable bird species like the blackbird have learned to live in close proximity to man and we have already seen that most of the birds in our gardens come from the woods. The commonest birds of woodland are chaffinches, wrens, robins, blackbirds and willow warblers. There are differences in the bird communities according to the age, type and situation of the woods. Broad-leaved woods are richer than coniferous ones and mixed woods are richer than either. I have written very fully about woodland birds elsewhere and so I do not propose to repeat the text here.

Another distinctive feature of the countryside around most of our towns and cities is that offered by large parks and parklands. Some of these may be in private occupation, belong to the local authority or be in the care of the National Trust. A considerable part of the countryside consists of parkland which I have described as 'a landscape which is a patchwork of small woods often enclosed as shelter belts or game coverts, ornamental clumps and groves, garden trees, orchards, avenues, hedgerows and lines of trees as well as the laid out parks of the manors and country mansions'. The birds of parkland are those like the rook, jackdaw and starling whose lives involve both trees for nesting and grasslands for feeding. Kestrels and owls may nest in a variety of parkland habitats where the green woodpecker is normally the commonest of the three woodpecker species. Stock doves will breed in parkland ecotones and, if small woods and dense hedges grow among the grasslands, there may be turtle doves as well. Mistle thrushes, greenfinches and goldfinches are common and there are also linnets, yellowhammers, tree sparrows, hedgesparrows, whitethroats, magpies and, much less commonly, woodlarks, red-backed shrikes and cirl buntings in southern England only. In keepered parkland the bird life may be noteworthy for a high density of gamebirds and a low density of predatory birds. Private parklands are not easy to census but J. D. Magee has studied the birds of one municipally-owned outer fringe park near Watford. This is Cassiobury Park which lies about seventeen miles from St Paul's Cathedral. It was found to be fairly typical of many southern parks and woodlands. Herons had managed to breed there and, as these birds normally need woods with tall trees in which to nest, some of the British heronries are in the parklands of large houses. I have seen herons' nests in oaks, elms, hawthorns, sweet chestnuts, Scots pine, Sitka and Norway spruces. The regular breeding birds of Cassiobury Park include mallard, kestrel, partridge, pheasant, stock dove, turtle dove, collared dove, cuckoo, little owl, all three species of woodpecker, skylark, swallow, magpie, willow tit, long-tailed tit, nuthatch, treecreeper, blackcap, garden warbler, whitethroat, willow warbler, chiffchaff, goldcrest, tree pipit, linnet, redpoll, and yellowhammer. A list of this kind with woodland, scrub, parkland, farmland and waterside birds gives a fair indication of the more rural and varied character of this park and it also includes a number of less adaptable birds which we have seen nest very rarely or not at all in many of our outer suburbs. Six species have recently been lost as nesting birds in Cassiobury Park which may be found in other country parklands – sparrowhawk, woodcock, barn owl, woodlark, rook and lesser whitethroat.

Patches of open land not used for farming such as commons and downland have a way of disappearing around big towns or being trod literally almost out of existence. Yet, according to the late Sir Dudley Stamp, 'Common land is of vital importance in Britain's nature conservation programme'. As it covers about 3·3% of the land surface of the country it is a habitat that should be guarded and not allowed to disappear by default. About 80% of common lands are grazed, 10·4% have an amenity or recreational purpose, 7·8% are scrub due to the absence of grazing animals, 1·9% are forest and 0·6% fen, bog and marsh. Where the atrophying of 'commoners' rights' to graze animals has taken place trees and scrub have grown up on many commons and here the bird community is clearly one of woodland or scrub. The development of estates has involved the destruction of many habitats and many commons and heaths, converted to agriculture during the 1939–45 War, have never recovered. In the case of London it was the conception of a green belt that slowed down the steady erosion of this scarce environment. Where heaths and commons are heavily used and the trampling of thousands of feet destroys their character and prevents plant regeneration, they need a very special protection. Around London one can see on Hampstead Heath and Wimbledon Common, Putney Heath and Mitcham Common, the effect of what Lord Molson called 'access in excess'. The bird community of heaths and commons is essentially one of ground or near-ground nesting species. Typical birds include meadow and tree pipits, whitethroat, stonechat, whinchat, skylark, yellowhammer, reed bunting, grasshopper warbler and, in a limited number of British and Irish localities, nightjar. The Dartford warbler, which is a bird of heaths, commons and downs, is now restricted to only a few localities in the south of England. Among the gorse and other shrubs there are usually linnets and, if the scrub growth is high enough, perhaps bullfinch, turtle dove, lesser white-throat and, in eastern or southern England after a great contraction in range and numbers, red-backed shrike.

There has been a decline near London in the total of nesting stone-chats, nightjars and grasshopper warblers. The ploughing up of Up-minster Common during the last war led to a reduction in the number of breeding linnets, reed buntings, yellowhammers, skylarks, stone-chats and some of the warblers. Where birch scrub has grown up, hawfinches, wood warblers, coal tits and sparrowhawks may establish themselves. The combination of heath and grass may suit the woodlark which breeds in most counties south-west of a line from Merioneth to Kent as well as in Nottingham and East Anglia. This bird with its beautiful melancholy song seems to have rather special habitat require-ments and it is also very particular about the exact choice of nesting site. Bracken cover has provided shelter not only for woodlark nests but also for those of reed bunting, yellowhammer, tree and meadow pipits but when the fronds grow into a miniature forest the bracken

GOLDFINCH and GREENFINCH, two seed-eating species of suburbia. *Above,* goldfinch preening itself on the nest; *below,* male greenfinch with young.

SISKIN and GOLDCREST, two rarer species occurring in the suburbs. *Above,* male siskin, a comparative newcomer to some suburban gardens; *below,* goldcrest, a tiny bird that may nest almost unnoticed in gardens and churchyards, especially if yew trees are present.

becomes much less attractive to nesting birds. In winter short-eared owls may become birds of heathland and occasionally remain to breed in the following year. Redpolls, siskins and house sparrows often feed in winter in the birch scrub. Severe weather may affect bird numbers and stonechats disappeared from many heaths and railway embankments after the bad winter of 1946-7.

Sometimes the outer fringe of countryside around towns includes some chalk downland which can be a mixture of short turf, perhaps grazed by sheep or worn down by human feet, and varying amounts of scrub. Much of this kind of land has already been built on – take Purley and Sanderstead near London – but small pieces are sometimes embalmed in golf courses and so saved from the developer. Here pipits and larks may share the habitat with scrub birds once more. I have seen cirl buntings on the lower slopes of the Chilterns while quarries in the chalk may hold nesting colonies of jackdaws and other birds. However, the red-backed shrikes that I used to watch in the early 1930s along the north slopes of the South Downs near Ditchling have gone and there have been other changes too with the ploughing up of the turf and the growth of weekend tourism. In 1900 the naturalist, W. H. Hudson, described a walk he made along the Downs when 'The little birds that live in the furze, the titlarks, whitethroats, linnets and stonechats, sprang upwards at frequent intervals and poured out their strains when on the wing.' These were the precious days of nature in downland. The South Downs were declared an Area of Outstanding Natural Beauty and recommendations have been made to turn them into a National Park. As an A.O.N.B., the region enjoys strict planning control and it is not easy to get approval for road or house building, for the erection of overhead cables and for the extraction of any mineral resources. This kind of protection is also given to the so-called 'green belts' around some of our major towns and to which I referred in chapter 1. There are some 3000 square miles of this type of country around London in a belt up to thirty miles deep in places (see figure 2).

David Thomas in his study of London's green belt showed that in 1960 the land use inside the belt could be divided up as shown in the table on p. 114.

It can be clearly seen that agriculture takes up the larger part of London's green belt with what Hugh Gaitskell called 'green ditches separating subtopia'. Woods and trees in the belt can be protected by the direct action of the local planning authorities and by the Forestry Commission which can enter into a Forestry Dedication Covenant with the owners. There are several areas of protected woodland around London – at Broxbourne Woods, near Gerrards Cross and Chalfont St Peter, by Epping Forest, near Brentwood and also on the chalk and greensand downs to the south of the capital. If the woods are declared

H

1. AGRICULTURE (grassland, arable, allotments, orchards and market gardens)	69·5%
2. WOODLAND (all types)	11·8%
3. RESIDENTIAL AND COMMERCIAL	6·2%
4. RECREATIONAL (playing fields, open spaces, golf courses, etc.)	6·2%
5. EXTRACTIVE (sand, gravel, chalk)	1·8%
6. TRANSPORT (road, rail, air)	1·5%
7. INSTITUTIONS (with large gardens: hospitals, schools, colleges)	1·1%
8. PUBLIC SERVICES (utilities, services, cemeteries)	0·9%
9. WATER	0·6%
10. MANUFACTURING	0·2%
11. UNUSED	0·2%
	100·00%

of Special Scientific Interest then the Nature Conservancy can be involved as well.

The residential and commercial area is a zone of semi-urbanized land, substantially built over and with a human population that is rapidly becoming conditioned to urban ways of living and attitude. In 1953 a housing estate was built on green belt land at Hainault in Essex and this greatly reduced the feeding and dispersal zones available to an old-established rookery. Alan Parker traced the decline of rooks in the district and found that 'being "immediate countryside" to a huge urban development to the south and to a lesser extent to the north, illegal shooting was persistent throughout the year'. Land given over to recreation will be looked at in detail in chapter 8. The mineral extraction industry has led to abandoned pits, spoil heaps and unsightly disused buildings in many parts of the country and it is interesting to note that around London almost the whole of the extraction takes place inside the approved green belt. Aquatic and associated habitats will be the subject of a discussion in the following two chapters where they can be examined with more space. Unused land consists generally of land cleared and waiting to be afforested or of the surroundings of various mineral workings, or 'wasteland'. Transport and its variety of demands and effects will figure later in the present chapter.

Green belts are no longer regarded as a method of stopping the expansion of towns and, in fact, present planning opinion favours a succession of rural wedges to lead from the countryside into the very heart of the town, just as they do, for example, in Southampton. The National Trust, which in 1966 administered more than 350,000 acres of England, Wales and Northern Ireland, keeps large tracts of country undeveloped and maintains a number of nature reserves. The multiple land uses in green belts ensure a wide variety of habitats for birds and their ornithology has been documented by Ronald Lockley. Modern ecologists have shown beyond question that it is essential to preserve the widest range of natural and semi-natural habitats as possible.

An interesting attempt was started in 1972 to create a country park from a four-mile wide crescent of agricultural land that lay between Leeds and Bradford, but it met with opposition from many of the local farmers. Both cities with their civic societies and the four local authorities were anxious to preserve the fields and woods between Holme, Tong and Cockers Dale from development and to keep them as a recreational amenity for the one million people living in the area. The two cities owned a great deal of the land and were ready to undertake footpaths, signs, picnic zones, car parks and even a nature trail. The farmers said that there were already enough footpaths and too much public access to their land and they thought that urban users did not know how to behave in the countryside, which was hardly a new argument. One of the difficulties today is that local parks are no longer regarded by many people as adequate substitutes for what they call the 'real' countryside and so the pressure on well-known beauty spots and attractive regions away from the towns is growing all the time. Sir Dudley Stamp urged us to understand that 'the maintenance of the peace and security of the countryside as an antidote to urban hustle and stress has become an essential part of natural life'. What is difficult to avoid is the destruction by thoughtless and massive intrusions by us of those very features that attracted us there in the first place.

Two kinds of land use on the edge of the countryside are concerned with road and air transport. We looked at something of the birdlife along the rail tracks in the last chapter and we saw how the abandonment of lines had provided an extension of wildlife habitats, but this has meant a heavier use of the roads and a general rise in road traffic. Roadside verges are often interesting environments for birds and other animals while the hedges nearby may be used as nesting sites by a wide variety of different species. Between 1950 and 1959 chemical sprays were widely used to kill vegetation on the verges and this had a devastating effect on the flora and the associated fauna. The extensive cutting of the grassy edges has an important effect as well. For me there is something rather special about untouched roadside verges. I can remember many July journeys along Cotswold roads when, as I once wrote, 'For miles the roadsides were a soft blue with drifts of meadow cranesbill, a bright gold with lady's bedstraw or a royal purple with the rayed crowns of knapweed.' 'Fire risks and traffic hazards,' say the sprayers and cutters but there are many places where these arguments are not strictly valid and scarce plants, butterflies and birds all suffer from the destruction of the habitat. In Lincolnshire roadside nature reserves have been set up by the County Council and the County Naturalists' Trust, but road verges constitute a problem for conservationists in many other districts.

It appears that there are favourite patches of road or roundabout where birds are able to gather food in a plenty that does not seem to exist elsewhere in the immediate neighbourhood. Dick Bagnall-Oakeley, in a broadcast in a Radio 4 *Living World* programme, advanced the theory that passing traffic creates in certain circumstances a vibration in the ground which will bring earthworms and other members of the soil fauna to the surface. He first noticed birds feeding in favoured spots in the Cambridgeshire Fens about 1968. Two lapwings were on the roadside among the grass. When he approached they flew a short distance away but came back as soon as he had passed on. He watched the patch of grass very carefully. A large sugar beet lorry with a trailer went past and at once three worms came up to the surface and were picked up by the birds. Birds normally have to hunt and search for food but if they are seen returning to the same place there must be a reason for it. Bagnall-Oakeley found that one of the best places for this activity was on the roundabout at the south end of the King's Lynn by-pass. Despite the heavy load of traffic there are always birds to be seen there – lapwings, redwings, fieldfares, song thrushes, blackbirds, starlings and gulls. It seems that the critical factor is the consistency of the soil which then vibrates in a certain way under the wheels of the lorries and cars. This type of feeding is apparently not seen along motorways because, although there is plenty of vibration with the enormous volume of traffic, the soil is not properly consolidated along the verges. It would be interesting to have observations on this from other parts of the country.

The rising speed and volume of the traffic on Britain's roads pose a serious threat to birds which are often struck by fast-moving vehicles. Most birds are hit for one of three reasons – they just fail to see an oncoming vehicle, they take no notice of it or they misjudge its closing speed. A number of co-operative enquiries have been undertaken in Britain to find out about these avian casualties. One experiment involved the ringing of all nestlings from hedges and buildings to a depth of some one hundred feet on each side of a road in Wiltshire. The casualties recovered with their identity rings from a mile-long piece of roadway showed that traffic had killed one third of all the pied wagtails, one fifth of all the chaffinches and about one tenth of all the blackbirds and song thrushes. About three out of every ten birds killed had died from shock through impact chiefly with vehicles but also to a lesser extent with overhead wires and cables. House sparrows, blackbirds, song thrushes, hedgesparrows, chaffinches and partridges suffer particularly badly from traffic but I have also seen pheasants, various warblers and pigeons in quite large numbers. I can well remember parking my car in King's Lynn during a filming session and seeing the remains of a pair of hedgesparrows lying flattened on the grille of the car in the next space. Near the coast herring gulls are regular casualties and I counted sixteen corpses, mostly of young birds, on a six-mile stretch of road between Aberdeen and Peterhead. Investigations have shown that many birds are consciously aware of traffic and can get out of the way in time. Rooks often walk along the edges of motorways and dual carriageways only a couple of feet from the wheels flashing by in the slow or the overtaking lane. In my experience this habit becomes more frequent the farther north one drives from London. It has been suggested too that birds can avoid cars travelling not faster than 25 m.p.h. I drive many thousands of miles each year on Britain's roads and there are countless occasions when my 'tooting' of the horn was the only way to alert birds to the growing danger and to get them to fly away in time. Crows and gulls are loath to leave the remains of the road victims that they are feeding on and they become victims in their turn. Song thrushes also use the hard road surface as an anvil for smashing snail shells and may be so engrossed in their activity that they fail to appreciate the approach of a vehicle. Gamebirds, finches, pigeons and house sparrows may be struck when collecting grit, usually in the early morning, and when sunbathing, dust bathing or drinking from puddles. At night headlights can temporarily blind birds and I have seen tawny owls only too frequently lying dead on the road. For me it is a matter of regret that with careful and thoughtful driving techniques many of these deaths could be avoided, but the modern 'press on' style of driving, revealed only too clearly by the cavalier disregard of motorway speed limits, leads to the many unnecessary deaths not only of birds but also of ponies, deer, badgers, hedgehogs and an increasing number of cats and dogs.

The 1965 Road Deaths Enquiry mounted by the British Trust for Ornithology found that the old type of busy 'A' road, or arterial link, running through rural areas, had the highest casualty rate of birds, while well-used 'B', or secondary, roads came a close second. The Enquiry came to the conclusion that two and a half million bird casualties is 'a reasonable and perhaps a conservative annual total'. A similar survey made by the United States Automobile Association suggested that in the United States something like a million animals a day are killed on the roads and the annual total was thought to be greater than the combined toll taken each year by American hunters. It is much more difficult to obtain any figures for rail deaths in Britain. However, in 1957 on a $2\frac{1}{4}$-mile length of track, the deaths occurred of 66 birds, including 19 partridges, 15 tawny owls, 8 barn owls, 6 pheasants and several birds of smaller species.

The widening and re-alignment of older roads sometimes results in pieces of closed highway being left more or less untended; these can become small but valuable sanctuaries for hedge and scrub birds. Where these lopped-off sections of road are turned into car parks and lay-bys – and they are now a common feature of the country areas around towns – the bird community is formed from scrub birds able to put up with the disturbance and from scavengers that come to feed from the litter baskets and containers and on the scraps thrown out by drivers. I have found that the commonest scavengers in lay-bys are crows, rooks, jackdaws, magpies, starlings, feral pigeons, house sparrows and gulls. I have seen black-headed gulls at work in lay-bys all the way from the green acres of the New Forest north to the Sutherland floes, while common, herring and lesser black-backed gulls have flown to greet me on my arrival in many northern stopping places. In recent years during extensive car drives through northern England and Scotland hordes of chaffinches have alighted on the roof, the bonnet, the side mirrors and even the edge of the lowered window glass as I slowly came to a stop in a lay-by. Most were hand tame and ready to take food from my fingers. The largest numbers I have come across have been in the Lake District and in Wester Ross where great tits have come to feed from the hand as well.

By the mid-1970s there will be 1350 miles of motorway in Britain. On the M1 for every mile of road there are something like 17·1 acres of land between the hard shoulder and the boundary fence. Each mile of motorway itself occupies more land than this. When the motorway plan is completed the total area of verge will be equal to about 20,000 acres. This land is comparatively isolated and is disturbed only by the sound of passing traffic and an occasional grass cutter. It forms a very useful conservation area. Michael Way led a Nature Conservancy study into the verges of the M1 Motorway. It was carried out at mile intervals from Hendon to Leeds and at each interval point a 50-yard-wide transect was made to record the physical and vegetational characteristics. Dr Way believes that the verges could provide a valuable chain of wildlife habitats, and with a grass or clover ground zone and some bushes and trees they could form 'reservoirs of populations of wild plants, invertebrates and small vertebrates that are increasingly under pressure from loss of habitat in lowland agricultural and industrial England'.

I have seen many grassland birds on the embankments of the M1 and M6, including crows, rooks, jackdaws and starlings and, in autumn, small parties of finches looking for the seeds of various weeds. Constant cutting tends to make the verges better feeding than nesting grounds and that is why planting with shrubs and trees is very much to be desired both for amenity and conservation purposes. The planting scheme for the M6 between Carnforth and Penrith is very welcome. There is also a lack of overhead wires and cables and often tall bushes from which birds such as the stonechat, whinchat, whitethroat and tree pipit can sing their territorial songs. Judged by the number of occasions on which I have seen kestrels sitting contemplatively on motorway signs or hovering and pouncing along the verges, there must be a fair number of small mammals available as food. In the late summer of 1971 I drove up the M1 from Mill Hill to the junction with the M18, and my son David kept a record of the changing landscape and the birds that we encountered on the way. The commonest species were rooks and jackdaws, particularly on the Newport Pagnell section, followed by sand martins, starlings, swallows, magpies, carrion crows and black-headed, common and lesser black-backed gulls. An interesting example of how birds can make quick use of a new motorway has been given by T. C. E. Link; in April 1962, at Upper Strensham in Worcestershire, a new bridge over the M5 from Bristol to Birmingham was completed and opened to the public on 20 May 1962. On 24 October 1963 a house martin's nest was found on a ledge at the top of one of the pillars and against the underside of the bridge at a height of 19 ft 6 ins above the overtaking lane.

Some of the countryside around our towns may be taken up with meeting the needs of aviation – military, commercial and private. Airfields provide wide, open habitats which can attract a number of bird species. I was stationed from November 1943 until July 1944 at the operational No. 1 Group Bomber Command Station at Wickenby, some twelve miles from Lincoln. On the airfield itself I recorded 47 different species and, when I included a small amount of wood and scrub, I added another 11 species to the total, including the nightingale. R. K. Murton in his book, *Man and Birds*, reported that C. J. Bridgeman had recorded a total of 43 species on 3 British airfields over a year of study. Stone curlews and ringed plovers, which I did not observe in Lincolnshire, have bred on a Suffolk airfield. When I was flying in Florida in 1942 the attractive killdeer plover was the typical species, rather like the lapwing in Britain. Corn buntings, which I did see at Wickenby, have been heard in song on London Airport near Staines. Heathrow covers a large expanse of ground and it is difficult to know what species do occur there. A melanistic male Montagu's harrier was seen between 18 and 21 May 1960, and a pair of red-legged partridges was recorded in February 1971. In winter the airfields often prove attractive to rooks, jackdaws, starlings, pigeons, lapwings, golden plover and gulls which come to feed on the grass. In November 1973 I landed in a BAC 1-11 at Luton Airport in the dark and in the landing lights I could see lapwings and small gulls as well as a barn owl moving just in front of the aircraft. Up to 600 golden plover were recorded at London Airport Heathrow in January 1950, and 80 were seen there in January 1970. In August 1950 ten dotterel were seen with lapwings and golden plover on some gravel between the newly finished runways. At Baginton Airfield near Coventry I have seen winter flocks of golden plover up to 250 in size and lapwings in assemblies of over 2000 birds. Hendon once used to hold lapwings and small numbers of golden plover but with the development of this historic airfield the birds come no longer. Other waders such as redshank, ruff and oyster-catcher have been seen on airfields from time to time. Kestrels can often be observed hovering over the grass between the airfield runways and a pair succeeded in rearing three young on a ledge above a large hangar door at Weybridge. On 27 June 1973 a black redstart was heard singing on Jumbo Hangar 002 at Hatton Cross, Heathrow Airport. Summer-visiting yellow wagtails may nest in the patches of rough grass on airfields, and whinchats bred at Elstree Airfield in 1964 and at Hornchurch in 1969. Wild geese may graze on airfields and up to 400 have been known to come to the airfield at Campbeltown. There are several instances of birds actually nesting in parked or old aircraft and involving jackdaw, blackbird, robin, pied wagtail, starling and house sparrow. For me one of the pleasantest records is that of a red-backed shrike which used an aircraft at Park Street in Hertfordshire as a look-out post!

Some of the most obvious winter visitors to the grassy parts of air-fields are gulls. They come in search of food and may even use the hard runways or the perimeter track for resting. Although up to 300,000 gulls roost on some of the reservoirs within ten miles of London Heathrow Airport few of them actually interfere with the movement of aircraft. They can be a greater danger elsewhere and the problem of birds on airfields is not unique to Britain. I have seen turkey vultures rise up in front of the aircraft that I was piloting in Florida and bob-whites in Alabama, while a closeup view of buzzards at Basel and kites at Khartoum during aircraft landings has proved rather unnerving. Gulls are attracted to our airfields by the food resources. In 1962 J. D. R. Vernon investigated the food taken by common gulls coming to Colerne Airfield in Wiltshire between the months of July and April. The birds chiefly took earthworms, craneflies in late summer, small numbers of other insects as well as wheat seed and a certain amount of broken-up grass leaves. Gulls sometimes 'paddle' up and down with their feet to bring worms up to the surface and at Coltishall Airfield it seems that the down-draught from helicopter rotor blades will also bring up worms. Gulls come in from the surrounding area as soon as a helicopter gets airborne and pick up the worms from the grass without actually landing.

During the autumn of 1943 I was flying in a Lancaster of No. 1 Group which collided at a height of 2400 feet with a starling – one of a party of several hundred flying straight and level. The impact of this small bird completely crushed the metal housing of the radiator on the port inner engine. On another occasion a colleague of mine in another Lancaster had his skull fractured by a black-headed gull which crashed through the windscreen. Birds can prove a hazard to aircraft, not only when flying at comparatively low altitudes but especially when the machines are taking off or landing. In 1970 a Buccaneer from Lossiemouth RAF Station hit two gulls over Buchan while flying at 300 feet and at 560 m.p.h. The Perspex cockpit canopy was shattered; the navigator, covered in blood and feathers, ejected successfully and the pilot landed his million-pound aircraft but rather the worse for wear. Once aircraft have got above a certain height the danger decreases. During some 225 hours of daylight flying over the British Isles in the last war and, despite many flights up to 25,000 feet, neither I nor any of the airgunners who were in a very favourable position to see, spotted any birds above 3800 feet. The problems tend to be low down and the Royal Air Force's annual bill for damage caused by air-strikes by birds may be as high as a million pounds.

Several hundred bird strikes are reported each year and 70% of the incidents involving civil aircraft take place near airports. A Vanguard at Edinburgh flew into a large flock of gulls resulting in the failure of one engine and a loss of power in the other three. A second engine then stopped, leaving only two in operation but one of these was in a critical condition. After a brilliant piece of airmanship the aircraft was landed safely and 125 dead gulls were later found on the airfield. At Renfrew another aircraft struck a flock of gulls, killing at least four hundred of them and suffering itself £100,000 of damage. There is always the possibility of a bird strike in flight but most civil aircraft cruise far above bird height and multi-engined machines have a reasonable chance of survival.

All engines of British manufacture are designed to meet the requirement that no emergency should arise after an engine has been hit by a four-pound bird, like a large gull, or by ten 1½-pound birds or up to sixteen small birds. Ninety-five per cent of the birds involved in collisions with aircraft do not, in fact, weigh more than four pounds. The standard is being raised to that for an eight-pound bird, but it is not possible to increase the strength indefinitely of an engine or airframe without bringing the weight of the machine above an economic level. It is sensible for both civil and military aircraft not to fly low over bird reserves and wildlife sanctuaries and the siting of new fields should be most carefully considered. At existing airports and fields it is also prudent to try and persuade the birds that these are places to be avoided. Nevertheless, it is worth recording that London Heathrow has a rate of only one bird strike for 10,000 aircraft departures and arrivals – one of the lowest figures in the country. Peregrine falcons have been used to clear fields of birds but they cannot be used in rain and high winds. I assisted with experiments at Heathrow to broadcast distress calls to certain species while shell crackers, Very lights and allowing the grass to grow to lengths that the birds find unattractive have all been tried but birds may soon become conditioned to the new situations very quickly. E. N. Wright has described the effect of putting ten automatic bird scarers that gave vent to loud acetylene-induced explosions along an airfield runway. For one week these devices were a great success but the birds then began to use them as perches.

Of the actual species of bird that have been reported in Europe as having flown into flying aircraft the most important are black-headed, common and herring gulls, lapwings, golden plover, pigeons, rooks and starlings. Homing pigeons were responsible for 23 air strikes at Colerne Airfield. At most fields runway patrols are carried out and reports passed on to the control tower. At night searchlights may be used to disperse birds on or near the actual runways. One evening in July 1973 I was at Aberdeen Airport at Dyce waiting for a Viscount that was bringing my wife from London. Scores of black-headed gulls and lapwings were flying in to settle on the grass for the night quite close to the operative runway. A few minutes before the plane was due to arrive a vehicle drove several times up and down the runway and along the perimeter track firing off crackers which went off with a bright flash and, to me, a deafening explosion. The birds rose up from under the crackers, flew a hundred yards or so and settled again. The effect of the crackers could only be described as a chivvying and not a clearance. However, the Viscount landed without incident. Radar can play a valuable role in giving plots of roosting flyways and migration paths among birds and these can be given to pilots. The problem is, however, both serious and worldwide and it can be especially acute in coastal regions. This would be a matter for concern if London's proposed third airport were built at Maplin Sands. The Roskill Commission reported that 'there must be a greater risk of a major disaster due to bird-strikes at Foulness than at an inland site'.

While on the subject of aerial hazards to birds I ought to say something about the effects of overhead power lines, cables and telegraph wires, since some birds die by flying directly into them. R. K. Murton reported that 'of 400 ringed swans recovered dead, 95 had died through colliding with overhead wires'. In the Broxbourne area of Hertfordshire nine swans died in a fortnight in 1971 from this cause. In my own experience I have known a number of species to fly into telegraph wires including moorhen, corncrake, tawny owl, swan, pink-footed goose, and Canada goose. I once saw a goose fly into wires, crash into the road, walk about for several minutes and then take off apparently none the worse for the experience. In Britain there are about ten thousand miles of from 132 kv to 400 kv transmission lines maintained by the Central Electricity Generating Board. Where these run close to estuaries, between lakes and reservoirs, across well-used bird flight lines and in areas of heavy nocturnal migration the death rate may be quite high. Teesmouth and Carlisle have proved especially to be regions of high mortality.

Between 1964 and 1970 a survey was jointly carried out by the Royal

Society for the Protection of Birds and the C.E.G.B. to find out by weekly searches at Dungeness in Kent how birds might be affected by the powerlines in the district. More than a thousand birds of 74 different species were found dead at this focal point of bird migration in southern England. Most of the casualties were gulls flying to and from their roosts or night migrants such as starlings, thrushes, warblers, rails and turtle doves. Although large birds the size of swans and cormorants have been electrocuted by causing a short circuit, most of the deaths arose from direct impact with the single earthing wire which runs from the top of one pylon to the top of the next. This single wire is apparently much less visible than the conductors. In an attempt to reduce the mortality luminous orange tapes were wrapped around the earthing wire at four-foot intervals but the results of this experiment have proved inconclusive. In some areas corks and silver and coloured balls have also been fitted to the lines to mark them more clearly. In the Teesmouth area the addition of black tapes to the earthing wire at six-foot intervals brought down the death rate practically to zero. The survey suggested that if cables were hung parallel to well-used bird flight paths the danger could be lessened and that marking the earthing wire was likely to have positive advantages.

It can be seen from this chapter that there are many varied uses of the land along the edge of the countryside but I have made little mention so far of the importance of water as a habitat for birds. This may be water that occurs in rivers and streams, canals, sewage farms, reservoirs, lakes and ponds and in the flooded pits that form after the extraction of sand, gravel and clay from the land. Man has increased the areas of water to meet his growing demands and this has had a considerable effect on aquatic and waterside birds. We have also seen how the countryside fringe to our outer suburbs is under continuing pressure. Max Nicholson and A. W. Colling in their notes to *The Chart of Human Impacts in the Countryside*, prepared for The Countryside in 1970 Conference, drew attention to 'the very heterogeneous nature of the activities and operations responsible for impacts on the countryside, and the apparent lack of awareness among those concerned of their role in this respect'.

CHAPTER 6

Rivers, Lakes and Reservoirs

A PROPORTION of the land in the suburbs is occupied by water in the form of natural rivers and man-made canals, of ponds and lakes and of artificially created reservoirs. As man has extracted minerals from the face of the earth he has left it pock-marked with pits some of which have become filled with water. In other places the land has sunk to produce more wetland habitats. All these stretches of still or flowing water can provide valuable environments for birds, particularly at the present time when natural wetlands in so many parts of the world are being drained and developed for housing or agriculture. Some of these waters have both commercial and recreational uses and many of our inland lakes, pools, reservoirs and disused gravel and other mineral workings experience a multi-purpose exploitation by commerce, boating, fishing and bathing interests and by students of wildlife. The character of all these watery habitats is a very varied one. Some rivers are tidal, others are dammed. There are also slow-flowing lowland streams with rich vegetation and clear fast-moving torrents with a poor one. The banks of some rivers are regularly scoured by draglines and excavators which destroy the fringe habitats and bank heaps of spoil along the water's edge. Some waterways are polluted by heated water or by organic and chemical wastes which de-oxygenate the stream and kill both plant and animal life or encourage the growth of fungi and algae. Canals which are no longer maintained or have been drained are a loss to wildlife. Man-made pits may be rehabilitated or left as depressing barren pools in a desert of waste and spoil. The banks of some lakes and reservoirs are rich in plant growth while others are paved in concrete or stone. Some pools and lakes are deep, others are shallow. Some waters are rich in natural foods and others are rather poor, and all these factors can influence the kinds of birds that can be found there.

For convenience it seems better to divide all these watery habitats into two groups. In the present chapter the discussion will be confined to the birdlife of rivers, docks, lakes, pools and reservoirs, all of which have certain general features in common. Marshes – both salt and fresh-water – sewage farms, flashes and gravel pits will be examined in the next chapter since again there are factors in all but the first habitat which are very similar. It also seems more logical to hold over a comparison between the birds of the two kinds of marsh to a later point. Many migrant birds as well come to patches of water to rest and feed and these will be discussed in chapter 10 which is devoted to migration among suburban birds. Gulls and some other species use reservoirs in some areas as roosts and their communal roosting behaviour will be one of the subjects investigated in chapter 9.

Before looking in detail at the various types of habitat it might be useful to say something in broad terms about the vegetation and wildlife associated with water. 'Freshwater habitats', wrote R. S. R. Fitter, 'range all the way from Loch Ness to the puddles in the town-hall car-park'. Rivers, ponds and lakes contain a vegetation that differs chiefly according to the rate of flow and the stagnancy of the water and to the amount of silt that covers their beds. Mountain lakes and highland rivers in a land of hard insoluble rocks accumulate very little silt and so their vegetation tends to be rather sparse. On the other hand, lowland rivers flow over much softer rocks and remove a lot of material from their banks and beds which is deposited as silt on which a varied and rich plant life can establish itself. Silt can also be moved along the shores of lakes in a similar way and these banks can carry a very luxuriant vegetation. If a river drains well-manured land or a pond receives rainwater enriched locally from nearby farmland then again the plant growth can be very good. However, the drainage of chemicals and waste products into the water can have a correspondingly adverse effect. There is a zonation of plant life in ponds and slow-flowing rivers from the wholly submerged species in the deeper parts, such as *Elodea*, to those nearer the banks with floating leaves, such as pondweeds, and finally to others growing on the margins and wet ground, such as reeds, reed-mace and other waterside species. This type of succession has been very well described by the late Sir Arthur Tansley.

It is the speed of current flow and the corresponding character of the bottom which are the most important factors influencing the animals and plants that occur along a river. Local variations are also very significant. It is not really possible to state any very clear biological distinctions between a river, stream or rill and a pond or lake. For example, the first 60 miles of the River Tees from its source consist of rapidly flowing waters with only a few fish species such as trout and grayling. Downstream the river begins to slow and here rooted plants are growing and coarse fish are common. The Tees then reaches a town which is responsible for some pollution and a loss of oxygen in the water. Finally, a brackish stretch of river enters the saline and dirty waters of the estuary. The Tees must be considered in four different lengths. In contrast, a lowland chalk river rich in calcium and with a slow fall towards the sea is richer in nutrients and consequently plants, insects and fish.

Some suburban rivers may have been fed by smaller streams and rivulets which joined them in more rural surroundings. These small water-courses in highland areas may hold breeding dippers and grey wagtails. In a lowland region they may still attract a few grey wagtails but their community is likely to consist of mallard, moorhens, sedge warblers, yellow wagtails, reed buntings and kingfishers, and, in marshy places, redshank and snipe. The main river, still flowing in rural calm, is now broader and slower and may harbour little grebes, coots, swans and perhaps reed warblers. Herons come to fish along the margins of the river. In winter, if there are alders growing along the banks, red-polls and siskins may arrive to hang acrobatically in the branches as they feed on the seed.

Around London, on some of the fresher rivers, watercress beds have been established for commercial cropping. They were set up at such sites as Carshalton on the River Wandle, at Fetcham on the River Mole, at Denham on the River Misbourne and near Watford on the River Gade. These beds have proved a special attraction to moorhens, little grebes and kingfishers. In one place at least kingfishers began to use the hats of people working on the cressbeds as look-out posts! Pied and grey wagtails may find their food on the beds and nest close by. Mallard and moorhens may do some damage to the watercress and blackbirds have been seen rooting up plants as they searched for insects and other invertebrates. In winter, and particularly during severe weather, the watercress beds can become an important refuge for a good number of species. On the beds along the River Gade the regular winter visitors include snipe, redwings, starlings, grey and pied wagtails and meadow pipits. Also, since 1965, there have been up to four water pipits present during each winter.

It was during the winter of 1962–3 that the discovery was first made that small numbers of water pipits from the marshy Alpine meadow-lands were wintering in south-west Hertfordshire. One of these pipits was first identified by I. G. Johnson on a watercress bed near West Hyde. After that, other birds were observed not only there but at a number of other similar sites. On 7 February 1965 a total of thirteen birds was recorded. In 1971 there were up to five water pipits in the valleys of the Colne and Gade. The birds seem to be very closely linked with cressbeds which never freeze and are fed by springs which remain at relatively the same temperature even in very cold weather. The water pipits are much shyer birds than the meadow pipits which are common on the beds and they will not allow an observer on foot to come closer than fifty yards. This species of pipit is now being reported more regularly as a winter visitor to Britain but it is not wholly restricted to watercress beds here. It also occurs in coastal situations and in 1971 I tape recorded a bird at Minsmere in Suffolk. Some individuals favour inland reservoirs, and I have watched birds at Chew Valley in Somerset, while others frequent sewage farms and freshwater rivers and marshes. K. C. Osborne analysed the records of the water pipit in the London area and found that 90% occurred on watercress beds, at sewage farms and 'associated water systems'. The two main wintering areas are the River Wandle at Beddington Sewage Farm and the Colne Valley from Harefield Moor to Cassiobury Park. The watercress beds in that park have also been visited since 1963 by bittern, spotted crake, jack snipe, woodcock, redshank, curlew sandpiper and ruff.

In 1970 the Hertfordshire and Middlesex Trust for Nature Conservation acquired some old watercress beds at Lemsford Springs in the neighbourhood of Welwyn Garden City. This reserve consists of 'a series of shallow lagoons fed by springs and previously used as watercress beds, a stretch of the River Lea, some marsh, and small areas of wet and dry woodland'. T. W. Gladwin, whose description I have just quoted, has taken a leading part in the development of this reserve. The marsh is made up of tall herbage with reed-grass, marsh woundwort, meadow sweet, hemp agrimony and various *Carex* sedges. Over the whole reserve there are from forty-one to forty-two breeding bird species including little grebe, kingfisher and grey wagtail, while the winter visitors may involve such species as snipe and jack snipe, redshank, dunlin, common and green sandpipers and water rails.

If suburbia is residential, affluent and little disturbed then the waterside birds of the area may be varied and interesting. If, however, the river becomes embanked, entombed, industrialised and polluted then the bird life is limited to the hardiest and most adaptable species. On a grubby, urbanised river the breeding birds consist of the typical town community – just a small nucleus of birds with perhaps a few pairs of mallard nesting on a ledge or the pier of a bridge. A few feral pigeons, starlings, crows and house sparrows may feed along the banks and muddy verges while during the winter months gulls may turn up to scavenge alongside their urban companions.

If a town stands on the banks of a tidal river the suburban stretches, which are covered and revealed by the tides, may prove very attractive for birds. The character of a 'suburban' length of a well-used tidal river is unlikely to be very different from that of an 'urban' one. For this reason a study of two sections of the River Thames carried out by Stanley Cramp and W. G. Teagle in 1955 is of interest. In the winter months they found that all five species of the commoner gulls were present and fed regularly from the exposed mud and shingle banks when the tide was out. Floating morsels of food were picked off the water by the gulls in flight. Mute swans and mallard were common and there were also small numbers of tufted duck, pochard and, more rarely, little grebes, coot, woodpigeons, common sandpipers, house martins, grey wagtails, one species of tern and examples of American wigeon and ruddy shelduck which had presumably come from St

James's Park. Where the outfall of power stations runs into rivers, terns may assemble in the migration seasons and up to thirty have been observed at Dartford lower down the River Thames. P. J. Strangeman, who watched the river at Westminster from 1968 to 1970 saw great crested grebes, Canada geese, starlings, meadow pipits, and pied and grey wagtails. At various times other watchers have reported such odd vagrants as a gannet, grey phalarope and guillemot, while a razorbill seen flying upstream was only able to clear Westminster Bridge at its second attempt. The Thames at Woolwich, which was studied by P. J. Grant in the winters between 1968 and 1970, proved capable of holding very high numbers of surface-feeding and diving ducks. There were 700 each of teal and mallard, 330 pintail, 400 tufted duck, 2500 pochard, 1600 shelduck as well as smaller numbers of gadwall, wigeon, shoveler, scaup, goldeneye, smew and goosander. Since the numbers continue to be sustained, this must surely be a sign of a much less heavily polluted river. There are other factors as well which may have contributed to this build-up, such as bad weather and disturbance on the continent of Europe.

The Thames does offer some hope for the future but no salmon has been seen in it since 1833, so there is still some way to go. Other rivers that flow through the suburbs are subject to varying degrees of pollution and these can occur within the whole range of industrial and sewage effluents. Any pollution of rivers and streams must affect the flora and fauna. If fish and invertebrate life are reduced or damaged by chemical and other wastes then there will be an adverse effect on the birds. In recent years somewhere between 10,000 and 100,000 fish died on two miles of the River Lea – a river near London once respected and admired by the great Izaak Walton himself. A strike by municipal workers resulted in raw sewage being discharged into the River Thames near Swindon and killing between 10,000 and 20,000 fish. Only conditions of semi-flood that diluted the sewage prevented more fish from dying than actually did. One expert thought that it would take at least a year for a polluted river to become clean after the sewage works started operations again, while it might take up to ten years for the complete recovery of mature fish stocks. Other kinds of substances may clog the plumage of birds and I have seen both mallard and kingfishers on the River Brent with their feathers matted by some foreign matter that had been discharged directly into the water. The Welsh Harp Conservation Group has suggested that booms be placed across the tributaries of the Brent to hold back unwanted substances both from the river and the reservoir. If pollution goes on too long a river or canal may be 'killed' and then the only birds that will come to it are scavengers searching for scraps of food that man has thrown into it and any other organic rejectamenta of our twentieth-century society. In 1973 Dr A. L. Downing, director of the Water Pollution Research Laboratory estimated that by 1980 there would be significant reductions in the length of grossly polluted rivers to about 200 miles and of poor quality rivers to 670 miles at a cost of around £700 million.

Where towns have been established on rivers large enough to be navigated by commercial shipping then the areas of dockland provide, just off the river, a number of large artificial lakes filled with river water. Although these have not been studied in as much detail as those other artificial areas of water around towns – the reservoirs and sewage farms – the closure to ships in 1970 of the Surrey Commercial Docks at Bermondsey provided an ideal opportunity for investigation. We have already seen how the wasteland formed near these docks attracted many birds. Between August 1970 and March 1971 P. J. Grant made at least fifty visits to this area of disused docks and found that in cold weather the docks might be visited by more than 2500 ducks of ten species of which the commonest were mallard, pochard and tufted duck. Wigeon were seen there too and it is interesting to recall that as long ago as 1941 the late James Fisher saw a score flying over Bermondsey. Other ducks that were reported were pintail, scaup, goldeneye, red-breasted merganser, shelduck and a pair of ferruginous duck. Wading birds were also seen feeding on the mud and of these the most regularly observed were ringed plover, common sandpiper, redshank and dunlin. There were also little grebes, up to forty moorhens, some three thousand black-headed gulls and smaller numbers of herring, common, lesser and great black-backed gulls. A first winter Mediterranean gull was recorded on 15 December 1971. Trevor Stroud (*in litt.*) described for me a visit that he made to the dockland area in October 1972. He wrote: 'Saw six grey herons in a secluded mooring bay which, not having been dredged for two years, has developed a sloping mudbank the higher level of which has dried and cracked. The herons were standing on this feature. There was also a considerable coming and going of carrion crows, gulls and flocks of thirty or more tufted duck, mallard and quite a few moorhens.' Some of these species may also appear in other dockland areas such as those in Southampton, Liverpool and the Clyde but the variety in these ports is smaller than that at Bermondsey because their waters are more disturbed and there is little or no dereliction to produce peaceful lakes and mudbanks. I have seen mergansers, cormorants and shags in several English docks and guillemots, black guillemots, razorbills and long-tailed ducks in some Scottish docks and harbours. Fishing ports attract gulls in very large numbers. Their capacities are quite remarkable as I once had occasion to observe in Peterhead in Aberdeenshire. A few feet from me was a basket of fish and, above it, beating and hovering was a herring gull. At last he came down and in less than a minute he had gulped down seven herrings. He stood rocking gently on the basket's edge with the

tail of a fish protruding from the corner of his bill. Two Buchan
fishermen shouted at him and he began to thrash the air with his pearl-
grey wings. But his vastly increased all-up weight would not allow him
to take off. Out of his gullet shot two herrings and, as he staggered into
the air, out came two more. Relieved now of more than half his meal, he
was at last able, like an overfull vulture, to get airborne. One of the best
places that I know to watch gulls is at the waste outlet of a fish canning
factory; here I have seen seven species of gull feeding at the same time,
including kittiwakes and the rare little gull. In those docks where grain
is unloaded feral pigeons gather in numbers and may live in this habitat
with very little seasonal change.

Upstream the rivers may be less commercialized and disturbed and
here the bird life is often quite varied, especially among the wildfowl
and wading birds. In one year, for example, thirteen species of duck
appeared on a stretch of suburban river; these were shelduck, mallard,
gadwall, wigeon, shoveler, pintail, teal, tufted duck, pochard, goldeneye, scaup, goosander and smew, and I have also seen common scoter
and red-breasted merganser there in another year. Between Putney and
Teddington on the River Thames there may be as many as a thousand
mallard, two or three hundred mute swans, fifty or more Canada geese
as well as small numbers of teal and tufted duck. Glaucous and Iceland
gulls have also been known to visit this part of the Thames and there
are sometimes great crested and little grebes, herons and cormorants
and I have also noted lapwing, redshank, green and common sandpipers
feeding among the hordes of grubby feral pigeons, starlings and house
sparrows on the mud. Meadow pipits can sometimes be seen on the
river mud and in colder conditions redwings as well. On 8 March 1947,
towards the end of that bad winter, Miss M. Curtis saw two crested
larks on the foreshore of the river at Hammersmith. Sections of the
River Clyde, despite their proximity to Glasgow and its industrial and
mining operations, still attract wildfowl and so also do parts of the
Tyne. In the winter of 1970–1 there was a flock of 5450 pintail on the
River Mersey, surely one of our most polluted rivers.

In many suburban areas there are canals wandering through the
landscape, following the contour lines, running through tunnels and
dark cuttings, under bridges, past the gaunt tall backs of Victorian
terraces and sometimes opening up into basins to form lagoons in front
of gracious houses or grey wharves. These slow-flowing man-made
rivers are a feature of the lowlands where they link up with the main
river systems. In 1800, at the height of the Canal Age, there were about
4000 miles of navigable canal in use. Now some of these waterways have
disappeared, others hold water but are rarely used, while a few still
survive with some commercial exploitation of their channels. Today the
cabin cruiser and the canoe have largely replaced the narrowboat. The
water in the canals tends to be rather hard and quite rich in nutrients

which are steadily replaced by the gentle flow of water. Each canal has to have a large supply of water at the summit level and so reservoirs were constructed to hold the reserves. Those at Tring which help to keep the Grand Union Canal filled are famous for their bird life. The fauna of the suburban canal lengths is very similar to that of the urban sections. A disused canal may prove to be a most important wildlife reserve and is often rich in aquatic insects. Whenever I wanted specimens of *Dytiscus* water beetles or *Notonecta* water boatmen for television programmes a disused part of the Basingstoke Canal was always able to yield up specimens in a hurry. On these neglected canals mallard, moorhens, mute swans and even little grebes may flourish. Some canals are now protected or leased by County Naturalists' Trusts, others are being redeveloped for recreational use and many are being guarded from too much indiscriminate chemical spraying.

On the more built-up suburban sections of the canals the commonest bird is often the mallard, but occasionally a few tufted duck or even a teal may turn up. Mute swans sometimes try to rear cygnets close to the paths and a few pairs of moorhens may be able to breed by building their nests high off the ground in hawthorns and other trees. I have also known pied wagtails sometimes to nest under the arches of canal bridges. At other times grey wagtails, herons and kingfishers may drop in to surprise the observer walking along the bank. In winter black-headed gulls often join the carrion crows to look for scraps in the usually opaque and discoloured water.

The rest of this chapter will be devoted to those more or less static pieces of water such as ponds, lakes and reservoirs which may be in some instances very similar in their bird life whilst in others they may be very dissimilar. A pond is a small area of water but it is not just a tiny lake. Most ponds are artificial, having been dug for cattle, but they can also arise from surface workings that later become filled with water. It has been suggested that a 'pond' is any piece of water that is so shallow that attached plants can grow all over it, but it is, in fact, the clarity of the water itself which most controls the spread of such plants. The water of a cattle pond may be dark because of the clouds of small organisms living in it. Another feature that is sometimes used to distinguish a pond from a lake is that the former does not suffer from wave action. I am sure it is better to use the terms in their popular sense; after all, some quiet parts of lakes have all the characteristics of ponds. On the whole, ponds are rather still and this favours the growth of a surface flora, such as duckweed, and a varied fauna. If there is regular fouling of the pond by manure, the water may become very rich in algae and also possess a large and thriving population of Chironomid larvae.

A typical pond has its pair of moorhens, perhaps some wild or domestic ducks and perhaps a pair of visiting pied wagtails and spotted flycatchers. The insect production of such a piece of water is high and so it will attract swallows and house martins, migrant warblers and other birds. Swifts will come sweeping low over the water on warm thundery evenings and a kestrel or sparrowhawk may come in search of small unsuspecting birds drinking at the water's edge. In Cheshire the drinking pits for cattle were largely formed from marl diggings made when marl was extracted to improve the land. Pondweeds, sedges, yellow flag, purple loosestrife, sallows and alders often grow around their margins. Here the breeding bird community consists of moor-hens, reed buntings and perhaps sedge warblers with a few of the scrub birds such as robins and hedgesparrows. In winter perhaps mallard and teal will come to the more secluded ones. As ponds are small they contain rather rigid food chains and the overcropping of the food resources is always a possibility. In hot weather a pond may evaporate to such an extent and the sunken plants decompose, that all the available oxygen is used up.

The characteristics of lakes have been closely studied by T. T. Macan and E. B. Worthington; they described three categories – eutrophic (rich in nutrients, with a varied flora and fauna; shallow, dark and usually in a lowland situation), oligotrophic (low in nutrients as well as plants and animals; clear and usually in wild, rocky sites), and dys-trophic (rich in organic peat; beer-coloured with a rich plankton but few large invertebrates). Many lowland eutrophic lakes have a fine flora of *Elodea*, various types of pondweed, arrowhead and water plantain, white and yellow waterlilies, reedmace, bulrush and common reed. Oligotrophic pools and lochs often lying in rocky basins may contain plants such as *Nitella*, shoreweed and, where the soil is less organic, a fringe of reed swamp. Thick reedbeds slow down the move-ment of water and they also deposit layers of organic matter on the lake bottom as the reeds die down each year. Some lakes are rather in-hospitable for birds and, when I have driven about the British country-side, I have often passed these pieces of water which always seem devoid of birds except in very bad weather or during the seasons of passage. Some of them have little vegetation or cover and others may have to endure disturbance from water skiing and power boating. Large lakes where the human pressures are more or less confined to the week-ends may have an improved fauna, but oligotrophic waters often hold little more than some mute swans, mallard, coot and perhaps grebes, while a quiet bay may afford breeding sites for a few pairs of tufted duck or pochard.

On the other hand a lowland eutrophic lake, lying in a shallow saucer of land, will allow reeds and other plants to grow thickly around its margins and here there is a much richer bird population. Good examples of this rich kind of lake are provided by the meres of Cheshire. A. W. Boyd studied three of these large meres – Marbury, Pickmere

TAWNY OWL, the typical owl of suburban parks and gardens.

GREENFINCH and BULLFINCH. *Above*, greenfinch at a water tank. This is generally the best known of the suburban finches; *below*, bullfinch, a species that has spread remarkably in recent years into town parks and suburban gardens.

and Tabley – for more than forty years. Here he found a regular breeding community of reed bunting, reed warbler, sedge warbler, kingfisher, heron, mute swan, Canada goose, mallard, teal, tufted duck, great crested grebe (known as '*the* Cheshire bird'), little grebe, common sandpiper, moorhen and coot. There were also summer records of the garganey and the black-necked grebe. In winter the meres were visited by cormorants, shelduck, wigeon, shoveler, pochard, goldeneye, goosanders, black-headed, common, herring, great and lesser black-backed gulls and water rails. The migrants that appeared in most years generally included dunlin, sanderling, green sandpiper, and both black and common terns.

Many lakes in Britain which at first glance seem natural have been created by man. These include flashes, subsidences and the landscaped pools in the parklands and on the estates of the outer suburbs. We have already seen how urban and suburban parks can provide mallard with food throughout the year. In outer London alone there are some forty lakes of this kind that together form about two hundred acres of open water and where there is a winter population of around two thousand mallard. These ornamental pools play a very important part in the ecology of wintering ducks. Grovelands, Broomfield and Alexandra Parks, Waterlow, Clissold and Finsbury Parks in suburban London hold almost half the total of mallard on these lakes, and there are also numbers in Kew Gardens, Grange Park, Carshalton Grove and elsewhere. Tufted ducks also come to many of the larger pools while there may be pochard and sometimes gadwall on the others. Pen Ponds in Richmond Park are still a haunt of the handsome goosander and I have also seen between fifty and sixty meadow pipits and a curlew sandpiper on their banks. There are lakes of this kind in many suburban situations throughout the country and similar reports might be made from many of them. The public park lake at Stapleton on the northern fringes of Bristol attracts up to a hundred mallard and there are often up to three hundred and fifty mallard and two hundred teal on Roath Park lake on the outskirts of Cardiff. Another favourite haunt of mallard is Wollaton lake on the eastern side of Nottingham. On the northern edge of Newcastle-upon-Tyne lies Gosforth Park with a lake which offers sanctuary to mallard, teal, wigeon, shoveler, pochard, tufted duck, goldeneye and mute swan. Pochard and tufted ducks can often be seen in the Edinburgh parks in winter while Duddingston Loch has a breeding colony of pochard. Many smaller lakes in less pretentious parks hold small numbers of the common ducks and they help to form a chain of wildfowl refuges at a time when the pressure on these birds is growing all the time.

A great deal of what man does in developing the land, in extending the facilities for transport and communications, in draining wetlands and marshes has a direct and adverse effect on water birds through loss of habitat. In recent times, however, urban man has demanded more water, more concrete and more sewerage and these have benefited large numbers of wildfowl, waders and gulls. To satisfy the first demand he built reservoirs, to meet the second he excavated gravel pits and to fulfil the third he laid out sewage farms. The most important of these new habitats were those provided by the reservoirs and these we shall consider next. The other two environments will be reserved for the next chapter. Reservoirs are kinds of lake but the other two habitats fashioned by man tend to be more complicated with the presence quite often of scrub, marsh, open waste ground, as well as water and, in the case of the sewage farm, settling tanks, sprinklers and so on. According to figures published in 1963 in the Wildfowl Trust's survey for the Nature Conservancy of wildfowl in Great Britain, there were just under five hundred and fifty reservoirs in England and Wales, providing 35,000 acres of water or about 55 square miles. These were constructed primarily to satisfy the needs of domestic and industrial users and, to a smaller extent, to supply the canals with 'topping up' water.

About seventy-five per cent of the reservoirs have little or no significance for wildfowl because they are too small, too high above sea level or too poor in food resources and cover. Some of the least productive are situated along the Pennine Chain and even such big tracts of water as those of Ladybower, Catcleugh and those in the Elan Valley in Wales, all of which I have visited, can be very unrewarding. When the total of unpromising sheets of water has been subtracted from the full total of 550 reservoirs, the actual number of valuable ones sinks to as low as 140 with an acreage of about 20,000. Of these remaining reservoirs 50 are known to harbour more than 250 ducks each and so should be looked upon as important refuges. Three of them lie in North Wales and North-West England, eight in South-West England and South Wales, ten in North-East England and the Border Country, twelve in Central and Eastern England and seventeen in Southern and South-Eastern England. The most important reservoirs are grouped in Southern and Eastern England, especially in Essex, Northamptonshire, Leicestershire and Somerset, and in the outer suburban ring of London itself. In this region are 24 of the 29 reservoirs in this country which can support over 500 birds, as well as all but one of those capable of carrying 1000 ducks or more. In this part of England the waters seem to suit the birds and many of the migrants arrive here first after their journeys from Europe. After these reservoirs had been built they offered safe roosts for the surface-feeding ducks which were able to explore new areas from them, and they also provided food resources for the diving ducks. The suburban reservoirs of London too can reveal assemblies of duck species equal to many others that can be found in other parts of Great Britain.

The first reservoirs to be constructed were built in the early part of the nineteenth century around London – at Ruislip, Elstree and Hendon. These joined with the reservoirs that now form the National Nature Reserve at Tring in Hertfordshire to keep up the level of the Grand Union Canal. For half a century or so these were the most extensive sheets of water in the area. Since canal reservoirs store water that is not used for drinking purposes, they are often made available to the public for recreation. They then become subjected to such pressures as arise from sailing, canoeing, rowing, hydroplane racing, vandalism, pollution, rubbish dumping, fires and the encroachment of estate and factory building. The canal reservoir at Cannock in the West Midlands has suffered a lot of disturbance and its value to birds correspondingly reduced. This piece of water is situated one mile to the north-west of Brownhills and is bordered by a hinterland of gorse, heather, rough ground, marshes, slag heaps, flashes and pools, small fields and a railway embankment. In 1955 M. J. Rogers reported that 'the surrounds of the pool are the unofficial park for the local population' but mallard, redshank, skylark, whinchat, sedge warbler, yellow wagtail and reed bunting were still able to nest. In winter grebes, coots, mute swans, black-headed, common and herring gulls, lapwing, golden plover, merlins and small numbers of some ten species of duck were regularly recorded while of the migrants the most frequent were oystercatchers, turnstones, snipe, curlews, whimbrels, common sandpipers, greenshanks, dunlin, sanderlings (which 'could be described as almost common'), black, common and Arctic terns, wheatears, redstarts and willow warblers. Among the interesting and rare vagrants that appeared at Cannock were a great northern diver, a Slavonian grebe, a Leach's petrel, a long-tailed duck, a kite, a Temminck's stint and a Lapland bunting. The other midland canal reservoirs at Gailey and Belvide, situated as they are on the edge of an industrial region, also suffer from considerable disturbance.

The Brent Reservoir, known locally also as the Welsh Harp from its original shape, has also suffered from increased development. In 1913 about ten per cent of the immediate area around it was urbanised but by 1930 the amount had trebled. Now as high-density housing estates and other changes are pressing in on the reservoir from all sides Leo Batten, who has made a long study of the region, finds it 'difficult to feel optimistic about the effects these will ultimately have on the bird life'. A Welsh Harp Conservation Group has been formed to try and prevent residential and industrial encroachment on the area, and to improve the facilities for human recreational needs as well as preserving part of the region as a marshland nature reserve. The initial broad response to the Group's proposals has been very encouraging and volunteers have already joined together to clear the water of rubbish and litter and to take part in an extensive tree-planting scheme. Much of the disturbance at the Brent occurs at the weekends and so the comparative respite granted to birds during the week gives some small encouragement to duck in winter, especially mallard, tufted duck, pochard, and up to 30 smew, but the combined wildfowl total is now rarely above 300. In autumn, little grebes and gulls of all five common species are regularly seen and it is also possible to observe passage of great crested grebes (one pair is often present in summer), teal, gadwall, shoveler, dunlin, redshanks, greenshanks, green sandpipers, common sandpipers, curlews, snipe, black and common terns, sand martins, meadow pipits (some winter), grey wagtails, chiffchaffs, whinchats and wheatears. On 2 September 1956 I flushed a female ortolan bunting – the first in Middlesex for 88 years. In April of that same year two little buntings were seen at Staines Reservoir by D. I. M. Wallace. At the Brent herons, wigeon, pintails and jack snipe are now only scarce visitors but water rails sometimes overwinter and I heard one 'sharming' in the winter of 1972–3.

Unlike many of the drinking water reservoirs that were to be built later in the nineteenth or in the twentieth centuries, these reservoirs made to serve the canals had natural-looking banks where vegetation could grow and flourish. At Elstree and Ruislip it was possible, according to R. S. R. Fitter, to find lesser spearwort, bur-marigold, water forget-me-not, flowering rush and the rare foxtail grass *Alopecurus fulvus*. This orange foxtail also grows at Tring. I have seen the flowering rush in a small pool on the edge of the Brent Reservoir. The waterside vegetation is important as it provides a food resource, nesting sites and cover for several species. At Tring the water level is continually changing, but it is at its highest in winter. The water comes from the Chilterns and from springs and wells. The opening of a lock on the canal for the passage of a boat moves some fifty thousand gallons of water and a whole day's consumption might be as high as twenty million gallons. The maximum depths of the four reservoirs at Tring vary between eighteen and twenty-two feet and fluctuations in levels during the spring and autumn can affect the number of wading birds using them. Besides the waterside vegetation at Tring, which is formed largely from reeds, reed-grass and sedges, there is also some willow and hawthorn scrub and larger trees such as ash, elm, poplar and horse chestnut. As a result communities of lakeside and scrub birds can be found breeding there in the summer. In spring and autumn various waders and wildfowl appear on passage. It was at Tring that in 1938 the first pair of little ringed plovers was proved to nest in Britain.

The Brent Reservoir in suburban north-west London and its bird life have both been well documented from its early days when J. E. Harting and F. Bond walked round its shores with their guns and recorded squacco heron, night heron, little bittern, spoonbill, avocet and Temminck's stint, to the present time when it is regularly visited by bird watchers who are carrying out many different kinds of research.

Once an attractive beauty spot it is now dominated by factories and tower blocks but still preserves some banks with an almost rural charm. One frosty December morning in 1972 I toured the northern shores of the reservoir. The sky was a pale shade of blue, there was still some warmth in the low sun and the rime-encrusted stems of the dead sedges, willowherbs and thistles crackled under my feet. The water was a still silent mirror, reflecting in itself the slopes of Dollis Hill wreathed in a faint and ghostly mist. High overhead an aircraft glinted in the sun. It was a perfect morning for bird-watching – so still, in fact, that I could hear a Tannoy from a factory on the North Circular Road demanding 'Mr . . . , wanted on the telephone!' For two hours I walked along the water's edge and in that time I had logged no fewer than 41 different species of bird. There were flocks of finches, tree sparrows and red-wings near Birchen Grove while gulls of three different kinds sat in serried ranks and preened on the wooden pier near the sailing club. In the bay near Cool Oak Lane – marked as Cold Duck Lane on my nineteenth-century maps – there were a pair of swans, a hundred coot, some of them noisily engaged in aggressive encounters and splashing after each other across the surface of the water. The number of duck was disappointing; only six pochard and four tufted ducks with one black and white drake. However, I did see up to eight little grebes all busily slipping under water without a fuss and reappearing many yards away from their point of entry. Another visit two weeks later disclosed several hundred pochard and tufted ducks, a dozen smew and a water rail.

Leo Batten, whose researches into suburban bird life have already figured in this book, wrote a fascinating paper on the birds of the Brent Reservoir in the *London Naturalist* and I am indebted to him for most of the following information. The reservoir has a thin fringe of reed grass (*Phalaris arundinacea*) which separates much of the water from the playing fields and grassy swards on the northern and southern banks. At the western end is a dam. At the northern and eastern limits of the water are some silt banks bearing a more extensive growth of reed grass, willows, patches of *Typha latifolia* and a one-acre bed of reeds (*Phragmites*). In this region of willow swamp and reed grass are found all the moorhens, coots, great crested and little grebes, tufted ducks and reed warblers that hold territories and actually breed. Although reed buntings and sedge warblers can be found outside this habitat, the majority of birds appear here. In 1970 a grasshopper warbler held a territory. In the willow swamp there are also territories of mallard, blackbird, song thrush, wren, hedgesparrow, great and blue tits, robin, greenfinch, pied wagtail, willow warbler, magpie and skylark, while the reed grass marsh supports territories of mallard, song thrush, wren, whitethroat and yellow wagtail. Mute swans some-times try and breed, a gadwall laid eggs in 1957 and other species occur in the scrub and woodland nearby. The level of the reservoir can alter considerably and after heavy rain the swollen streams that flow into the reservoir may raise the water level by as much as a foot – enough to flood the nests of coots. Rafts have been provided for waterfowl to nest on and a pair of scaup occupied a raft one spring but, as one might have expected, they did not breed.

Rafts can play a most important part in the conservation of water birds. For many years common terns bred on a marsh in the River Dee in Cheshire but their numbers steadily dropped over the years because of tidal flooding and growing disturbance from the public. Then a few pairs nested on the walls of a reservoir in the Shotton steelworks. To encourage this disappearing species a raft of telegraph poles and railway sleepers, topped with a layer of slag and turves and given buoyancy with polystyrene blocks, was floated out on the reservoir. Terns quickly adopted the raft and brought a new freshness and delight to what was described as a very 'blighted environment'. As a result more rafts were added and by 1972 at least ninety pairs of common terns were nesting and the rafts were also visited by Sandwich and Arctic terns and even a single roseate. There is still a threat to the Dee estuary from a barrage scheme but the raft experiment has been encouraging, just as similar experiments on flooded gravel pits have brought rewards.

Swifts are often seen over the Brent Reservoir, flying low during warm and cloudy evenings when they can be mist-netted and ringed. House martins also come from their colonies on the estates nearby to forage over the water. A full list of Brent birds can be found in appendix 6.

As man's way of life began to change from that of a rural to an urban being, so it became increasingly necessary to satisfy his need for fresh drinking water. As the industrial revolution gathered pace, factories and power stations began to consume growing quantities of pure water. London's demands were looked after by the Metropolitan Water Board which stored water largely through reservoirs in the valleys of the Thames and Lea. These new artificial lakes were to bring about some remarkable developments in the history of suburban bird life around the metropolis. The first reservoirs were built at Stoke Newington in the 1830s, at Kew in the 1840s and at Walthamstow near the end of the century. In 1902 a huge reservoir, occupying some 424 acres, was completed at Staines and during the next 25 years there followed Island Barn, Queen Mary at Littleton and King George in the Lea Valley. After the 1939–45 War King George VI was added at Staines, the William Girling at Chingford, the Hilfield Park near Watford, and Queen Elizabeth II at Walton. At a time when true marshland had virtually been cleared from the River Thames the construction of these reservoirs and the gravel pits was to compensate in no small way for the loss of this natural habitat. In many other parts of the country other reservoirs were also being built and land flooded to provide more water reserves. In Essex there were Abberton in 1940 and Hanningfield in 1954; in Leicestershire Eyebrook in 1940; in Northamptonshire Pitsford in 1955; in Somerset Cheddar in 1938 and Chew Valley in 1953 and in Staffordshire Blithfield in 1952. It is thought that fifteen of the most important reservoirs, shown in appendix 5, give refuge to three per cent of all the country's mallard, four per cent of the teal and from fifteen to twenty per cent of the pochard and tufted duck.

The reservoirs for drinking water vary to some extent in their methods of construction as well as in their shape and depth. Many of the London ones have concreted or paved banks which do not allow for the growth of sedges and other plants which occur by the Brent. The upper banks are sometimes sown with grass and may be ornamented with bushes which can give some protection to such nesting ducks as mallard, tufted duck and, more rarely, pochard. The islands on the reservoirs at Walthamstow give some security to nesting tufted ducks which have raised young there since 1905. In *The Birds of the London Area* R. C. Homes noted that great crested grebes and coots sometimes tried to anchor their nests to wooden booms and stone projections in the absence of natural cover. Meadow pipits and yellow wagtails may nest on the embankments and at Walthamstow, where herons breed on a wooded island, reed warblers used to nest in elders and privet bushes before the last war. Sand martins have also been known to turn drain pipes in aquaducts into artificial nest burrows. The reservoir at Bartley, some six miles to the south-west of the centre of Birmingham, is a pure water resource and the wildfowl population there has declined in recent years since the Birmingham Water Department has been using explosives to disperse the gulls coming there to roost.

On the other hand those reservoirs which have been formed from dammed and flooded valleys may have considerable areas of marsh and shallow. A good example can be found at Chew Valley which, by the end of only its second season of life, held a total of 3500 duck. Since then an even bigger flock, composed of fourteen different species and numbering nearly five thousand birds has been recorded. I remember visiting a small sheltered bay at Chew in March 1959 and here I counted sixteen wigeon, and eight pintail with larger numbers of mallard, tufted duck and pochard on the water and with a party of lapwings feeding on the bank. In this same bay in autumn I have also watched more than two hundred shoveler and up to sixty pintail. The reservoir at Abberton in Essex is partly natural and partly faced with concrete, and its floor slopes from a shallow zone which is attractive to wading birds down to a depth of fifty feet just behind the dam. Here there are normally quite good numbers of mallard, wigeon, pintail, shoveler, teal, pochard, tufted duck, goldeneye, goosander, smew and mute swans, while the visitor may be thrilled by the sight of a shelduck, gadwall, red-crested pochard, Bewick's swans and perhaps whooper swans and white-fronted geese. The natural situation of the reservoir and its proximity to the coast have made it a very good haunt for wild-fowl. It was on this 1200-acre expanse of water that Major-General C. B. Wainwright started his ringing station; between 1949 and 1962 a total of 28,740 ducks was trapped and ringed here. In a single season more than 4000 teal have been ringed and released. At various times Abberton has held up to 4000 mallard, 12,000 teal, 5000 wigeon and 3800 pochard.

Other reservoirs may carry important congregations of ducks. Barn Elms has attracted up to 2300 tufted ducks and Chew Valley over 1000 shoveler. The Staffordshire reservoir at Blithfield may afford refuge in December to as many as 2800 ducks, while in summer it provides nesting sites for great crested grebes, shoveler, tufted duck as well as redshank and many woodland or scrub birds. I have seen many hundreds of mallard, wigeon, teal, pochard and tufted duck on the 800-acre reservoir at Pitsford in Northamptonshire as well as smaller numbers of goldeneye and mute swans. Eccup Reservoir, on the out-skirts of Leeds may carry all these species besides Canada geese and goosanders. These areas of water may show exceptionally high numbers of wildfowl but smaller reservoirs also play an important part in the general pattern of conservation. For example, the 200-acre Balgray Reservoirs to the south-west of Glasgow may have a winter population of about a hundred mallard, fifty teal, two dozen tufted duck and a few visiting wigeon, goldeneyes and goosanders. Within the local con-ditions of the urbanized River Clyde, where lowland waters are scarce, Balgray has a very vital role in affording habitats for ducks.

Despite some differences in situation and climate there seem to be some reservoirs which attract ducks because of their intrinsic qualities. The incidence of peak numbers must be expected to fluctuate from year to year but, even after making allowance for this, there appear to be certain consistent features of the habitat which influence the choice by ducks of particular reservoirs. These artificial expanses of water vary in their depth and those around London are no exception. More than eighty per cent of the city's area of reservoirs is more than twenty-eight feet in depth. The surface-feeding ducks such as mallard, teal and wigeon find their food on nearby grassy banks, on waterside vegetation and on neighbouring farm and marshlands. They use the deeper waters of Staines, Walton and Littleton Reservoirs for resting and they are not incommoded by the lack of shallow water for dibbling. Diving ducks, especially the tufted duck and pochard, prefer the shallower waters and resort to Walthamstow, Barn Elms and even the Brent. Pochard seem to favour water not deeper than fifteen feet, while tufted duck like water less than twelve or even ten feet deep.

GOLDFINCH and CHAFFINCH. *Above,* goldfinch about to drink. This bird favours orchards and gardens and may nest in small numbers even in the inner suburbs; *below,* chaffinch at nest in a pear tree against a wall. A common bird in the outer suburbs that also breeds in parts of the inner ring.

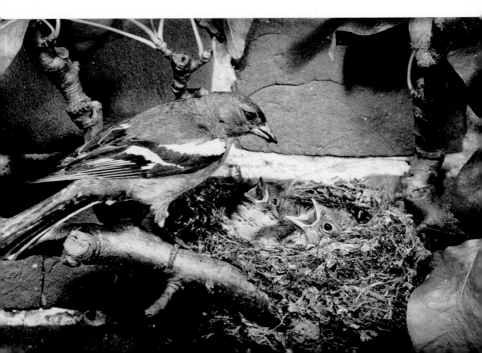

STARLING, a common suburban breeding bird that also roosts communally in trees or on buildings. *Above,* flocks at pre-roost assembly point; *below,* birds settling in tree roost at dusk.

Goosanders often choose to rest on the deep waters and then move to the shallower ones to fish and the shallow waters of the Brent Reservoir have long been a favourite haunt of the smew. That this scarce but attractive bird avoids the deeper water was well illustrated in 1948 when a drop in the level of the Staines Reservoir brought about the largest influx of birds there ever recorded. Both shoveler and tufted duck can sometimes be seen feeding around the inflow pipes.

Storage reservoirs that are filled with nutrient-rich water from a lowland river often develop a good plant and animal growth similar to that of natural lakes. On the other hand storage reservoirs in Scotland, Wales and the Lake District may hold much more 'pure' water. The depth of these man-made lakes is governed by the height of the dam but from a water engineer's point of view the ideal storage lake should be deep and with so small a surface area that light, which stimulates plant growth, can be reduced to a minimum. In lowland reservoirs algae may be introduced with river water and it has been estimated that a Thames-fed artificial lake of 7000 million gallons' capacity could contain up to 110 tons dry weight or 1000 tons wet weight of an alga known as *Fragilaria crotonensis*. Filtering equipment and copper sulphate are generally used to fight the advancing algae. There can also be a bottom fauna of insect larvae, particularly of midges, and of molluscs and annelid worms. The diving ducks exploit the food on the reservoir floors and coot will dredge up and eat the underwater growth of plants.

In the London area the peaks for wildfowl seem to average out at about 4000 to 5000 ducks in early October, rising in mid-December to between 5500 and 8500, depending on the severity of the weather in a particular winter. According to *The Birds of the London Area*, a winter maximum in January of say 10,000 ducks on the reservoirs and smaller waters in the region might be composed of some 4000 mallard, 2750 tufted ducks, 1200 pochard, 500 teal, 300 wigeon, 150 goosander, 100 smew and not more than 100 each of gadwall, shoveler, goldeneye and pintail with a few of the rarer species such as red-crested pochard, scaup, ferruginous duck, long-tailed duck, velvet and common scoters, red-breasted merganser, ruddy duck and shelduck. All nine of these rare ducks were recorded on the London reservoirs in 1971. Wild geese and swans are very rare but in most winters it is possible to see all three kinds of diver and five species of grebe. In 1971 black-throated and red-throated divers were seen on the King George VI reservoir as well as great crested, red-necked, Slavonian, black-necked and little grebes. Cormorants turn up at some of the better-known waters and in one recent year there were at least sixty-five at the Queen Elizabeth reservoir. The regular bird watcher may also see perhaps a shag swimming on one of the reservoirs, or even such rare vagrants as the Manx shearwater seen at Barn Elms, the gyrfalcon at Queen Mary's reservoir, the sooty tern at Staines, the osprey at King George V and the fifteen bearded tits at Walthamstow. Of course, most reservoirs have restricted access and permits are required from the local water authority to visit them. It is this limitation on visitors that adds immeasurably to the peace of these important bird habitats.

Although wildfowl make up the larger part of the winter bird communities on the reservoirs, wading birds may be attracted to them for short periods, since the concrete slopes and the algae growing on them may offer a little food and an opportunity for rest. Common sandpipers are regular on migration but, if the reservoirs have areas of exposed mud such as Blithfield in Staffordshire, then up to thirty different species of wader can be recorded. These migrations of wading birds and their occurrences at reservoirs will be described in more detail in chapter 10.

From being an occasional visitor in bad weather the gulls later established themselves in inland habitats and today more than half a million roost inland. R. A. O. Hickling, after studying a population of gulls wintering in Leicestershire, which were using Cropston and Swithland reservoirs for roosting, found that the birds, which were chiefly black-headed gulls, were spending their time in the valley of the River Soar and around the city of Leicester. They foraged for food over the industrial sites, parks, houses, playing fields and refuse tips. Much of the feeding activity was truly social and the birds spent a great deal of time together feeding and resting. The gulls used regular flight lines to and from their roosts where a number of social behaviour patterns began to emerge. One of the most impressive social activities consisted of massed formation flights before settling in the roost and it was thought that these aerial manoeuvres might help to strengthen the social bond.

Reservoirs often attract bird watchers by the very wide range of species that they may be able to see at them as well as the countless opportunities for studying behaviour and display in individual groups or kinds of bird. I was first drawn to Staines reservoirs as a schoolboy in the 1930s after spending a great deal of time watching pochard, tufted duck, mallard and other species at close range in St James's Park – a study that was to prove invaluable when I came to observe ducks on lakes and reservoirs at much greater range. It was at Staines that I came to know my first goosanders and red-breasted mergansers before I saw them on their northern or western breeding grounds. My first long-tailed duck was seen with A. Holte Macpherson one January day in 1939 long before I listened to other drakes 'cahooing' across the waters of Budle Bay or Scalloway Harbour. There were not many inland places in Britain where on a December day I could watch ten golden-eye, a dozen shoveler, three scaup and a black-necked grebe on the same stretch of water. One September I stood on the causeway at

Staines and in the field of my vision, on the hard slope, were a knot, a
greenshank and a ringed plover, while behind me I heard the notes of
what I still believe was a bearded tit.

In 1951 I was fortunate enough to work, and even sleep, in the new
William Girling reservoir near Chingford as it neared completion. In
collaboration with E. R. Parrinder I was collecting tape recordings of
the vocabulary of the previously unrecorded little ringed plover for the
BBC's Sound Archives. A full account of this undertaking was given in
Voices of the Wild but I would like to reproduce a passage from it as it
recalls my very first visit to this uncompleted reservoir which I was
later to come to know so well. It marks the stage in which a short-term
habitat can come into existence before being finally overwhelmed by a
man-made flood. This is how I described my impressions as Parrinder
and I climbed up the earth wall one May evening in 1951 and stood on
the top.

'The sight before us took my breath away. Lining the inner surface
of the wall was a concrete shell which carried a broad road all the way
round the reservoir. In front of me stretched 300 acres of gravel,
shallow pools and uncleared patches of tough sedge and willow. In neat
and silent rows lay numbers of enormous bulldozers and mechanical
excavators. I had a rapid vision of these great machines roaring and
rumbling from one end of the reservoir to the other, and I could hardly
believe that any birds bred safely on that gravel desert. Beyond the
reservoir and behind me lay Brimsdown Power Station and Epping
Forest; to my right a main-line railway betrayed itself by the steam
and sound which rose above the concrete wall; to my left were serried
rows of houses and, in the distance, Alexandra Palace. As we stood on
the wall we could hear far-away bird calls. Inelegantly but safely we
crawled down the shelving concrete slope to the gravel. Several redshank and lapwing got up calling as we made our way round the first
shallow pools and ridges of uncleared shingle. A solitary curlew went
in search of quieter places. Sand martins were everywhere, sweeping
and dipping above the pools; pied wagtails fussed among the pebbles;
skylarks poured out their passion from above; a sedge warbler bom-
barded us with song from a willow and a reed bunting churned out his
mechanical little ditty from a marsh. As we came closer two pairs of
mallard and a heron rose from the water. Suddenly in the distance we
heard a faint, high "pee-oo", and Parrinder spotted a little ringed
plover circling above a pale grey patch of stone and gravel.'

We also saw three wheatears, a pair of whinchats and scores of yellow
wagtails. A red-legged partridge was calling like a traction engine from
the reservoir wall. Later in the season we were to find at least four pairs
of little ringed plover with small young. Four months after our first
visit we watched W. H. Girling, the Chairman of the Metropolitan
Water Board, press a button and 3400 million gallons of water began to

flow into the reservoir and over the breeding haunts of six pairs of little ringed plovers. In the following summer at least seven pairs, with perhaps two more, nested at four sites in the Lea Valley. These rare birds had fortunately found themselves new summer homes, and I had been glad of an opportunity of watching them at close range in a unique habitat in the heart of suburbia.

CHAPTER 7

Marshes, Sewage Farms and Gravel Pits

IN the last chapter we looked at a number of different open water habitats, both natural and artificial, including rivers, canals, ponds, lakes and reservoirs. I would now like to consider those remaining aquatic and semi-aquatic environments which are rather more specialized and complex in their ecosystems. In this group I include both salt and freshwater marshes, sewage farms, flashes and gravel pits all of which may experience periodically fluctuating levels in the amount or quality of the water and be linked with closely associated habitats which can influence the bird life in the area. We shall meet again some of the species which we discussed in the preceding chapter but there will be a number of fresh ones as well.

Throughout the lowland areas of Britain there are sometimes regions of land, based on a mineral soil, that become waterlogged and these are known as marshes. This is a distinct type of land which should not be confused with fen which, although also waterlogged, occurs on a peat soil with a lot of lime in solution. Marsh conditions can appear around the edges of lakes and large ponds and in the flood plains of rivers where water meadows, marsh scrub and woodlands of birch, alder, sallow and other willow species may form. Man-made sewage farms have certain characteristics resembling those of freshwater marshes and these will be considered later in this chapter. On the other hand some suburban areas can be found as settlements on river estuaries; here the influence of salt water and the accretion of land can result in the growth of salt marsh plants which may stabilize the silt and form quite recognizable plant communities. Some river sections are subject to regular tidal scour and inundation which prevent the growth of many plants but still provide important feeding areas for birds.

Tidal rivers that flow through suburban areas include those in London, Great Yarmouth, Hull, Newcastle-on-Tyne, Glasgow, Bristol, Southampton and Aberdeen. On these rivers the activities of birds is very much regulated by the daily rhythm of the tides. At high tide, on those rivers where the banks are revetted, built up or heavily disturbed, gulls and wading birds are forced to resort to more quiet sections of the coast or to small islands and rocky outcrops. At low tide on the estuary of the Cheshire Dee there are many square miles of exposed sand and mud. The tides, which may be as high as thirty feet, cover everything except the Hilbre Islands where the birds have to pack on the only land left above high water. The nearby shores of North Wales and the Wirral are generally too busy and noisy for the birds to enjoy any peace. On one occasion I spent a day between tides in a hide lent to me by Eric Hosking on Middle Hilbre and I noted that within twenty yards of me at high tide 'there were at least 5000 knot (probably more, but I erred on the conservative), 300 oystercatchers, 250 redshank, 200 dunlin, 100 sanderling and the same number of turnstone, and 40 purple sandpipers. In the middle of the flock, head and shoulders above the knot, was a single bar-tailed godwit'. The waters on other rivers often carry ducks, geese and swans. On the River Thames between Tilbury and Gravesend there may be up to 1200 shelduck, 1000 mallard, 500 wigeon, 500 pintail, 135 scaup, 130 teal, 40 common scoters and 25 mute swans.

On Southampton Water John Crook made an interesting study of the way in which gulls feed along the tidal part of the river. Black-headed gulls exploited the muddy shore on the ebb tide as well as a shallow zone some two to four inches deep below the tide line, certain patches of calm water about two feet deep over thick mud and any waste and carrion which they could find by 'beach-combing' above the tide line. They found other food resources in open water such as fish and shrimps as well as 'floating waste from ships, sewage outfalls, floating carrion, food from philanthropists and pleasure steamers and other miscellaneous sources'. Some food materials were also stirred up by the passage of ships. The gulls also found quite high shrimp concentrations in some nearby salt pans. Like the waders that I watched in the estuary of the Dee the gulls had to look out for 'high water resting places' and these they found on sheds and buildings, on log piles and in parts of Dibden Bay. Estuaries such as these may also attract marine birds – skuas on migration, auks, cormorants. The death of large numbers of sprats through pollution in the Tees estuary in August 1962 brought in large numbers of birds including over 30,000 fulmars, 6000 kittiwakes, more than 50,000 other gulls, 2000 terns as well as several hundred Arctic skuas and great skuas. Other birds can also be seen scavenging on tidal estuaries and Michael Clegg has described how carrion crows not only fished in tidal pools but at West Ferry, Dundee, regularly took mussels and periwinkles from the inter-tidal zone. I have also watched starlings and feral pigeons busily searching the mud of the Thames estuary for morsels of food.

Salt marshes can form at the mouth of many estuaries and here the vegetation, according to Sir Arthur Tansley, 'occupies the mud and sand of those marginal parts of tidal estuaries and bays which are protected from swift tide races and currents'. The first plants to colonize the mud below the level of high water at the neap, or lowest range tides, are green algae and eelgrass. These are important food plants for wigeon and Brent geese which is one of the reasons for the present concern about the future of Maplin Sands – an area which is also able to support up to 40,000 wading birds at a time. On the seaward edge of the salt marsh it is possible to find glasswort with perhaps some sea blite, sea manna grass and sea aster. In some estuaries, such as those of Southampton Water, Poole Harbour, Bridgwater Bay, the Severn and the Cheshire Dee, *Spartina* has colonized the deep mud. There are places on the east coast such as Blakeney Harbour where the growth is very extensive and at Parkgate on the Dee it stretches like a meadow almost half a mile from the quay into the estuary. Where *Spartina* is missing, sea aster replaces glasswort and at the higher levels scurvy grass and sea plantain may grow. These plants all form the lower salt marsh community; they are largely succulent and undergo at least fifty hours' total inundation every month.

The middle salt marsh is often uncovered for long intervals during the summer and here one can find sea plantain, shrubby sea purslane, sea spurreys and the common sea lavender with thrift flourishing towards the upper levels. Sea rush often grows here among the community of middle zone plants. Sea lavender and thrift are often separately dominant at different levels but Tansley thought that the following six plant species were most commonly represented in the general or mixed salt marsh community – sea lavender, thrift, sea manna grass, sea spurrey, shrubby sea purslane and sea arrow grass. If fresh water flows into the salt marsh then plants such as reed, lesser spearwort and water dropwort that can tolerate some salinity can often be found as well.

One of the areas of salt marsh most intensively studied lies between Gravesend and Whitstable in Kent. The results were published in a book by Eric Gillham and Richard Homes who explored and described those 'bleak tidal marshes with their intricate pattern of innumerable serpentine creeks and gutters'. On the *Spartina*-covered mudbanks of tidal ooze they found no breeding birds other than two colonies of black-headed gulls and small numbers of mallard and shelduck. The nests of the gulls and mallard were bulky structures built above the mud and supported on the strong stems of the *Spartina* plants. Higher up the marsh mallard and redshank were the dominant species and there were also smaller numbers of shoveler and lapwing breeding as well. Skylarks and meadow pipits were nesting in the shorter plant growth nearer the sea walls and there were several pairs of reed buntings, linnets and yellow wagtails. Some common terns and oystercatchers had also succeeded in establishing themselves as breeding species. In winter and during the seasons of migration the mudflats formed valuable assembly and feeding grounds for wading birds and in bad weather these birds would seek shelter in the salt marshes.

John Wilson has pointed out how rich estuarine habitats can be used by waders as wintering areas, as staging posts on migration and as moulting areas in the late summer. In his study of Morecambe Bay he found that from 145,000 to 165,000 wading birds were present there in the winter months. This total might include 77,000 knot, 45,000 dunlin and 38,000 oystercatchers many of which used the Bay as a moulting zone. There were also bar-tailed godwits, curlews, redshanks and turnstones. A joint 'Birds of Estuaries' enquiry was staged by the British Trust for Ornithology and the Royal Society for the Protection of Birds, and this showed that in 1971–2 the top twenty estuaries for waders were, firstly, as one might expect, Morecambe Bay, followed in order by the Solway, Wash, Ribble, Cheshire Dee, Humber, Firth of Forth, Severn, Strangford Lough (Co. Down), Chichester Harbour, Burry Inlet (Glam.), Duddon, Swale (Kent), Langstone Harbour, Foulness, Lindisfarne, North Bull (Co. Dublin), Blackwater/Dengie, Teesmouth and Exe. In January 1972 almost 1,410,000 waders were counted in Britain and a further 110,000 in Ireland. The International Waterfowl Research Bureau has declared that any area that holds more than 20,000 waders is an area of international importance and the twenty estuaries just listed all qualify for this status. Since both the Wash and the Dee appear in the top five on the list the plans for water storage reservoirs in both areas take on a special significance. Besides the wading birds large numbers of ducks were found in the estuaries at Lindisfarne and Strangford Lough with over 20,000 wigeon each, on the Mersey with nearly 7000 pintail and over 5000 teal, on the Firth of Forth with more than 22,000 scaup and 550 velvet scoter, and on the Tay with some 15,000 eider and 4200 goldeneye, while 22,000 Brent geese were reported in Britain with nearly a third based at Foulness. Estuaries represent a very vital habitat for birds and in the event of growing pollution and reclamation schemes they need special safeguards. The mudflats are attractive to waders, geese and ducks, but the saltings are not frequented by these birds to such an extent, although small numbers of birds may be seen at low tide on the salt marshes with herons, crows, gulls, finches, buntings and other birds.

Salt marshes are now being widely reclaimed for industrial, agricultural and urban use. How does this affect the birds? Fortunately some answers have been provided in two papers by David Glue and M. E. Greenhalgh which were published in *Bird Study* in 1971. Glue examined a reclamation scheme at Dibden Bay on Southampton Water and Greenhalgh traced the changes to the salt marshes on the Ribble estuary in Lancashire. The Southampton study lasted from 1950–70 and followed the various stages in land reclamation each one of which was dominated by a different bird species. The meadow pipit achieved dominance in the area of salt marsh and brackish pools, the reed bunting of the soft mud pans, the yellow wagtail of the hard mud pans

COOT, a pair at the nest with male standing upright. These birds need larger sheets of water than moorhens but they will nest on many park lakes, reservoirs and gravel pits with suitable marginal cover.

GREAT SPOTTED WOODPECKER, TREE-CREEPER and GOLDCREST. *Above left,* female great spotted woodpecker – the most frequent of the woodpeckers in the suburbs, but needs mature timber; *right,* treecreeper, a very marginal species of parks and outer suburban gardens where pollution levels are low; *below,* goldcrest, a very local breeding species in suburbia, nesting here in ivy.

and the skylark of the subsequent stabilized grasslands. The enclosed salt marsh held, besides the meadow pipits, a community that included reed buntings, lapwings, redshanks, yellow wagtails and skylarks. One third of the bird territories was found on the retaining dykes built during the first stage of reclamation. On the enclosures of soft mud in the polders, where the reed bunting was dominant, there were also yellow wagtails and meadow pipits on the marshy fringe and – in different years – single pairs of both ringed and little ringed plovers. The oldest reclaimed polder consisted of rough grazing, sallow and bramble scrub; here the skylark was the most abundant bird but there were also breeding lapwings, redshanks, reed buntings, meadow pipits and yellow wagtails as well as a scrub community of blackbirds, white-throats, hedgesparrows and wrens. Ruffs were seen on the poorer pasture in summer but breeding was never proved. On the waterlogged sections of this polder there were also mallard, moorhens, redshanks and sedge warblers, while a few reed buntings and yellow wagtails also held territories. Altogether 27 species of wildfowl were seen in the area as well as a dozen species of avian predator including kestrel, sparrowhawk, hobby, barn owl, little owl and tawny owl which hunted over the study area but nested outside it. A vole plague on the North Kent marshes in 1955 resulted in an assembly of some forty short-eared owls and half a dozen hen harriers. On the Ribble estuary the embanked salt marshes acquired a land flora and wet pasturelands where the bird community, according to Greenhalgh, included the following species which are typical of freshwater and salt water marsh and farmland – coot, moorhen, lapwing, redshank, skylark and yellow wagtail. It seems clear that the salt marsh bird community is very similar even in areas as far apart as North Kent, Southampton Water and Lancashire.

Salt marsh habitats and estuaries are subject to a certain amount of pollution and of these oil spillage is one of the most likely. From experimental work carried out by Dr J. M. Baker of the Field Studies Council Oil Pollution Research Unit it appears that there can be an ability to recover but this may be removed by subsequent and repeated dosages. Sea rush is very severely affected by only two coverings with oil while white bent grass can recover after as many as twelve oilings. This wide difference in reaction to oil makes it rather difficult to generalize but Dr Baker, writing in *Environmental Pollution No. 4* in 1973, suggested that the vegetation on a salt marsh has powers of good recovery from up to four successive oil spillages, although the dominant plants may be different from those present before oil came ashore. After four oilings bare mud will appear in those regions which were once covered by *Spartina* and sea meadow grass. Oil terminals have been developed in Milford Haven, the Thames estuary, Southampton Water, the Mersey, Humber and Tees with further proposals for the Firth of Forth, the Cromarty Firth and elsewhere. We have also seen that the discharge of crude sewage can affect rivers and such great conurbations as Liverpool and Edinburgh still resort to this practice. Other forms of pollution may also affect estuaries – dumped chemicals like cyanide, industrial effluents and so on. The Don estuary in Aberdeenshire, distinguishable in the summer of 1973 by a remarkably pungent smell, was described by the Geography Department of Aberdeen University as 'inevitably a pollutant trap', and the Dee and Don River Purification Board called for meetings with the owners of industrial sites along the Don to achieve a greater control over the effluents reaching the estuary, which starts in suburban Aberdeen.

Fresh water marshes occur much less widely than they once did and those regions called 'marshes' today consist largely of low ground, drained by dykes, and used for farming and perhaps rather miscellaneous purposes. In North Kent the three really common breeding birds of the fresh water marshes and which were also widely distributed were the mallard, skylark and common partridge. The range of many other species was, according to Eric Gillham and Richard Homes, 'governed by the nature of the fleets and dykes, by the effect of livestock on the type of pasture, by the distribution of rabbits, by the presence of buildings, by the mounds and by various other odd nest-sites or song-posts'. Shelduck held their social gatherings and bred there while other nesting ducks included shoveler, garganey, pochard, and more rarely wigeon, pintail, teal and gadwall. The fleets were the homes of coots, moorhens and little grebes while lapwings, snipe and redshanks – the last species sometimes breeding also on marshy industrial sites – reared their young on the marshlands. It was possible to find numbers of reed buntings and both reed and sedge warblers along the waterways and yellow wagtails, corn buntings and skylarks on the grassy regions. The old buildings attracted kestrels and stock doves while carrion crows built their twig nests in the low trees that often grew close to the huts and sheds where swallows were already established. When I have walked over these marshes in summer I have also seen starlings and flocks of non-breeding gulls on the pastures and an occasional heron standing motionless on the bank of a fleet. These fresh water marshes have formed an invaluable sanctuary for wildlife.

An interesting example of a fresh-water marsh transformed from a rather dull and unproductive habitat into an attractive environment for wading birds and ducks is provided by Rainham Marsh in Essex on the north side of the Thames estuary. In 1959 the Port of London Authority began to pump Thames-dredged mud on to this marsh and Keith Noble recorded the changes that this activity brought to the ornithological value of the marsh. Much of it consisted of a chequerboard of pastures and small drainage channels where skylarks and meadow pipits were the typical birds with smaller numbers of reed buntings, sedge warblers and reed warblers. The pumped mud was deposited in artificially made earth reservoirs which turned into fresh-water marshes with shallow pools and grass or rush-covered borders which proved 'particularly attractive to teal, garganey, greenshank and wood sandpiper'. The drying mud was later invaded by plants but this mixed habitat held nesting meadow pipits, yellow wagtails and reed buntings. In 1971 a pair of oystercatchers nested on a strip of bare earth alongside a newly cut drainage channel. In winter several hundred bramblings and a few twites may come to feed on the plant seeds.

Areas of fresh-water marsh are now rather rare and regions such as the Ouse Washes represent internationally important reserves for wildfowl. However, the bird watcher who visits some of the surviving sewage works and farms, the gravel pits and mining subsidences may still be rewarded with a glimpse of a habitat that was once much more common in the British Isles. Sewage farms, in particular, have formed a valuable retreat for birds, providing feeding areas for many species and nesting sites for others. The old-style farms were large, often occupying 200 acres of land or more and, although their system of working was an economic one, they were considered to be taking up too much valuable land especially in suburban areas. The newer chemical plants were smaller and so released land for development. Even now the famous Perry Oaks sewage farm near London Heathrow is being considered as an alternative to Maplin Sands since more runways could be laid across the site. 'The modernisation', wrote A. W. Boyd, 'of one after another of these artificial marshes is little short of a calamity, necessary though it may be for the community as a whole.'

Sewage used to run from many of our towns directly into the rivers but during the second half of the nineteenth century sewage farms were established in different areas to improve water sanitation. At the beginning their significance as bird habitats was not understood and so little is known about their early ornithology. Reading Sewage Farm was laid out in 1875, Cambridge began active operations in 1895 and Altrincham came into being between 1900 and 1905. Farms now began to appear in many different areas – Penrith, Darlington, Liverpool, Nottingham, the West Midlands and London, for example. In the outer zone of London they were built among other places at Bedding-ton, Epsom and Brooklands in Surrey, at Chigwell and Romford in Essex, at Edmonton and Ponders End in the Lea Valley and at Perry Oaks in the valley of the Colne. In recent times some of these farms have been closed as part of a centralisation programme or modernized but reduced in size.

The actual processes of purifying sewage can bring into being a very varied series of bird habitats. The crude sewage arrives at the works in fluctuating quantities throughout the day and is pumped into rows of what are called sedimentation tanks. Here the larger solid matter is removed by the aid of screens while a considerable part of the suspended material sinks slowly to the bottom of the tanks. The semi-liquid sludge that has been trapped in the sedimentation tanks is pumped into prepared settling beds where it can dry out and be turned by bacterial action into a sort of compost which can be later removed. The liquid effluent may then be carried to filter tanks and allowed to evaporate and filter through the soil which becomes enriched with a growth of algae that assists in the filtering operations. These tanks are often drained and may then be left alone, sown with ryegrass and other crops, or reflooded. Donald Parr has described how at Weylands sewage farm in Surrey the liquid effluent, after being fed by moving rotary arms over a series of percolating filters, sinks into 6-foot deep and 60-foot diameter beds of clinker, full of 'a great mass of plant and animal life forming a gelatinous matrix called *Zooglaea* – a complex association of Algae, Bacteria, Fungi, Protozoa and dipterous larvae. The biological activity of this mass aerates and purifies the applied liquid, the organic wastes are oxidized or converted into the living matter of the Zooglaea'. The liquid, after passing through the filters, then moves on to some small humus tanks and finally into long shallow humus beds where the last traces of suspended humus are removed. The final purified effluent then flows into a local river.

The initial tanks carry no vegetation and little life but, after they have been flooded, gulls may snatch up some of the floating debris and, when they are empty, starlings and pied wagtails may be attracted to the muddy floor. The sludge tanks are a different proposition since they may contain muddy pools where many insects, including *Diptera*, can breed and these are food for small insectivorous birds which, as the pools dry out, can alight on the surface. As the tanks continue to dry out, plants begin to take hold and the compost becomes very rich in bacteria, spiders and dipterous larvae especially those of the *Chironomidae*. The varied plant life includes usually such species as persicaria, mugwort, fat-hen, bur marigold and, interestingly enough, tomatoes which were introduced as seed through the sewage. In summer the dipterous flies often attract starlings, wagtails, swallows, house martins and swifts, while in winter meadow pipits, chaffinches, pied wagtails, moorhens and snipe are frequent visitors. On some sewage farms the chickweed growth is often luxuriant and woodpigeons and stock doves regularly fly in for the food. As the lagoons produce their seed crop in the autumn large numbers of finches and sparrows come to feed and flocks of over a thousand have been recorded at certain farms.

It seems that the sludge can sometimes form a trap for unsuspecting birds. In 1965 G. L. Webber reported that large quantities of sludge were pumped into lagoons at the Swindon sewage farm in Wiltshire and that a thin crust then formed over quite deep mud. Many birds

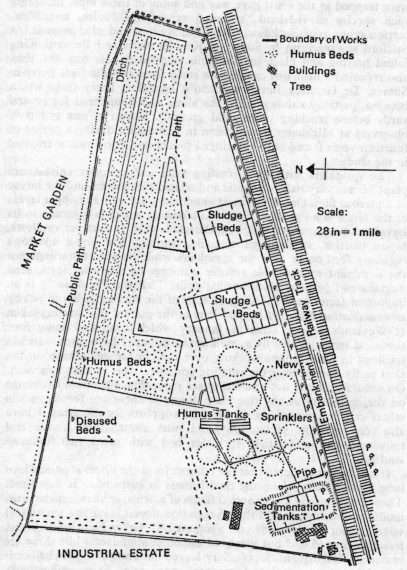

FIG. 8 Weylands sewage works. Reproduced from the *London Bird Report* by kind permission of D. Parr.

were trapped as the crust gave way and some of these died, including such species as redshank, common sandpiper, dunlin, kingfisher, carrion crow, rook, jackdaw, blackbird, starling and pied wagtail. At Saltford sewage farm in Somerset Ken Hawkins and Bernard King found herring and black-headed gulls trapped in this way and they also reported a little owl caught at a small farm at Sidlesham Ferry in Sussex. Dr Geoffrey Beven watched a kestrel at Perry Oaks which became 'partially submerged in the slime and floundered for several yards before reaching more solid ground'. However, one group of observers at Mickleton sewage farm in Lancashire during a period of fourteen years found only one ringed plover and one swallow trapped in the sludge.

The sprinklers with their rotating arms and complex animal and plant life are very rich in aquatic and oligochaete worms and the larvae of dipterous flies. One of the most abundant animals in the upper layers of the filters is a fly called *Psychoda alternata* which is common in its larval and adult stages throughout the whole year. In summer swallows, house martins, swifts, pied wagtails, starlings and house sparrows regularly feed on or over the sprinklers while in winter starlings are the dominant species with smaller numbers of meadow pipits, pied wagtails and perhaps black-headed gulls. That the *Psychoda* fly is an important factor in the feeding ecology of the starling is borne out by an examination made by Donald Parr of the gizzard of a starling taken at Weylands sewage farm in January which contained some four thousand larvae of this fly as well as ten pupae. I have often watched starlings in busy groups working over the clinker but always on the alert to fly up and over the rotating sprinkler arms as they approach. On some farms it is not unusual to see more than a thousand starlings on the sprinklers at any one time. Some of these are feeding while others can be seen resting on the wire supports for the arms. I have also seen meadow pipits, grey and pied wagtails, blackbirds and redwings sharing a single sprinkler bed with some two hundred starlings.

It will be remembered that the effluent from the filters is passed into long banked beds where the final humus in suspension is deposited. These beds contain a very varied fauna of worms, spiders, crustaceans, molluscs and insects and their vegetation depends on the amount of water flow or the dryness in each humus bed. Green filamentous algae, lesser duckweed and bur marigold are often abundant while there are sometimes large quantities of celery-leaved buttercup, fat-hen, halberd-leaved orache, creeping buttercup, persicaria, hairy willowherb, nettle, couch and meadow grass. In the summer months it is possible to see the food resources being exploited by mallard, coot, moorhen, snipe and other wading birds, wagtails, warblers and finches.

On the older sewage farms the liquid used to be run over open fields which formed marshes where many kinds of wading bird could be found. As a matter of fact the first record of a wader on a sewage farm which was reported to the journal *British Birds* was described in Volume 2 by A. W. Boyd when 'the third recorded specimen of Little Stint for Derbyshire was shot out of a trip of a dozen on the sewage-farm at Eggington, September 26th, 1908'. In 1912 Boyd himself reported at Clifton Junction sewage farm, just five miles north of the centre of Manchester, observations of ringed plover, turnstone, ruff, knot, curlew, sandpiper and bar-tailed godwit – 'an inland movement of which we had had no previous suggestion'. These new marshes formed from flooded fields and settling beds sometimes resulted in some fascinating wader records. On one day in 1950 on a single marshy pool at Perry Oaks were a pectoral sandpiper, two little stints, a Baird's sandpiper, eleven curlew sandpipers, several ringed plovers, a dunlin and a sanderling. Wading birds often rest during the migration seasons at sewage farms and their movements will be discussed in more detail in the account of migration in suburban areas in chapter 10.

T. W. Gladwin has given a description of how at Rye Meads Sewage Purification Works in Hertfordshire which was opened in 1956, purification is now achieved by 'sedimentation and bio-aeration. Sludge is digested and run into drying beds and lagoons to de-water. Methane given off in the sludge digestion plants supplies power for the works. Some of the water effluent is passed through sand filters and is then run directly into the river, whilst the rest of the effluent is pumped into gravel banked lagoons from which disposal is effected by natural percolation'. More than a million gallons a day finds its way vertically into the underground water system. Many birds feed over the lagoons, especially birds of passage, while larks, pipits, pied wagtails and starlings feed on the sludge lagoons and drying beds often in consider-able numbers. The nearby water meadows are often saturated and even flooded and these conditions may attract numbers of gulls, lapwings and snipe as well as woodpigeons, herons, jack snipe, golden plover, skylarks and meadow pipits.

So far I have been talking primarily about the feeding opportunities for birds provided by the various habitats on the sewage farms. But how effectively do they offer nesting sites for birds? The answer to this will depend on the type and size of sewage farm. From February 1947 to July 1948 I carried out a survey of Rugby sewage farm – a small works some three eighths of a mile long, equipped with sprinkler beds and situated in the suburban part of the town between two railway lines and the River Avon. Here I observed 69 different species of bird including common and green sandpipers, snipe, curlew and mute swan but there were only single records of mallard and black-headed gull; it was clearly not a wader or wildfowl farm. The total of breeding species was 24 – carrion crow, starling, greenfinch, goldfinch, bullfinch,

chaffinch, yellowhammer, tree sparrow, treecreeper, spotted flycatcher, willow warbler, garden warbler, whitethroat, song thrush,
blackbird, robin, hedgesparrow, wren, lesser spotted woodpecker,
stock dove, moorhen, pheasant and partridge. This was very much a
scrub and parkland avifauna. Linnets, reed buntings, pied wagtails,
swifts and a barn owl were present in summer but breeding could not
be proved. Rugby was a small farm but the famous Perry Oaks sewage
farm near Staines, according to *The Birds of the London Area*, boasted a
total by 1952 of only 26 annually breeding species but these included
the black-headed gull colony discovered by Lord Hurcomb in 1946.
Blackbrook sewage farm, which lay some five miles from Wolverhampton and was closed in 1961 produced some thirty-seven breeding
species including curlew, redshank and yellow wagtail, none of which
nested at Rugby.

Weylands sewage works at Hersham in Surrey between 1961 and
1962 was able to support some twenty nesting species of which
mallard, reed bunting, reed and sedge warblers were among the more
interesting records. Some of the birds such as moorhens, coots, reed
and sedge warblers and reed buntings bred on the humus beds
themselves while other sedge warblers and mallard built their nests on
the banks. Pied wagtails and wrens nested in the walls of the sprinklers –
at Beddington this was also a favourite site for tree sparrows. A laurel
hedge at Weylands was the site for the nests of blackbird, hedgesparrow, chaffinch and house sparrow and hedges of this kind are a
frequent ornament of many sewage farms. The only breeding site for
the goldfinch at Rugby was in a hedge of this type. Pollarded poplars
proved a valuable breeding site and here at least nine species were
observed nesting. Between 1954 and 1955 some forty species were
recorded nesting at Beddington sewage farm in Surrey. Mallard,
lapwing, snipe, redshank, little owl, skylark, meadow pipit, sedge
warbler, whitethroat and yellow wagtail bred in both years and little
grebe, water rail and reed bunting in one only. In 1964 and 1965 a small
colony of spotted crakes summered at Beddington and it is likely that
breeding took place in both of those years.

Rye Meads sewage works, where T. W. Gladwin logged 170
different species between 1957 and 1962, held a breeding community
of 50 species of which the dominant birds in the vegetation around the
lagoons were mallard, tufted duck, coot, sedge warblers, yellow wagtails and reed buntings, while smaller numbers of little grebes, meadow
pipits and marsh warblers were also present. Reed buntings, yellow
wagtails and a few whitethroats were breeding around the sludge-
drying beds. On the water meadows the nesting community here
consisted of redshanks, snipe, lapwings, yellow wagtails and reed
buntings. It is interesting to note here that the London Natural History
Society's enquiry into the breeding distribution of the lapwing in the

COMMON and RED-LEGGED PARTRIDGES. *Above,* common partridge. A few pairs of this declining species may nest on arable and grass lands, golf courses and sewage farms; *below,* red-legged partridge. This introduced gamebird breeds in small numbers in open country, on wasteland, by sewage farms and gravel pits east roughly of a line from the River Tees to Exeter.

MUTE SWAN and CANADA GOOSE. *Above,* mute swan on gravel pit. This bird, which breeds on river, canal and lake banks, has benefited from the flooding of gravel pits; *below,* Canada goose at the nest. First introduced over 300 years ago, this goose breeds in public parks and by lakes and reservoirs and is most common in central and northern England.

London area showed that of all the nesting pairs reported nearly twenty-four per cent were on sewage farms. At Rye Meads there were also birds of scrub and parkland nesting in the hedgerows while a wide ditch provided a sanctuary for nesting moorhens, reed buntings, sedge and reed warblers and perhaps even a few water rails.

Sewage farms have thus provided a unique habitat for birds which come to feed on their resources of insects, invertebrates and seeds. These man-made fresh-water marshes have also provided breeding sites for a recognizable bird community threatened by the enforced contraction of their riverside environments. There have also sometimes been rarities nesting in the shelter of these refuges, like the spotted crakes at Beddington, the two pairs of black-winged stilts at Nottingham sewage farm in 1945 and the little ringed plovers at Ham Fields in Berkshire. Of 154 sites used by these attractive plovers in 1967 four were at sewage farms. Common terns and lesser black-backed gulls have also bred at Nottingham, teal at Epsom and shoveler near Perry Oaks. Wading birds of many species may occur on migration while surface-feeding ducks visit the beds at night and large numbers of passerines appear outside the nesting season. Water pipits have wintered at some of the sewage farms, especially those at Beddington and Maple Cross in suburban London. On a small farm such as Rugby a total of some seventy species may be recorded while a larger one such as Minworth in Birmingham's suburbs may produce a total of 90. We have already seen how farms like those at Rye Meads can muster much larger totals thus revealing their great importance as specialized and indeed unique bird habitats.

There is also another interesting and very assorted group of environments in which water plays an important part. This includes such sites as the slurry tanks of power stations, ash lagoons, mining subsidences, flashes, ings, brickworks and clay, sand or gravel pits. Here there is often some standing water generally in association with bare gravel or sand, waste ground, scrub and a varied ground zone flora. If there is no contamination of the water then many of these sites can provide suitable nesting places for a wide number of species as well as feeding or resting grounds for others, particularly waders and wildfowl. The ash-filtering lagoons or ponds at Littlebrook Power Station near Dartford have been regularly visited by such wading birds as turnstones, little stints, curlew sandpipers, ruffs, dunlin, and ringed and little ringed plovers. Little ringed plovers have also been nesting on ash lagoons and by open-cast mines in the West Midlands; in 1958 a family party of two adults and two flying young were seen at ash lagoons at the Hams Hall Power Station in Warwickshire. In the north of England, according to E. R., and E. D. Parrinder, 'industrial wasteland and areas associated with coal mining are frequently used'. Open-cast mines may provide a temporary area of wasteland habitat in which birds may breed in only single seasons. It is perhaps of interest to note that five pairs of sand martins nested in a coal heap at Stockton in Warwickshire in 1957.

Subsidences caused by mining operations occur in many parts of midland and northern England and these may lead to the formation of shallow pools or 'flashes' of permanent or semi-permanent water. There are good examples of these at Stodmarsh in Kent, at Fairburn Ings in Yorkshire, in the Cheshire plain and in the valley of the River Anker in Warwickshire. Since open-cast mining is now widely employed to work shallow seams it seems rather unlikely that many new areas of the 'flash' type will be formed in the future. Subsidences at Stodmarsh Colliery in the 1930s led to the appearance of some five hundred acres of reed-fringed lagoons; here at least twenty species of wildfowl have been recorded, including both whooper and Bewick's swans, Brent, pink-footed and white-fronted geese, goldeneye and smew. Among the rarer visitors were marsh harrier, bittern and avocet. Alvecote Pools near Polesworth in east Warwickshire occupy about a hundred acres and these were formed over the last fifty years, according to H. Lapworth, by the 'flooding of meadow land and by subsidence of this land into old colliery workings'. The area is now a non-statutory nature reserve and is locally maintained in a state that will continue to prove attractive to wildfowl and wading birds. It has a field study centre which arose from the practical work of children at Polesworth High School. The pools are nesting sites for such birds as great crested and little grebes, mallard, shoveler, pochard, redshank, water rails and other marsh and water-loving species. It was here in 1959 that the little ringed plover was first proved to have nested in Warwickshire. In winter at Alvecote there are sometimes up to 200 mallard as well as 400 teal, 315 pochard, 220 wigeon, 130 tufted duck and smaller numbers of shoveler, goldeneye, Canada geese and mute swans. Rarer visitors have also been recorded and these have included white-fronted geese, scaup, pintail, common scoter, ruddy duck, shelduck and Bewick's swan. Many waders drop in to feed – curlew, whimbrel, greenshank, spotted redshank, wood sandpiper, green sandpiper, curlew sandpiper, ringed and little ringed plovers, golden plover, black-tailed godwit, knot, dunlin, ruff, jack snipe, avocet and up to a thousand lapwing. Other birds of passage in many years include black, common and Arctic terns, little terns and white wagtails. Certainly over the last 28 years I have seen Alvecote Pools grow in size and importance as bird haunts.

When I lived in Rugby I regularly used to visit Brandon Floods which formed between 1949 and 1952 when mining subsidence took place along the River Avon, creating an area of open water and marsh. Alan Richards, who studied the birds of this interesting region of 'river, floodwater (level much affected by amounts of rainfall), adjacent marsh, small pools and rough ground left after earlier sand extraction', found that the breeding community was made up from four to six pairs of great crested grebes, three or four pairs of little grebes, mallard, shoveler (in 1957), tufted duck, pochard (in 1955), partridge, moorhen, twenty to thirty pairs of coot, lapwing, snipe, redshank, skylark, sand martin, carrion crow, rook, jackdaw, magpie, great, blue and long-tailed tits, treecreeper, wren, mistle and song thrushes, blackbird, whinchat, robin, reed and sedge warblers, blackcap, whitethroat, willow warbler, meadow pipit (in 1960), yellow wagtail, goldcrest, hedgesparrow, starling, greenfinch, goldfinch, bullfinch, chaffinch, yellowhammer, reed bunting ('very common'), corn bunting and house sparrow. During the three years of the study there were also visiting birds, many of which were quite new to the district, such as cormorants, two of the rarer grebe species, a spoonbill (the first record for Warwick-shire), 14 species of duck, 3 of wild geese, 3 of swans, 4 of terns and 23 of wading birds. The waders included little ringed plover, both bar-tailed and black-tailed godwits, green and wood sandpipers, spotted redshank, little stint, ruff and red-necked phalarope. In winter there were sometimes flocks of up to 400 mallard and teal, from 30 to 40 pochard, 300 lapwings and 400 tree sparrows.

Many of the mining subsidences are close to centres of population and may suffer from a certain amount of disturbance. In northern England the flooded lands are known as 'ings' and occur in various parts of the coalfields. Fairburn Ings which lies along the River Aire has undergone regular tipping and the reinforcement of the banks with slag which has largely prevented vegetation from getting much of a foothold. Yet this area, which is now a local nature reserve, and a sewage farm nearby can hold between them an estimated total of one thousand five hundred ducks in the course of a winter. There are often several hundred mallard, parties of up to a hundred wigeon, pochard and tufted duck, fifty shoveler and smaller numbers of swans and golden-eye. Even in this apparently unpromising industrial region it is not unusual for mallard, pochard and tufted duck to breed regularly, and teal, shoveler and garganey occasionally. One summer two juvenile wigeon were also reported. Farther to the south around Doncaster and Barnsley are other colliery subsidences but these seem to be much less popular with the ducks, whose flocks are usually less than ten in size, but they seem to have some appeal for whooper, Bewick's and mute swans. On the western side in south Lancashire Pennington Flash can hold up to 85 pochard and 25 tufted duck while the bird watcher visiting Astley Flash in winter may find as many as 250 teal, up to 100 mallard and small flocks of wigeon and shoveler.

In Cheshire the subsidences there are also known as 'flashes' and these have arisen from the mining of rock salt from the 1750s onwards and the subsequent falling in of the workings. As water flowed into the tunnels the columns of salt holding up the roofs dissolved and the land above began to collapse. In later years the pumping out of the brine also increased the danger. Salt works and flashes have then been known to plunge downwards and water has again filled the cavity. Many of these pools have a certain amount of derelict land and chemical spoil around their margins. In a study of Cheshire bird life A. W. Boyd recorded the breeding community of the 'flashes' as consisting of such water-loving birds as the great crested and little grebe, redshank, common sandpiper and reed bunting. Summer visitors might also include kingfishers, herons, mute swans and Canada geese while in winter gulls and some of the rarer ducks and waders used to come from the Mersey estuary. The broken ground around the flashes attracted both scrub and wasteland birds. 'The yellow wagtail in particular abounds;' wrote Arnold Boyd, 'there alone in the district the meadow pipit breeds.' In the course of time some of the flashes have become filled with industrial lime waste, offering a very bare habitat to which only the gulls would come. When the pumping stops the local streams may spread mud over the lime and then migrant waders can be found on the flash once more.

The extraction of minerals from the land is a growing and important activity. It has affected both the countryside and many suburban areas around our towns and cities. Besides the open-cast mining of coal and ironstone there have also been many operations to remove chalk, clay, sand and gravel from the surface of the land. For the manufacture of bricks enormous grabs are used to dig out the clay which runs on conveyor belts to be ground, graded, pressed and dried. This is a big industry employing about 25,000 men and producing some 7000 million bricks every year, as well as tiles, earthenware pipes and building blocks. Sand martins are often associated with brickworks and fields. They nested early in the present century near London's White City and Charles Dixon reported that 'they nest in other brick-fields to the west of the exhibition site'. Similar sites have been used by sand martins near Coalville in Leicestershire. Clay pits and cement works sometimes provide a sort of lunar landscape and may be rather devoid of birds; when they become overgrown with scrub or flooded and clothed with sedges they may then form a most valuable habitat for birds. Chalk quarries may hold kestrels, stock doves, red-legged partridges, sand martins and a number of scrub or water birds. In the London area B. S. Nau found that the largest sand martin colonies were established in chalk pits, followed by sand and gravel pits. In fact, sand pits which 'accounted for only 35% of all the colonies in the area, nevertheless contributed 48% of the total number of burrows'. Some of the sand martin colonies in sand pits are quite large and *The Atlas of Breeding Birds in the West Midlands* reported 144 pairs nesting in a sand pit at Claverdon in Warwickshire and 160 pairs at Whittington in

Staffordshire. Many sand pits are often colonised by martins soon after they have been dug.

We have already seen in our review of suburban growth how, after the First World War, concrete was very much more widely used as a building material. To meet the rising demand it was necessary to expand the sand and gravel extraction industry. By 1938, according to E. R. Parrinder, 'the output in the London area was more than four times the pre-war figure for the whole of England and Wales'. By 1963 the annual demand for gravel had risen to 35 million cubic yards or 50% more than that required just before the 1939–45 War. Although it was difficult to follow all the activities of a rather transitory industry, it was estimated at that time that of the 730 gravel pits listed by the Ministry of Housing and Local Government about 300, or 40%, were filled with water. At the present time working for sand and gravel appears to take in some 4000 more acres of land each year and during the next decade the extraction industry will probably excavate enough new land to provide another 30,000 acres of new water. More than three fifths of the gravel workings and abandoned pits are situated in the southern and Midland regions of England while more than half of the water-filled ones lie south-east of a line from the Wash to the Bristol Channel. Around London almost all of the extraction takes place inside the approved green belt where it occupies 1·8% of the available land. Gravel pits can be found in the valleys of the Ouse, Nene and Trent, in south-west Yorkshire, Lancashire, Durham, Northumberland, the Scottish Lowlands and Wales as well as in other localities in Britain.

The gravels and sands around London which are the most in demand form part of the higher level glacial drift or plateau deposits such as those near St Albans in Hertfordshire and near Beaconsfield in South Buckinghamshire. There are also 'solid' deposits in the Lower Greensand where one can now find the dry sand pits that occur in Kent and Surrey. At a lower level in the valleys of the Thames, Colne and Lea are valley gravels under alluvial deposits where the excavations fill with water and it is these 'wet' pits that provide the greatest interest to the ornithologist as well as opportunities for human recreation and sport such as sailing, powerboating, water-skiing and skin-diving. When very heavily exploited in this way they tend to be rather poor in birds and other animals. Abandoned pits, half filled with water and ringed with disused plant and heaps of spoil can, if they remain undisturbed, become valuable bird sanctuaries, and even working pits can provide very interesting bird records. The larger pits are deep enough to attract such diving ducks as pochard and tufted duck while the shallower ones are more favoured by the surface-feeders like the mallard and teal. Some counts made in the Thames Valley suggest that a peak population of some forty-five ducks per pit is a good average figure. With at least a hundred pits in the London suburbs these must therefore make a significant contribution to the status and conservation of wildfowl around the metropolis.

Between the two world wars some of the pits near London were visited in connection with censuses being then made into the numbers of grebes and ducks. In 1944 a pair of little ringed plovers was discovered breeding in a gravel pit in south-west Middlesex. The continuing growth of gravel and sand extraction induced the London Natural History Society to institute a Gravel Pits Survey which also included a detailed study of the bird communities of four selected pits. The fieldwork for this survey was carried out between 1948 and 1951. Much of what follows in this chapter is based on a description by K. P. Keywood and W. D. Melluish in the *London Bird Report, No. 17*, of the material gathered from the study, which included mapping of all pits both from the ground and from the air.

Two of the survey pits lay in suburban areas and two in rural. The former were located at Mayesbrook Park at Barking in Essex, nine miles to the north-east of central London, and at Walton-on-Thames, fifteen miles to the south-west. The two rural pits selected were at Moor Mill and Feltham. The actual areas of water at the pits varied from $6\frac{1}{2}$ to $77\frac{1}{2}$ acres and the depth from 6 to 30 feet. At two of the pits the banks were perpendicular while those at the others were shelving and there were differences in the vegetation as a result of these features. At Mayesbrook there were large stretches of reedbed and scrub while at the other pits there were various forms of algae, sedge, reed, rush and such aquatic plants as arrowhead and water crowfoot. All the pits were encompassed by some waste ground, dumped spoil and scrub, and they all contained fish. Roach were recorded in all four pits, pike, perch and sticklebacks in two and dace and carp in one each. The suburban pits tended to suffer from a greater amount of disturbance.

As one might have expected, the breeding populations of the four pits showed some differences as well and only three bird species – skylark, yellow wagtail and reed bunting – nested regularly at all the pits. Other summer birds which bred less regularly were mallard, tufted duck, moorhen, coot, blackbird, whitethroat, sedge warbler and linnet. At three of the pits tree sparrows and partridges were recorded nesting in several of the years. Broadly the survey showed that the characteristic breeding species of the watery areas are great crested grebes, moorhens, coots, mallard, tufted ducks, reed and sedge warblers and reed buntings – species which have appeared over and over again during our discussion of fresh water marshland habitats. On the surrounding dry areas the typical birds were partridges, blackbirds, skylarks, yellow wagtails, whitethroats, linnets, reed buntings and tree sparrows. Less common were yellowhammers, pied wagtails, little grebes and willow warblers. The pits which had sloping banks held a higher density of breeding birds. In addition to the breeding community 66 species came to the pits in the summer months and these included gulls, finches, swallows, martins, swifts, snipe, lapwing, common sandpipers, herons, kingfishers, teal, pochard and tufted ducks.

When gravel pits are first excavated the vegetation is absent or slight and there are exposed areas of both worked face and waste ground. Power draglines and excavators are at work and washing and grading machinery is installed. Sand martins may set up colonies in the pits and one in Kent held over 700 pairs. Of the 3859 burrows located in the London area in 1960, 1848 were in sand pits, 1284 in chalk pits and 673 in gravel pits, but more colonies were discovered in gravel pits than in any other kind of site. The shallow pools and sandy gravelly deserts that appear in the early stages of gravel working are often attractive to little ringed plovers. These colonists from Europe, which first bred in Britain at Tring in 1938, have steadily increased their hold on the country. At first the spread was rather slow. In 1945 two pairs bred at pits in Middlesex and at least one pair in 1946. Their progress over the years has been documented by E. R. Parrinder. By 1947 the number of breeding pairs had risen to about a dozen and new sites were found in Essex, Berkshire and Kent. As some of the pits became overgrown and unsuitable the birds moved to some of the reservoirs then under construction. By 1950 there were 29 pairs and by 1956 the total had risen to 74. New gravel pits were constantly being dug and the figure of 230 pairs for 1967 may well have been a conservative one. What was interesting was that the 'proportion of pairs north of a line from the Welland to the Severn increased', according to E. R. and E. D. Parrinder, 'from 41% in 1962 to 49% in 1967 and the species spread to north Yorkshire and Durham (as well as to Northumberland and Scotland in 1968)'. As gravel production goes up in Scotland and northern England new areas may appear, suitable for the little ringed plover to colonize. The 1967 survey revealed that of 154 breeding sites 108 were found in quarries, sand and gravel pits.

As a gravel pit ages, plants begin to grow on the waste areas, particularly willowherbs, scentless mayweed, goose grass, nettles and various grasses, and these, in turn, are replaced by scrub. Such a succession in the growing plants has an appreciable effect on the bird life. The little ringed plovers leave and the rough herbage and damp ground begin to attract reed buntings, yellow wagtails, whitethroats and willow warblers. The development of a growth of sedges and reeds provides cover for breeding great crested grebes, coots, moorhens and mallard, reed and sedge warblers. A ten-year census of great crested grebes in six counties in south-east England showed that out of a total of 190 adults recorded, 129 were seen on flooded gravel pits. This species of grebe has also been taking advantage of increased gravel working and open-cast mining in Staffordshire and Warwickshire over the last 25 years, and, according to *The Atlas of Breeding Birds of the West Midlands*, 'these two counties are now the most densely populated of inland Britain'. Mute swans nest on many of the gravel pits and black-headed gulls bred in 1966 at Stretton Gravel Pits in Staffordshire. Common terns have also bred at both Stretton and Branston Pits and there is now a tendency for small numbers to breed at gravel pits in eastern England. John Parslow noted that 'Such records have come from twelve or more different counties from Kent to south Yorkshire.'

Between 1963 and 1968 David Glue carried out a survey of a 100-acre gravel pit some four miles from the centre of Southampton which offered all the intermediate stages in development from bare gravel to grass and willow woodland. Eight acres had been bulldozed, leaving bare gravel and shallow pools rather like the floor of the William Girling Reservoir before completion. Here eight species nested in the first year – little ringed plover (no surprise!), redshank, lapwing, mallard, pheasant, skylark, sedge warbler and yellow wagtail. The wooded pools began to attract little grebes, coots and moorhens, while the spread of willow, rush, sedge and reed brought an increase in the numbers of reed and sedge warblers. With a rise in the water level and the willow scrub becoming dominant, ground-nesting birds ceased to breed. When water covered the whole area the total of nesting little grebes, mallard, coots and moorhens rose, while teal, tufted duck, pochard and mute swan started to breed as well. Eventually the willow scrub began to inhibit the reed growth and consequently fewer reed warblers held territories.

In the winter months the actual number of different species present on the gravel pits goes down but the total is often higher than that of summer. There are normally more duck, although the flocks are not as impressive as those on some of the reservoirs, more coots and moorhens, gulls, little grebes and perhaps snipe and lapwings. Less common visitors may include jack snipe, cormorants and shags. A glance through the *London Bird Report for 1971* showed that birds seen during that year at London's gravel pits included black-throated and great northern divers, red-necked and Slavonian grebes, purple heron, bittern and twelve of the rarer duck species. In the seasons of migration the pits will attract various waders but these tend neither to be so regular nor to stay as long as those on the sewage farms and reservoirs. The sandy, gravelly banks of a pit cannot be as attractive to waders as the muddy shore of a reservoir with its much higher population of invertebrate animals. A most interesting piece of behaviour among spotted crakes at a gravel pit in Somerset was reported by R. H. Ryall. Birds were actually seen to pick up worms thrown to them by anglers

and one individual was so persistent in subsequent raids on the anglers' supplies of worms that 'one of the men had had to shoo it away from his worm box, and once in doing so the bird had run on to his keepnet and had fallen into it'.

Serious attempts have been made to improve the value of gravel pits as wetland habitats and to develop their multi-purpose use as recreational assets. Let us deal with this latter development first. At Holme Pierrepont, near Nottingham, there is a 1½ million pound leisure park of some two hundred and seventy acres where derelict gravel workings have been converted to a National Water Sports Centre and park with a 2000-metre rowing course and facilities for canoeing and water skiing. Grassy artificial hills have been raised and there is also a nature reserve of quieter pools lying between the rowing course and the River Trent. At Thorpe in Surrey other gravel pits have been turned into what has been called 'the largest leisure and water sports centre in the Home Counties'. This will be provided with a water slalom course of international standard, a 40,000 square foot sailing marina and landscaped lakes stocked with fish to provide breeding grounds for wildfowl and recreation for both naturalists and anglers. Since there are now in Britain some three million anglers, two million people who seek their pleasure in boats and 70,000 water-skiers, the pressures on these areas of water are growing all the time. More water-based parks are being planned in the Thames and Colne Valleys and there is also a scheme to develop some seven hundred acres of water at Newport Pagnell for recreation. Large projects of this kind must have some effect on the birds even when areas have been set aside for them since it is difficult to confine either noise or disturbance to set areas.

Nevertheless it is clear that with proper management many flooded gravel pits can be turned into nature reserves and one of the best known is the 250-acre Attenborough reserve near Nottingham. An interesting and successful scheme for a reserve at Sevenoaks in Kent was planned for joint running by the Wildfowlers' Association of Great Britain and Ireland (WAGBI) and the Wildfowl Trust. In 1955, with the backing of WAGBI, the late Dr James Harrison and his son Jeffery started negotiations with the Kent Sand and Ballast Company to form a reserve from some closely adjoining lakes in the Upper Darent Valley. In 1967 the reserve became part of the Redlands Group but it continued as before by agreement between the companies. Dr Jeffery Harrison has described how 'The prime purpose of the reserve was to provide for wildfowl, but it soon became apparent that as a whole new ecosystem became established, so a wider range of birds was being encouraged'. The lakes are shut in on three sides by houses and industrial development but on the fourth side there are water-meadows, hedges, scrub and woodland. The depth of water ranged from one to eight feet in two of the lakes to as much as ninety feet in the others and the shorelines were all rather straight and artificial-looking.

How could this area be improved? The answer was to create new islands both from gravel and by supplying rafts and this, with the shaping of spits to form secluded bays, increased the length of the shoreline. Since breeding ducks are territorial by nature this would swell the total of breeding pairs. Cover was also provided by brambles and rushes while more than 13,000 trees, shrubs and other plants were added to increase both the amount of shelter and the variety of food. In particular, such wildfowl food plants as alder, birch, oak, hawthorn, reed grass, water dock, marestail, hard rush, water pepper, persicaria, curled pondweed, orache, amphibious bistort and watercress were planted. Provision was also made for what were rather aptly named 'loafing spots' so that ducks could have 'adequate shelter and places where they can swim ashore to preen, sleep and sunbathe in security'. Nesting boxes were also added for the benefit of the small passerine birds.

An annual breeding birds census was started and, after a steady rise, there were by 1968 some 1300 pairs of 55 different species recorded nesting. The figures that Jeffery Harrison kindly sent me for 1972 showed a total of 1178 pairs of 57 species. More than half of the county breeding species in Kent were represented on this reserve. At the Hampshire gravel pit where David Glue had carried out his studies the commonest birds were blackbird, reed warbler, willow warbler and coot, compared with sand martin, mallard, blackbird and hedge-sparrow at Sevenoaks. Other researchers found that the dominant species at one pit in the Nottingham area were reed bunting, sedge warbler and reed warbler, while at another in Derbyshire the common-est birds were sedge warblers, blackbird and song thrush. David Glue also made it clear that the proper management of the water levels, the control and clearance of scrub and the putting up of nestboxes could greatly improve the condition of a gravel pit for birds. The success of the Sevenoaks project and its properly organized management of the habitat is reflected in the increase there over thirteen years of 500% in the wildfowl population. Waders and terns are also seen on passage at Sevenoaks and winter flocks of 2000 lapwings, 500 fieldfares, 250 linnets and 100 tree sparrows are not unknown. Rarities reported on the reserve have included serin, aquatic warbler, red-footed falcon, avocet, semi-palmated sandpiper and lesser snow goose. Appendix 8 gives the detailed breeding communities at Sevenoaks and at the gravel pit in Hampshire.

A properly cared for reserve cannot be 'left to nature' and so there has also to be some control of predators such as foxes, rats, magpies and carrion crows. Jeffery Harrison is of the opinion that there are 'many opportunities for wetland habitat creation, particularly in conjunction with companies working on mineral extraction, which creates the flooded sand, gravel and clay pits'. Wetlands, which can be formed even in suburban areas, represent one of the most valuable habitats for birds in Britain, but few of us are truly aware of their value as wildlife assets in an increasingly urban countryside. Not only may they be pleasing to the eye but they can also offer immense opportunities for recreation and leisure.

CHAPTER 8

Birds and the Pursuit of Sport

QUITE a surprisingly high proportion of suburban land may be devoted to the recreational needs of the inhabitants, and a study of London's green belt shows that 6·2% of that region falls into this category. Two thirds of this percentage is formed from parks and open ground such as commons; the birds of these habitats have already been featured in chapter 5. The remainder of the recreational land occupies just over 2% of the green belt and is made up of golf courses (1·6%), playing fields (0·5%), and race courses and miscellaneous land (0·1% each). All these facilities have been provided since the middle of the nineteenth century to satisfy the requirements of a population with ever increasing leisure. Before that period people did not have enough spare time to travel from their homes or work to those places where they could fulfil their recreational needs. There was also a shift of emphasis in suburban leisure away from such pursuits as the hunting and shooting of game, and even the casual weekend pastime of firing at anything that moved, towards such activities as organized sport and its watching, walking, car journeys into the country, nature study and so on. However, the number of anglers has risen since the last war although there has been a decrease in active game-keeping. Such presently suburban birds as carrion crow, jay and magpie have been growing steadily in numbers in many unkeepered woodland areas from which they were able to colonize the more marginal habitats such as green belts and suburban rings.

The creation of golf courses and playing fields is of comparatively recent date. R. S. R. Fitter has pointed out that, although the first golf course in the London area was laid out on Blackheath as early as 1608, there was no other before 1863. It was only during the next two decades that the cult of golf really began to catch on. By 1900 both Middlesex and Surrey could boast more than fifty courses each but, as we have already seen, some were soon to be covered with houses. The provision of open spaces for sport has meant that large areas of grassland are maintained quite close to built-up areas. Playing fields consist principally of pure grassland, whereas golf and race courses, can contain trees and scrub as well as a taller field layer. One may therefore expect a more varied avifauna on the courses, both in the breeding season and during the periods of migration.

The greater part of most playing fields is regularly and assiduously mown, rolled and scraped and scuffed by many human feet. By their very nature such open spaces cannot provide a very suitable nesting habitat and only if there is some rough grass on the margins which is fairly free from disturbance is there any hope of birds breeding. Playing fields which are open to the public, where dogs roam at large and children play, are poor, if not impossible breeding sites unless they adjoin some scrub or trees. Private playing fields offer more promise since they are in use for shorter periods and only a few ground staff are about. Sometimes in spite of the odds against them a pair of skylarks manages to rear a brood on the grassy fringes. I can remember as a schoolboy in the 1930s playing cricket on my school field near the White City in London and watching between the overs two pairs of yellow wagtails collecting insects and feeding their young in nests in the long grass near the boundary fence. In other years yellow wagtails bred on nearby Wormwood Scrubs with its extensive playing fields and during the last war they also bred in Regent's Park.

Playing fields do, however, provide a valuable food resource for quite a number of different bird species. Carrion crows, rooks and jackdaws may fly in from surrounding districts; the crows and jackdaws look for insects and other invertebrates on or near the grassland surface while the rooks explore the deeper levels especially for earthworms. There is one curious record of crows attacking and killing starlings on a playing field at Mitcham! Starlings also work the grassy swards very systematically, probing into the ground for leatherjackets and worms. At various times I have also seen blackbirds, song and mistle thrushes going over football and cricket pitches, particularly after rain, to feed on worms and other animals brought closer to the surface by the moisture. In many suburban areas the thrushes depend on these grassy areas for much of their feeding activity. I have often watched pied wagtails chasing flies over playing fields and they are also perhaps the commonest visitor to those smallest of playing fields – bowling greens. These tiny rectangles of green may attract the thrushes and I once saw a migrant skylark on a green in Gladstone Park in Brent. Spotted flycatchers will haunt grass tennis courts and it is not unusual to see a bird using a playing net or stop net as a vantage point from which to start and end its hunting sallies. Perhaps one of the most English of all scenes is that of swallows swooping and diving for flying insects among the players on a cricket field – a common enough sight on many grounds on the edge of the countryside. I wonder how many cricket matches have been temporarily suspended by the presence of woodpigeons, feral pigeons and house sparrows walking or hopping on some critical part of the pitch! Swifts and house martins may also be seen in summer hawking for flies above the cricket pitches and playing fields. If the uncut fringes of the ground hold a vole or mouse population it may be possible to see a kestrel hovering on winnowing wings above the field.

Besides providing a supply of food in the nesting season the sports fields may also attract migrants such as wheatears, meadow pipits, thrushes, lapwings, golden plover and various species of gull. I have watched wheatears on many football pitches and redwings are also often regular visitors to playing fields. Lapwings used to be regular on the Polo Field in Richmond Park and a peregrine was once seen using the crossbar on a goal in Regent's Park as a look-out point. Fieldfares, which are often grassland feeders, may also appear and I once saw a party of golden plover alight on a playing field by the school in which I was teaching in Stratford-upon-Avon. Mallard, crows and skylarks may also come in autumn in increasing numbers while common gulls may be regular if there is not too much disturbance. These gulls, outside the breeding season, are very much associated with playing fields and Professor E. H. Warmington found that they were the normal winter gulls on these sites in the Mill Hill and Colindale districts of north-west London. Certainly they are also very regular on the football pitches in Gladstone Park in Brent and these they share with a much smaller number of black-headed gulls. J. D. R. Vernon has shown how common gulls prefer airfields and playing fields 'where the grass is regularly kept short during the summer and early autumn by mechanical mowers'. He found that earthworms appeared in 93% of common gull stomachs, crane-flies in 29% (August and September only), earwigs in 7%, and grass-leaf fragments in 80%. In Gladstone Park it is not unusual to see between fifty and one hundred of these gulls spaced evenly over two or three football pitches searching for worms. Black-headed gulls are less frequent and herring and lesser black-backed gulls, outside the migration season, rather scarce. Lesser black-backs are now wintering in greater numbers in the London area and since 1937 golf courses and playing fields have been much more widely used. During the winter months if one travels, say, on the Central line out of London, or on the Piccadilly, it is quite usual to see mixed flocks of gulls feeding or resting on most of the sports fields in suburban areas.

Much more valuable in the variety of their bird life are the golf courses that can be set in some of the parklands or in the more open suburban regions of our towns and cities. Like many race courses the golf courses are usually on undulating grass and scrub land, especially of that formed from hawthorn, and to some extent they may preserve something of their original character. However the cutting of fairways, the fine mowing of the greens and the regular passage of many human feet may restrict the breeding bird community. The combination of patches of scrub, trees and rough grassland may help some species to maintain local and isolated pockets of population. On some golf courses, according to *The Birds of the London Area*, 'woodlarks seem to find the close-cut "fairway" for feeding and the "rough" for nesting an attractive combination'. Other ground nesters such as skylarks and perhaps meadow pipits may still breed and there may also be a few pairs of partridges which often manage to survive on golf courses in quite heavily developed districts. Sand martins have actually bred in the sand bunkers of one Suffolk golf course.

Besides hawthorn the scrub on golf courses may consist of gorse with a field layer of bracken and this may be able to support quite a few interesting species. Gorse is often an important factor in the habitats of stonechats, yellowhammers and linnets while bracken can provide shelter for breeding stonechats, whinchats, woodlarks, meadow and tree pipits, yellowhammers and even reed buntings. If there is thicker scrub and woodland close by then rooks, crows, jackdaws, magpies, jays, starlings, green woodpeckers, turtle doves, owls, various thrushes and finches may use the golf course for feeding. Many courses are laid out on sandy soils where birch trees flourish and these may attract redpolls. On one golf course a magpie was seen to remove a ball after it had been played and when a second ball was brought into use this was also taken away! Of course, it is generally only the more interesting of the birds observed on golf courses that find their way into the local and county bird reports – a hoopoe on Surbiton Golf Course, a pair of willow tits at Wimbledon, a cream-coloured courser at Minehead. We know much less about both the general use of this habitat and the bird communities which are able to reflect the individual topography and situation of each course; whether it is inland or near to the sea, isolated by housing developments or in the open country or green belt, well endowed with fragments of wood or scrub or bare and open to the elements. Any golfer will readily appreciate the difference between playing on a lush, sheltered 'country' course in southern England or on a wind-swept one on the Scottish coast where there are only turf and bunkers. On one Surrey course I have listened to a dawn chorus in May which was varied and powerful with many song birds performing all round the course. On the other hand an early morning visit in the same month to, say, the town course at Peterhead in Aberdeenshire will be rewarded by the constant mew of herring gulls, the trilling of oystercatchers from a distant green and a few snatches of linnet or pipit song. Sand dunes, as Sir Arthur Tansley has observed, provide an ideal situation for a golf course and 'the fairway is formed largely over the smooth fixed dunes, the putting greens are sown with a special grass-seed mixture and kept carefully mown and rolled, while the irregular contours of the semi-mobile marram dunes provide any desired abundance of bunkers and hazards'. Marram is sometimes planted on inland courses and the introduction of coastal turf may bring in such maritime plants as sea milkwort and sea plantain.

Outside the breeding season the golf courses, like the playing fields and race courses, are very attractive to grassland feeders – carrion crows, starlings, rooks and jackdaws. When watching television outside broadcasts of race meetings and golf tournaments I have seen all four species on the screen. This televisual branch of ornithology allows plenty of opportunity for identification both by field characteristics and by voice and does not have to be confined to the British Isles! There are often large numbers of gulls and perhaps ducks and waders as well. E. C. Rowberry watched a lesser black-backed gull on Osterley Golf Course that took 45 worms in 5½ minutes and, since more than 200 birds were feeding at the time, it was estimated that a total of 38,100 worms was extracted in only a quarter of an hour. I carried out regular watches on the town golf course at Minehead in Somerset over the whole of two Septembers in 1962 and 1963. My study was primarily to plot the patterns of visible migration over the Bristol Channel and the results will be described in chapter 10. However, it seems sensible to describe some of my observations here since they involve numbers of birds actually seen on the golf course itself. In 1962 I recorded a flock of 350 curlew and 200 lapwing as well as smaller flocks of 49 golden plover, 100 oystercatchers, 150 turnstones, 40 dunlin, 35 ringed plover, 33 redshank, 20 bar-tailed godwits, 9 sanderlings, 4 ruffs and a single black-tailed godwit all of which rested or fed on the grass. I wrote in 1963 that 'many of these waders stalked quite unconcernedly around the greens of the golf course until the greenkeepers came along to sweep the turf. On 20th September 1962 I flushed a great snipe from a tussocky piece of dry grass above one of the bunkers; it rose silently and dropped into a hollow about thirty yards further on. Here I was able to watch it for several minutes at close range'. In 1963 the maximum number of golden plover rose to 480. There was also a merlin present in both Septembers as well as many passerine migrants.

There are other sporting facilities that can affect the bird life. We have already seen that inland waters, lakes, reservoirs and gravel pits can be used for public recreation with their greatest exploitation in the summer months and weekends. Considerable and in some cases massive disturbance is limited to quite short periods during the year. The water sports include swimming, canoeing, rowing, sailing, motor-boat cruising, water-skiing and even hydroplane racing. All of these activities may cause some disturbance to the wildlife through erosion and swamping of the banks, the destruction of aquatic vegetation, pollution, the loss of land to shore-based facilities and noise. At the Brent Reservoir, for example, pollution now keeps away the kingfisher, sailing rapidly disperses the diving ducks to other waters and hydroplane racing has been known to wash out the eggs of coots and moor-

LITTLE RINGED PLOVER and GREAT CRESTED GREBE, two gravel pit species. *Above,* little ringed plover at the nest, this is an early coloniser of flooded gravel pits; *below,* great crested grebe, an attractive species, once persecuted, that favours gravel pits with islands and developed vegetation.

WATER PIPIT and WHINCHAT. *Above,* water pipit, a rare winter visitor to some sewage farms, reservoirs and watercress beds; *below,* male whinchat, a regular migrant appearing in many suburban parks and on waste ground and allotments.

hens and cause the great crested grebes to give up their nesting attempts. Angling can also be a source of disturbance, particularly during competitions when anglers are spaced evenly along the banks over long distances. Yet this particular pursuit has also brought about the safeguarding of many rivers and other stretches of water and often extremely vigorous campaigns against sources of local pollution. Herons and kingfishers have been known to suffer as the result of actions taken against them since they may be looked upon as direct competitors to the anglers. In Scotland red-breasted mergansers have also been shot by freshwater fishing industries and goosanders would have increased at a faster rate if a bounty had not been placed on their heads.

There are also many land-based sports and recreations such as hunting, shooting, riding, motorcycle scrambles, rallies and even walking which can lead to the destruction of or damage to habitats, to noise and irresponsible conduct ending in vandalism, pollution, fires and other unwelcome effects. The hunting of foxes is restricted to the more rural areas but there the attitudes to the fox may lead to the existence of dense thorn and other coverts which benefit other wildlife as well, especially the scrub birds which may roost or nest inside the islands of green. The shooting of wildfowl normally takes place along the coast, in estuaries and on a number of inland waters. Under ideal conditions arrangements are usually made to provide shelter for wildfowl in order to offset the number of birds actually killed and if the size of kill is properly restricted then shooting may help to prevent too high a concentration of birds in a particular habitat. Unfortunately protected birds are sometimes killed through carelessness or a mistake in identification and there can be excessive disturbance in areas where control is missing or merely perfunctory. On some reserves the shooting permits are carefully controlled, perhaps by the owner, the Nature Conservancy and the wildfowling interests. Where this happens, as at Caerlaverock, it is possible for all interests to arrive at an amicable agreement. The late Sir Dudley Stamp cited this reserve in Dumfriesshire as an example of 'a successful compromise between nature conservation and sport'. Wildfowlers often assemble here from more than forty-five counties in Britain and may take annually up to five hundred of wigeon, mallard, teal, pink-footed and grey lag geese with a few other species but the protected birds such as the barnacle goose are left alone. Undoubtedly those who shoot need also to be conservationists. The Wildfowlers' Association of Great Britain and Ireland have acquired sporting leases to try and ensure that shooting is conducted in a responsible manner; it controls over a third of a million acres and of these about twenty-three thousand are reserves. It is often the individual wildfowler who misjudges both the speed and height of flying geese and fails to make a clean kill. Birds may carry lead shot in their hind regions and in some places crippled geese remain until the following summer and may try to breed. The X-raying of geese and swans has shown how high a proportion of birds may in fact be carrying shot. Some of the birds may have been hit abroad but some were certainly shot in the British Isles. Indiscriminate and inaccurate shooting can be a hazard. A snowy owl and a gyr falcon were shot in Anglesey in the same year.

Wildfowl management can also mean the raising of duck for shooting and the re-introduction of some species to their former breeding places. In the eight years from 1954 to 1962 a WAGBI scheme led to the release of more than twenty-seven thousand hand-reared birds. Today almost twenty thousand mallard are reared annually for release on unshot reserves to supplement the population of wild birds. There are probably a thousand English and Welsh-bred grey lag geese carrying rings and breeding in the wild in regions to which they have been returned after a lapse of perhaps two centuries. Canada geese, mute swans and gadwall have also been artificially managed in this way. Many people and organizations keep collections of wildfowl, often for their amenity value, and birds may escape from time to time. Ruddy duck can be seen in the south and west Midlands and mandarin around Windsor, while exotic species may turn up on many different suburban waters.

The long period of game preservation that lasted for more than two hundred years brought many of our birds of prey and other predators to a very low ebb indeed. In Surrey, at the end of the nineteenth century, the buzzards and harriers had gone, the magpie was rare and woodpeckers, owls and nightjars were persecuted equally with crows, jays, sparrowhawks and kestrels. Norman Moore has clearly demonstrated that a direct correlation could be achieved between the decline of the buzzard in Britain and gamekeeping methods. But what was the effect of the marked decrease in game preservation during the two world wars? It was at this time that the buzzard showed its biggest recoveries. In 1900 the sparrowhawk was a scarce bird in the London area and its persecution was maintained in some districts until about 1940. In 1937 one keeper at Hayes alone shot seventeen birds. After the Second World War the bird began to increase and then after the mid-1950s declined once more after the introduction of dieldrin and other persistent organo-chlorine insecticides as dressings on spring-sown wheat. As fewer of these toxic chemicals were used the sparrow-hawk has shown signs of a recovery in the west but it still remains rather uncommon in the lowland east. The campaign against the kestrel was relaxed as well; it had been no uncommon sight to find as many as a dozen birds on a keeper's gibbet. As a result kestrels increased in the rural areas and after 1930 began to breed in urban districts particularly in Lancashire and London. There seems to have been an increase after the 1939–45 War but in the late 1950s a sharp decline was reported in eastern England where toxic chemicals were being widely used on the land. Barn owls were also sometimes shot by keepers but the destruction of habitats, chemicals and disturbance may all have combined to keep the bird rather scarce despite a lessening of pressure on this fine bird from keepers. The tawny owl has staged a recovery after nineteenth-century persecution. The little owl enquiry of 1936–7 showed that the staple diet of this introduced European species was primarily insects and mammals but the bird was still persecuted by some keepers. It has shown signs of a recovery around London as gamekeepers disappeared from estates and properties were broken up. The little owl population has suffered considerably in bad winters. Carrion crows, magpies and jays, which were rare in 1900, have all staged recoveries as the pressure on them was relaxed and after an increase in many rural areas they then began to colonize the suburbs, and later the central parks, of many large towns. Here they occupied the suburban ecological niches waiting for them.

The species of game normally preserved for sport are partridges, pheasants and grouse. The pheasant was possibly introduced to Britain by the Romans and again in pre-Norman times. The original stock consisted of the black-necked form but there has been a great deal of interbreeding with other introduced races. It is a bird of many types of woodland as well as forest edges, parkland, farmland with hedges, game coverts and belts of trees, large gardens and even reed-beds. Most large pheasant shoots now rear or buy artificially reared birds for release and John Young has found that 'most estates only shoot an average of 30 to 40 per cent of the birds they release'. With a pronounced rise in game shooting in recent years the cultivation of birds as a profitable crop has become a much wider practice. Young pheasants are vulnerable to attack by predators which then tend to fall victim to the keepers' guns. John Young has suggested that predation by sparrowhawks could be avoided by choosing the right time and place for giving the young pheasants their freedom. Perhaps in such ways as this can game farming, in the words of Dr R. K. Murton, 'ensure a balanced attitude towards the conservation of predatory birds and mammals on the one hand, and productive game management on the other, but this is not always easy to achieve'. The rapid growth of nature conservation has in fact coincided with a remarkable surge in interest in game shooting and game production.

The partridge seems to have decreased largely because of agricultural changes including a decline in cereal/clover crops and leys which carried some of the more important insect foods of the partridge such as the larvae of sawflies. Partridges have declined very markedly in numbers over the last forty years except on some of the preserved estates in the south and east. Partridges are not reared artificially to the same extent as pheasants but there has been some increase in this activity in recent years but it is not easy to say how effective artificial propagation has been in building up depleted stocks. In the London area partridges do not seem to reveal very wide fluctuations in population levels. The introduced red-legged partridge is very much a bird of sewage farms, reservoir banks, gravel pits and wild country. It may be overlooked in those parts of England and Wales where it occurs. Its rallying call, like the note of a steam engine, is very distinctive and when heard is a valuable guide to the bird's presence. Red-legged partridges and their eggs may still be introduced to Britain following on the pattern of release from 1770 onwards. It is possible that more game species may be set at large. Already the North American bob-white quail has been released in some localities but there may be hidden dangers in this kind of practice.

It is estimated that each year in Britain about sixty thousand game licences are issued and about one quarter of these go to the owners of shoots or to the heads of shooting syndicates. As long ago as 1962 the gun licences numbered 396,568 and that figure has shown signs of growing. There is a campaign for training gamekeepers and it seems a pity that for practical reasons it cannot be extended to those members of the public who also have lethal weapons in their hands. A glance at two copies of *Birds* – the magazine of the Royal Society for the Protection of Birds – shows a number of recent and successful prosecutions carried out by the Society against people shooting birds at will. The targets or victims included redwings, fieldfares, skylarks, kestrels, swifts, firecrests, shelduck, little grebes, greenshanks and other protected birds. One of these two issues also reported the taking of kites' eggs in Wales, the trapping of linnets and goldfinches and the use of both nets and bird lime for capturing wild birds. This is symptomatic of a so-called 'sport' executed for commercial ends which appears to be growing in parts of Britain after many of us had thought it was disappearing for good. Suburban areas may be just as vulnerable as rural ones. In my district in north-west London young kestrels were removed from their nest in a municipal park and in 1972 birds were being trapped close to the Brent Reservoir.

In recent years I seem to have seen more air guns and shot guns being openly carried by young people in suburban areas than there used to be, especially in northern industrial England and in Scotland. Our world has become increasingly violent and the use of guns in an ignorant and indiscriminate way may well reflect this world. Many users of air guns are unaware of the strict laws that apply under Act of Parliament and which can be properly explained at a local police station. At a time when education seemed to be having definite results in persuading young people to take a more humane and enlightened view of wildlife this growth in the uncontrolled use of guns is greatly to be deplored.

CHAPTER 9

Suburban Roosts and Flyways

So far we have looked at many different aspects of bird distribution and breeding behaviour in suburban areas. When we come to the roosting habits of birds we may find that these escape our notice unless the birds are large like crows and gulls, or noisy and social in their nightly gatherings. Long lines or V's of gulls and starlings passing overhead in winter may give a broad clue to the whereabouts of their large communal roosts but it may be very difficult, if not impossible, to say exactly where the local blue tit or robin in one's garden spends the night. For all birds the potential roosting sites are restricted to houses, factories and other buildings, to the ground, to trees and shrubs and to such watery habitats as marshes, lakes, reservoirs and rivers. This chapter is devoted to the roosting habits of suburban birds and particularly to the large communal roosts that some species use and the routes that they adopt to reach them from their feeding grounds.

Much of the character of suburbia derives from the blocks of flats, houses, factories and workshops that have sprung up inside it and so it is the way in which they can be used as roosts that we shall consider first. We have already seen that the feral pigeon can be found nesting from town centres outwards through the suburban zones wherever there are ledges and holes in brickwork and masonry, factory structures, drainpipes and hoppers, bridges and similar sites. The late Terry Gompertz found in Hampstead that 'the situation regarding roosting sites follows the same general pattern as that of nest sites'. The pigeons seem to prefer some sort of enveloping cover but many make out with weather protection only at their backs. Some use drainpipes on houses while others sit on flat ledges sheltered by wider ones above their heads such as you may find on churches, and shop and office fronts. Here communal roosting is generally the order of the day but pigeons that tend to live solitary lives in the daytime also seem to roost alone. On modern blocks of flats birds sometimes roost in the corners of bathroom and lavatory windows which are built in stacks one above the other. Terry Gompertz found that these sites may be regularly used provided that they are not disturbed by a 'new occupant with a passion for opening the small bathroom window that was left closed by the previous six tenants'. Other feral pigeons seek out lofts, church steeples, factory roofs, railway stations and bridges. Where the street illumination is good, birds can often be seen moving about and flying from ledge to ledge in the middle of the night. At Holland Park tawny owls have been observed taking pigeons in the dark.

Urban starling roosts are generally associated with those noisy agglomerations of birds that come into the centres of cities such as London, Birmingham, Newcastle and Glasgow. In London starlings were already commuting from the suburbs to roost in trees in St James's Park in the 1890's and between 1898 and the First World War they moved on to buildings as well. The town roosting habit undoubtedly arose among British resident starlings and not among Continental immigrants which form large country roosts from October onwards. A few birds from Europe may be drawn into the roost, but the great majority are British in origin. Many of the urban roosts on buildings are in towns and cities in the northern industrial belt. Many of our resident suburban starlings may fly into a central town roost but others prefer small local roosts or even their nest holes. A pair of starlings spent each winter night in the roof of my house after nesting there in every year from 1952 to 1972. In 1973 for the first time and for an unknown reason a pair did not breed in this site and no starlings roosted there in the subsequent autumn and winter. Some of the smaller communal roosts appear on the towers of bridges, church towers, the façades of buildings and if the street lighting is good it is often possible to watch birds flying about for much of the night. Neon signs are sometimes chosen and I have seen starlings that have been burnt by a short circuit. I have also seen roosts on cranes in Peterhead Harbour, on transformers in Cornwall, in disused aircraft hangars as well as in quarries and on sea-cliffs. At Clevedon in Somerset birds gather to roost on the end of the pier which is separated by a gap from the main stretch attached to the land. Much of what is known about the roosting habits of London's starlings was the result of a large ringing project carried out for three years by members of the London Natural History Society from 1949 onwards. During this period more than five thousand starlings were caught and ringed both at night in Trafalgar Square and by day in suburban gardens. Torrential rain sometimes soaks roosting starlings; in 1956 several hundred were found on the lawns and bushes in St James's Park wet and bedraggled and some of these later died. Other starlings have been found at night grounded after bathing and these may have been 'iced-up' in very cold conditions.

The third common suburban species that sometimes roosts on buildings is the house sparrow. Sparrows have the choice of roosting in their nest holes or flying to communal roosts which are normally in trees or bushes. A pair of sparrows regularly spends the night under the eaves of my house where the nest is located and this is not too uncommon a practice. The two birds can be seen still feeding on the bird table twenty minutes or more after the rest that feed in my garden have departed for the distant communal roost. Spending the night in the nest hole must surely convey some advantage. Communal roosts on buildings are rather rare but birds will often take advantage of creepers growing on the sides of houses, sheds and other structures. For many years a small winter roost at Dollis Hill was maintained in some Virginia creeper growing on the wall of a semi-detached house and there was another not far away on a factory wall.

The number of other species that have been recorded roosting on buildings is rather limited. Some swifts roost in the roofs where they nest while others are spending the night on the wing. I have described elsewhere how tired migrant swifts roosted one night on a window frame covered with mosquito netting at Salin de Badon in the Camargue and birds have also been known to use telegraph poles and walls. House martins also roost in the mud cups of their nests. I have also seen kestrels passing the night in their nesting holes and owls sometimes use chimney pots, cowls and other external features of buildings for roosting. Great and blue tits use cracks, crannies and holes in walls and masonry and wrens sometimes favour similar sites. Jackdaws may roost on buildings and the black redstart seeks out holes and cracks around the gasworks and power stations that it now seems to prefer. Pied wagtails will sometimes spend the night on roofs and there was an interesting report in 1945 of seven black-headed gulls roosting on a roof in Kensington. Factories, workshops and even greenhouses may prove attractive to roosting birds. In 1964 and 1965 a party of swallows roosted on the roof girders of a large engineering workshop near Corby in Northamptonshire. They stayed until November in the first year and December in the second, flying in and out of the main building during the daytime. Starlings and sparrows may use hangars and Jeffery Boswall reported that more than two thousand five hundred pied wagtails were roosting inside a power station at Ferrybridge in Yorkshire and more than a thousand 'settled to roost on steel-work and lagged steam pipes' in a factory at Preston. Another roost survived for several years in the roof of a factory at Sparkhill, drawing up to one thousand five hundred birds from a ten-mile radius. E. M. Nicholson has also described a roost of several hundred wagtails 'on the glass roof of a post office in Leicester', and over a hundred used the roof of a boilerhouse at Rye House Generating Station at Hoddesdon in 1966.

Pied wagtails have, of course, been recorded roosting in greenhouses since 1936. Boswall listed 22 sites in Britain and Ireland where these birds were roosting communally inside commercial greenhouses and he expressed the view that 'there can be little doubt that more exhaustive enquiries would reveal many other instances and it seems likely, therefore, that this use of glasshouses by Pied Wagtails occurs on a much wider scale than was previously suspected'. The wagtails sit in rows on the steel struts and the hotwater pipes and are often very close to each other. Springtime roosting is not so common but in autumn, when the windows of the houses are left open and plants such as tomatoes and chrysanthemums are well developed, the habit is much more widespread. The glasshouses provide warmth and some security from predators but the most likely explanation is that they offer shelter from the weather. At one greenhouse site in Hampshire, where carnations were being grown, some six hundred pied wagtails were deliberately killed by leaving the greenhouse closed after the birds had entered it for roosting. There is a record of a pair of greenhouses at Sunbury-on-Thames being used annually by several hundred wagtails over a period of thirty years.

Because of the danger from predators the ground is not a very secure roosting place but on parkland, farmland, commons, wasteland, sewage farms and other open spaces then meadow pipits, skylarks and partridges may spend the night on the ground risking attack from foxes, weasels, rats and cats. It has been suggested that partridges roost or 'jug' in a group with their heads all pointing inwards. This I have never seen and Esmond Lynn-Allen and A. W. P. Robertson thought that such an arrangement was neither safe nor comfortable; 'We think it to be most usual for a covey to roost either in a rough circle, facing outwards – the position of droppings often seems to suggest this – or else in a loose group, each bird being head-on to the wind, or oblique to it and partially sheltered by the body of another'. Some adult and many young pheasants roost on the ground on heathland, wasteland, fields and saltings. Airfields attract gulls, lapwings, golden plover and even oystercatchers and I have also come across fieldfares spending the night on the ground. It is possible to flush roosting crakes and rails during the seasons of migration and wading birds may often be disturbed at night.

Most roosting sites are in trees and bushes and the majority of suburban birds seek shelter in them. We have already seen how starlings may use buildings for roosts but they also favour conifer plantations, evergreen thickets, scrub and reedbeds. In suburban situations trees such as planes and poplars are often used and at various times small roosts may form outside the catchment areas for the central roost and occasionally within them. Towards the end of summer some starlings establish small communal roosts near their feeding areas and Leo Batten has reported a temporary late summer roosting assembly of several thousand juvenile birds in a willow swamp by the Brent Reservoir. In 1951 some three thousand five hundred starlings decided to abandon their regular flightline from the north-western suburbs of London to Trafalgar Square and chose to pass their nights from August until the fall of the leaf in some Lombardy poplars at Dollis Hill.

TUFTED DUCK and GREAT NORTHERN DIVER. *Above,* drake tufted duck, a resident nesting duck increasing on lakes and large gravel pits as well as a winter visitor; *below,* great northern diver, a rare winter visitor to reservoirs, especially those with deeper waters.

SEDGE WARBLER, REED BUNTING and YELLOW WAGTAIL. A group of wetland and marsh birds. *Above left*, sedge warblers at the nest. These birds favour herbage near rivers, lakes, sewage farms, damp ground and sometimes drier areas; *right*, male reed bunting at nest. A bird of marshes, freshwater margins, gravel pits and sometimes drier ground; *below*, male yellow wagtail with young. This is a bird of damp pastures and open habitats near water, mostly in England and Wales.

In 23 years this was the only starling roost that I recorded in my study area, although Batten's roost is about a mile away. As starlings were flying into the poplar trees they often looked up to watch other starlings flying overhead from more outlying parts towards central London. In many outer suburban and more rural districts there are often tree and thicket roosts which are used primarily by Continental birds. They may come in such numbers that they damage scrub and plantations both by their physical weight and by fouling. A massive assembly of birds that I studied in the Midlands succeeded after five months of winter occupation in breaking well-developed hawthorns at least twenty feet tall right down to within four or five feet of the ground. In another roost in a conifer plantation in Norfolk the depth of slimy faeces at one end of the wood proved to be as much as twenty inches. It is, of course, above these more rural roosts that it is possible to observe best the remarkable pre-roost flights carried out by huge numbers of birds whose flocks rise and fall in giant waves, sweeping this way and that like corn in a fickle, changing wind, mingling and intermingling like the flowing outlines of some enormous one-celled organism and filling the evening air with the murmur of countless wings and the shrill chatter of their voices. Such roosts as these are not too difficult to locate but in suburbia the smaller ones may be less easy to detect while the leaves remain on the trees and the traffic roars on close to their sleeping forms. It is sometimes possible to find house sparrows sharing the same trees with the starlings but usually the sparrows occupy the lower branches.

House sparrows will also roost by themselves in communal gatherings and the roosts near my home have varied in size from about a hundred birds in a philadelphus bush and in hawthorn scrub along the railway to about seven hundred and fifty birds in four Lombardy poplars. The birds gather at certain favoured spots on their feeding grounds in the late afternoon in small groups and then they fly off, sometimes in one flock, but more regularly in small parties to the distant roost. In one year a roost formed in late July in a bush in my own garden and lasted until early November. I was able to watch from close range and noted the behaviour one early October evening. 'At about half past five the first sparrows begin to arrive in the top of a tall prunus. Within ten minutes or so about thirty birds have flown in from all points of the compass and from distances of up to three hundred yards or more. By ten to six I can count up to a hundred birds gathering like fruit in the top of the tree. For the next twenty minutes the sparrows sit about chirping quietly in their "chapel" as these pre-roost assemblies are called. Some birds will spar up to their neighbours if they get too close and an agonized shriek tells me that one sparrow has been tweaked by another. I can also see some of the birds idly tearing at the prunus leaves, pulling them off and allowing them to drift to the ground. This wanton and destructive behaviour is very like that of sparrows in the spring when they tear up the petals of yellow crocuses, primulas, polyanthus and celandines. The sparrows first made their "chapel" in this tree in late July and so the top twigs are now entirely denuded of leaves. From time to time a bird will fly out in a hesitant way to catch a passing midge or gnat. A woodpigeon suddenly flashes low over the sparrows like a passing sparrowhawk and all crouch down and "freeze" in momentary panic.

'At about ten past six the sparrows start to become very restless and one or two begin to plane down some six feet or so into the top of a neighbouring philadelphus bush where they will spend the night. Within a minute or so all are in the roost and suddenly a furious chattering and chizzicking breaks out and this racket goes on for minutes on end. Then they seem to settle except for an occasional call. A white cat passes below and they fall silent. Once more the evening chorus breaks out – a sound which I find rather pleasant – and then as the evening draws on they finally settle down for the night.' The very loudest house sparrow chorus that I have ever heard was in the Place du Forum in Arles in October where the sound was quite deafening. There is generally a fall in the number of birds coming to the roosts in April but some appear to be used by birds all through the year. In the more rural parts of suburbia the sparrow roosts may be quite large and several thousand have been reported in scrub and thickets in a number of places. Even on the edge of Ken Wood in suburban north London some 5000 birds have been counted and 2500 at Chingford to the east. There is sometimes an interesting summer phenomenon of short-term roosts in May and June which last for a few weeks only. One of these has been set up in my philadelphus in ten of the last fourteen years and another appears in July near the Brent Reservoir. The closely related tree sparrow which may hold on in suburbia in isolated pockets generally roosts in holes in trees as well as bushes and hedges; in Warwickshire, for example, roosts estimated at 250 birds were located in 1966 at Brandon, at 40 in Sutton Park and at 75 at Coombe.

I do not know of any feral pigeon roosts in trees but woodpigeons almost invariably spend their nights in them. Near my home there are roosts in the nearby park where up to a hundred birds come in winter and there are also smaller ones in tall elms, oaks, planes, sycamores and poplars. In some suburban areas woodpigeon roosts are confined to public parks where perhaps several thousand may gather and to the larger private gardens. The collared dove can also be found roosting in trees and W. G. Teagle, in a personal letter to me, has described how on 23 December 1970 he watched birds arriving at dusk on Southampton Common to spend the night in the oaks and other broad-leaved trees around The Lake.

Kestrels and herons sometimes spend the night in trees and sparrow-hawks do this very regularly. The adult pheasant is a ground feeder but it often flies up into trees to roost, often with a lot of noise. The little, tawny and barn owls will all select hollow trees and even branches where they will sit quite close up against the trunk. Tawny owls roosting by day are often discovered by small birds and mobbed with loud scolding calls. As I was tape recording a flock of robins and wrens in Essex the owl stirred himself and gave vent to a long strangulated hoot of annoyance. Tits, thrushes, blackbirds, chaffinches and other birds may join the mob. The swift is not normally regarded as a tree-roosting bird but R. A. F. Cox observed a bird entering a tree at Cromer. The three common species of woodpecker all roost in tree holes and both the green and great spotted have been known to make excavations especially for this purpose. Swallows sometimes spend the night in trees and pied wagtails, in addition to choosing greenhouses and factory sites, often select trees such as hollies, willows, planes and limes. About three hundred wagtails roosted in plane trees in London Road, Thornton Heath, in 1949, and there was also a roost of about a hundred birds at Hammersmith Broadway. The urban roost in Dublin's plane trees has been well documented and may involve almost a thousand birds. There is apparently a very interesting chorus among these birds which has been described by Jeffery Boswall as 'of a softer, sweeter character than the usual flight call, but each was almost certainly a double note, as is the flight call'. There may also be occasional song phrases in the chorus.

One of the dominant birds of our suburban scene is the carrion crow and our attention is often drawn to it by its loud, harsh caw and its predatory habits. Crows resort to large trees to roost and many of their gatherings are small, perhaps about half a dozen birds. There are often larger ones in parks which may number a hundred birds or more while others may form in tall trees on farm or other open land. Rooks and jackdaws tend to live in more rural areas and their edge-of-the-countryside roosts are often of considerable size. Tall elms are a favourite site and certain clumps or groves may be used for many years in succession. It can be difficult to assess accurately the numbers of birds using some of the large roosts but a method has been evolved to photograph the flocks as they pass in a stream on a series of consecutive pictures. Many of the largest rook assemblies consist of thousands of birds which are often joined by numbers of jackdaws as well. One jackdaw roost in the Merthyr Valley was in use up to late June. Some jackdaws in suburban districts will roost in their nesting places throughout the year.

The remaining bird species that regularly spend the night in trees and shrubs are comparatively small ones. One of the best-known birds in suburbia is the hedgesparrow and this shy, rather secretive little

bird usually roosts by itself in a shrub or hedgerow. Favoured spots in
my garden are a snowberry hedge and a thick privet hedge. The hedgesparrow has an interesting habit of breaking into song in the depths of
the night and I have, in fact, more records of nocturnal song with this
species than with any other diurnal bird. I do not include warblers
which may sing quite often at night such as the grasshopper, reed or
sedge warbler. The almost ubiquitous robin, like the hedgesparrow,
tends to pass the night alone in a hedge, shrub or tree but I have found
pairs sitting together in March. The diminutive goldcrest commonly
roosts in conifers in large gardens and churchyards while the spotted
flycatcher usually perches at night on the branches of broad-leaved
trees.

All of the five suburban species of thrush can be found at night in
trees or shrubs. Mistle thrushes in autumn may roost together up to
December, often in coniferous trees, and then they begin to split up
into pairs or individuals. The winter-visiting fieldfare also favours
pines as well as evergreens and tall hedgerows and I have seen reports
of quite large roosts with over a thousand birds at Hanchurch in
Warwickshire and at Leigh in Staffordshire. The redwing is rather
more of a shrubbery bird and seeks lower levels than its bigger relative,
making the air noisy with its harsh 'chittuck, chit-it-it-tuck' roosting
calls. I have seen one redwing roost where the birds flew into a clump
of rhododendrons in twos and threes giving the soft 'see-ip' call until
soon about fifty birds had arrived. Besides the harsh note there is also
a rarer whinnying call rather like the prolonged distress call of the
blackbird. Redwings sometimes sing at night from the depths of the
roost. Many redwing roosts are in thorns and I have also known birds
to spend the night in oaks in my local suburban parks. The song thrush
can be found roosting in shrubs and bushes sometimes singly or in
small discreet groups and even intermingled with large numbers of
blackbirds.

Outside the nesting season suburban evenings would not be the
same without the metallic, ringing 'chink-chink-chink' or 'mik-mik'
notes of blackbirds going to a roost. They may also be quite noisy as
they leave it in the early morning. D. W. Snow found that this kind of
calling was most intense at those places where good roosting places
brought in strangers from outside the area and my experience of roosts
at Dollis Hill tends to confirm this. Dr Snow reported that 'The
resident birds, chinking persistently, chase and chivvy the intruders,
who approach silently and furtively; but eventually they desist and
allow the visitors to settle down in their roosts.' I have found suburban
roosts in tall privet hedges, thorns, almonds, ornamental shrubs and
climbers such as honeysuckle. In winter some males and females roost
singly and are joined in spring by their mates. Other roosting sites may
hold from one or two up to a dozen birds. Of course, some gardens may

be unsuitable for roosting and blackbirds holding territories and feeding in them may be forced to pass the night elsewhere when they generally prefer the company of other blackbirds. Moulting birds may stay away from a recognized roost. Generally blackbirds are rather late going to bed. Some roosts are in use throughout the year. Some Continental roosts hold hundreds of blackbirds because the gardens in the area lack suitable cover. The largest roost I have found at Dollis Hill consisted of some fifty birds but close to the nearby Brent Reservoir is a scrub and woodland roost of perhaps two thousand blackbirds with smaller numbers of song thrushes, redwings and fieldfares in many if not all years. The highest numbers at this roost are found between late September and November. Leo Batten has studied this roost in which some six thousand blackbirds have been ringed. All but 4 of the 235 recoveries were in the London area and only one bird has been recovered abroad, and that was in Sweden. This suggests that Continental birds are scarce here but in September and October immigrants do come into the Dollis Hill area and Batten concluded 'that most immigrants which do arrive, stay only a short while to feed and/or do not roost with the residents'. By ringing and weighing the blackbirds in the Brent roost it became clear that these suburban birds suffer much less in winter than birds living in more rural surroundings. They also select the most sheltered and dense parts of their roosting bushes and hedgerows. Blackbirds are fairly light sleepers and birds will not only call in the middle of the night but will fly round my garden if disturbed by a car's headlights or passing cat.

The tits may be fairly conspicuous as a group while they feed assiduously during the short winter days, coming to artificial feeders and coconuts and hunting for aphids and other invertebrates in the garden. But how often do we see them going to roost? The long-tailed tit of the much more open, wooded parts of suburbia roosts in thick hedges and conifer plantations. It often huddles together with other members of the same species to keep warm at night. The male has also been known to roost in the nest when the female is sitting on eggs. Marsh, willow and coal tits often use holes in trees while the more common great and blue tits search out holes in trunks and branches, walls and masonry as well as drain-pipes, street lamps, nestboxes and even letter boxes. One October afternoon I pruned a laburnum branch by my lounge window which was tending in summer to obscure the light. At the end of the branch there was a tight little cluster of leafed twigs which had formed after the branch was cut during the previous year. Much of this new growth largely disappeared as a result of my gardening activities. As it began to get dark, I became aware of a rather distressed blue tit hovering around the end of the pruned branch. For 25 minutes it flew around until it became dark and then the bird disappeared. I was quite sure that the leafy cluster at the end of the branch had provided it previously with a very snug little roosting place! Treecreepers which often hunt for food in the company of nomadic parties of tits look for cracks and crevices behind the bark of trees and since 1923 they have been observed roosting snugly in small excavated holes in the soft bark of the Wellingtonia which was introduced to Britain in the middle of the nineteenth century. The nuthatch is also a tree rooster but it may sometimes use nestboxes as well.

The roosting habits of the wren have been closely observed by Edward A. Armstrong. He found that birds may use an old nest either of its own species or of others such as those of blackbirds, long-tailed tits, great spotted woodpeckers, house sparrows and house martins. Until cold weather comes along wrens usually spend the night alone but sometimes a large number of wrens will collect in a particular site. Roosting assemblies have included nine in an old thrush's nest, ten in a coconut shell, seventeen in another nest and Armstrong reported a total of forty-six entering a nestbox where they had to 'squat on each other's backs, forming two or three layers or tiers'. But these are not the biggest totals. W. U. Flower actually saw sixty-one going into a single nestbox!

In the more country areas, on sewage farms and at gravel pits, yellowhammers may be found roosting together and sometimes with finches and sparrows. Some of the sewage farm roosts may hold several hundred birds. During the breeding season the various species of finch tend to roost alone, in pairs or in small parties but after nesting some of the finch species gather into fewer and larger roosting assemblies. Ian Newton has described the roosting behaviour of these birds in his New Naturalist book and I intend only to summarize some of his findings. Greenfinches, which may share a roost with sparrows in suburban areas, favour bramble thickets and evergreen shrubberies formed from rhododendrons, laurel and box. One roost near Oxford held some three hundred birds but on certain nights the total might rise to well over a thousand and, exceptionally, even to two thousand. A December roost at Trickley Coppice in Warwickshire was formed from over a thousand birds. With chaffinches there is some difference in behaviour according to their provenance. Resident birds can usually be found in thorns, evergreens and other thick cover and roosting alone or in pairs, while immigrant chaffinches go to large communal roosts in woodlands and scrub, especially of conifers, evergreens and bramble where they sometimes mix with bramblings as well. In 1948 C. A. Norris and I trapped at night the first proven chaffinch of the Continental race in Warwickshire in a coniferous hedge just outside Stratford-upon-Avon. One night expedition to some bushes in Staffordshire, carried out in March, resulted in the netting of redwings, song thrushes, a hedgesparrow, a treecreeper, a chiffchaff as well as a haul of chaffinches. Hawfinches and bullfinches generally roost as feeding flocks in small numbers, perhaps not much above thirty in size. Siskins and crossbills like tall conifers but it is also possible to find siskins at night in thorns and alders. Redpolls roost in similar situations as well as in birches, and in willow scrub, and their gatherings may be as large as two hundred or more. Roosting sites for the goldfinch in summer include tall deciduous trees in parks, woodland ecotones and large gardens and, although the records are rather few, I have found them at night in suburban London in planes, Italian poplars and sycamores; in winter goldfinches often choose evergreens, broad-leaved trees that have retained their dead foliage and the branches of small trees. There are interesting records of a winter tree roost in a Kensington street in London which accommodated 105 goldfinches and another holding 14 in a holm oak in Richmond Park. Linnets have nightly gatherings which ranging in size from a few dozen to fifteen hundred or more can often be found among gorse bushes and in scrub. Numbers at any finch roost may vary a great deal and there is often considerable movement between the different sites.

Dr Newton has also described the 'communal displays' which may take place at finch roosts before the birds settle down for the night. Birds sometimes fly round the roost in a nervous, unsettled way and then land in the trees. Chaffinches can be seen using a bounding flight while greenfinches get up in a body and wheel round the roost before coming back to perch once more. 'The chief features of this pre-roost behaviour', wrote Dr Newton, 'are its conspicuousness, its noisiness and, in some species, co-ordinated flights in which the participants twist and turn in unison.' Then the birds drop silently and together into the roost. Perhaps a large group of birds could mean that an individual is less likely to be taken by a predator such as an owl or a mammal if they all act together and pack tightly into their overnight quarters. Certainly pre-roost restlessness and nervousness are features among many different birds. Communal roosting habits could also help birds in their search for food resources and also prevent birds losing heat at night by raising the local temperature. It was the chilling effect of wind that finally drove out my roosting blackbirds in the severe weather of 1962–3. To reduce heat loss many roosting birds also fluff out their plumage to increase the insulation available to them. However one of the clear advantages to birds roosting together is that one individual can alert the rest to danger from a predator.

Although communal roosts may be formed as a protection against predators, a certain amount of predation can take place from birds and small mammals. I studied a starling roost in Warwickshire which sometimes held over a million birds and where 'three sparrowhawks and a peregrine also roosted in the thorns, often sharing their branches with a dozen starlings or more, but they only took them in flight as they rocketed down into the roost at dusk when conditions were most difficult'. D. E. Glue has also described how hobbies, kestrels and sparrowhawks were taking starlings while a pair of barn owls gathered house sparrows, starlings and pied wagtails from a communal autumn roost at a Hampshire gravel pit. In suburban areas tawny owls often visit house sparrow and feral pigeon roosts and these owls came regularly to the blackbird roost by the Brent Reservoir. Foxes will feed on ground-roosting birds and stoats, weasels and cats on those in trees and bushes.

The last remaining habitat in which suburban birds can roost is that provided by marshes, lakes, reservoirs, sewage farms, gravel pits and their sometimes rather specialized environs. Waterfowl and gulls often spend the night on an island or on open water while other species seek out the reedbeds and sedgy growth along the water's edge. Most of the species that I have mentioned in this chapter so far could be found in roosts in trees and shrubs near water and pheasants may even show a preference for branches overhanging water. But the species that I wish to discuss are those that seek out reedbeds and waterside growth or roost on the open regions of water.

Reed beds form a most attractive shelter at night for quite a number of bird species. Areas of reed like those at Minsmere and near Christchurch in Hampshire can draw in thousands of immigrant starlings and there are reports of redwings roosting in similar situations. Outside the breeding season sand martins often roost together in quite large numbers in reedbeds, osiers and other marshy vegetation; a roost at Wiggenhall in Fenland contained over seventy-five thousand birds. Swallows are also great frequenters of reedbeds – in 1963 there were 20,000 in reeds at Northfleet in Kent – but house martins seem to find them rather less attractive. However, N. E. G. Elms between July and September 1970 saw from twenty to a hundred house martins settling in reeds with several thousand sand martins and a smaller number of swallows. Pied wagtails are familiar roosters in this type of vegetation and one reedbed at Snodland on the Medway held an estimated five thousand birds in the first half of September 1964. Grey wagtails sometimes gather in reeds but they will also spend their nights in trees and bushes near water. Dr Stuart Smith recognized that the reedbeds around the Cheshire meres were 'favoured as roosting places by the large flocks of Yellow Wagtails, composed of birds bred on the Cheshire plain'. A thousand of these wagtails were also recorded on Rainham marsh near London in 1956. Linnets, tree sparrows, reed buntings, warblers, pheasants and wandering bearded tits have all been recorded passing the night among reeds. The dense reedbed at Moor Mill gravel pit in Hertfordshire was used for roosting not only by the local breeding birds but also by starlings, meadow pipits, pied and yellow wagtails, swallows and sand martins. Beds of reedmace appear in some marshy spots and some of these are also used as roosts; there were, for

REED WARBLER. The favourite nesting site for this summer visitor is among *Phragmites* reeds by lakes, gravel pits and sewage farms in England and Wales.

KESTREL and GOLDEN PLOVER, two species that can sometimes be seen flying over suburbia. *Above,* kestrel hovering. A bird of open country that hunts over allotments, railway embankments, motorway verges and even gardens and parks; *below,* golden plovers in flight. These waders often frequent airfields in winter and may sometimes be seen flying over suburban areas.

example, 150 yellow wagtails at Alvecote in Warwickshire and a thousand sand martins at Hartshill.

We have already seen in chapter 6 how a wide range of wildfowl and waders occurs on or by various sheets of water and some of these birds are likely to roost there overnight as well. For the ducks the large expanses of many of Britain's reservoirs provide a reasonably safe and undisturbed roosting site. It is for this reason too that on winter afternoons thousands of gulls may be seen arriving in great flocks to pass the night on their surface. It seems that the first real increase in the number of gulls wintering in the London area was in the early months of 1895. The first gull roosts were at the Lonsdale Road reservoirs and on the River Thames by Chiswick Eyot. The reservoirs at Barn Elms, built in 1896–7, were also adopted quite early on by the gulls. An estimate of the number of gulls roosting around London in the winters of 1952–3 and 1953–4 suggested a total of somewhere between 80,000 and 100,000 birds. At this time there were some 10–15,000 common gulls, 10,000 herring gulls and 500 great black-backed gulls while the remainder was made up by black-headed gulls. By December 1963 the total of gulls roosting in the London area was put at about 221,000 – an increase of 135,000 birds or 157% over the figures for 1952–54. There was a marked increase in the overall population of black-headed and common gulls but, according to Bryan Sage, 'the most recent and startling development of all has been the increase in the numbers of greater and lesser black-backed gulls wintering in the London area'. The counts were repeated in December 1968 and January 1969 and showed a 7·27% decrease in the great black-backed numbers but further rises of 178% in those of lesser black-backed gulls, 55% of common gulls, 16% of black-headed and 12% of herring gulls.

An interesting indication of the rising gull population was given by Bryan Sage in his description of a new reservoir in Hertfordshire which was filled with water in the summer of 1955 and first used for roosting by gulls in the following winter. In January 1956 there were more than eight thousand gulls of four different species using the reservoir as a roost. During the next two years the roosting total nearly doubled. Some gulls, of course, fly out to estuaries from suburban districts to roost, not only on the River Thames but on other parts of the coast. Something of the order of 100,000 common gulls roost on the Solway for example, and in 1955 the total estimate of inland-feeding gulls using the Wash was put at 120,000. Some gulls will also roost on the sea. Not all inland reservoirs are used for roosting and some like the Brent have been used only by occasional birds and during an August night in 1969 when several hundred black-headed gulls stayed overnight.

So far I have discussed the London gull roosts because they have been studied and censused over so long a period but a report in 1967 by R. A. O. Hickling to the British Trust for Ornithology on the inland wintering of gulls in England referred to a number of other roosts. Hickling recorded an increase in the country between 1953 and 1963 with new roosts accounting for a rise of 252,000 birds, old roosts absorbing another 113,000 and disused ones representing a loss of 186,000 gulls. The grand total of gulls roosting in winter in England was assessed for inland sites at a figure of 504,000, compared with 333,000 only ten years before. In the Manchester area there was an increase of some 20,000 gulls and around Birmingham one of 10,000. Some of England's most favoured gull roosts are on such reservoirs as Chew Valley in Somerset, Queen Elizabeth II and Barn Elms in Surrey, Hanningfield, King George V and the William Girling in Essex, Hilfield Park in Hertfordshire, Queen Mary in Middlesex, Belvide in Worcestershire, Eyebrook in Leicestershire, Longridge in Lancashire, Eccup in Yorkshire and Colt Crag in Northumberland. Other well frequented waters include Ellesmere Lake in Shropshire, North Hykeham gravel pits in Lincolnshire, Rostherne Mere in Cheshire and Ullswater in Westmorland. Cannock and Blithfield Reservoirs in Staffordshire have been known to hold several thousand roosting black-headed and herring gulls, while Bartley in Warwickshire has been used as a roost by herring, lesser black-backed and black-headed gulls. This last species has been known to use Bittell Reservoir in Worcestershire with several thousand birds coming in to spend the night there. Out of a total of 58 inland roosts 3 contained fewer than 100 birds, 14 carried from 100 to 1000, twenty-five from 1000 to 10,000 and 15 from 10,000 to 100,000. Only one roost exceeded the 100,000 figure. There is sometimes a very large roost on the Ouse Washes; this fluctuates in size but has contained over 100,000 birds.

The perhaps rather dull statistics do reveal, however, an astonishing rise in the numbers of gulls wintering and roosting inland – an increase made possible by the waste food produced by urban and suburban man and the provision through the reservoirs of safe roosting places. The largest number of gulls pass the night on the open water but some roost on the causeways or filter beds and on some of the concrete baffles. Although gulls prefer solid ground such as islands or the edges of ice sheets they generally settle on the water. To prevent the fouling of some drinking water reservoirs the birds have been moved on by the noise from explosions. C. J. Cornish's description of the scene at Barn Elms reservoirs early in the 1900s has always impressed me. It was, he said, 'as sub-arctic and lacustrine as on any Finland pool, for the frost-fog hung over river and reservoirs' while in the centre of one of the stretches of water an acre of apparently heaped-up snow 'changed into a solid mass of gulls, all preparing to go to sleep'. A new night viewing device has recently been evolved; it is based on image intensification and should prove invaluable for counting roosting gulls at night.

The behaviour of gulls at a roost has been studied by R. A. O. Hickling who examined the birds at two Leicestershire reservoirs over the course of two winters. There are sometimes massed formation flights which take place before roosting when 'the flock moves as an entity, as a coherent whole' with a great mass of wheeling gulls flying back and forth across the water. This kind of activity may be useful in strengthening the social bond between the birds and in persuading any nervous, reluctant birds to settle down in the roost. Each gull performs as an individual bird inside the scattered flock whereas starlings and wading birds such as knot appear to move as a compact, single unit. In the morning the gulls rise fairly early and may then indulge in another massed flight; they have usually all left the roost by full daylight.

The times of day at which birds actually go to their roosts or leave them are adapted to how and when they feed. For many species roosting is a nocturnal feature but those birds such as wildfowl and waders which choose to feed at night may be seen sleeping in the daylight hours. There is also some variation among the day feeding species in the times at which they rise and go to bed. The early rising and late retiring robin or redstart have comparatively larger eyes than those of the sleep-demanding house sparrow. It is thought that sparrows manage to get at least an hour's more rest at night than, say, blackbirds. As the times of both sunset and sunrise change throughout the year so also do the times of waking up and going to roost. J. M. Cullen has found that awakening is 'almost always at a lower light intensity than the roosting'. There are also some seasonal changes as well as day-to-day fluctuations due to weather conditions that may have affected the light intensity. At Dollis Hill starlings and black-headed gulls which fly over my house on their way to roost may show differences of up to half an hour in the first departures on two consecutive afternoons. For example, between 1 January and 6 January 1974 the earliest departures for starlings and gulls were respectively at 1434 and 1444 hours, while the latest were 1506 and 1526. The earliest departures occurred on dark, often wet afternoons while the latest took place on dry and very light ones. Grey-black clouds at the famous Dublin pied wagtail roost used to bring forward the arrival of birds at the roost by some twelve minutes.

The arrival of fog and smog can influence roosting times very considerably. I can well remember how a sudden smoggy darkening of a February afternoon in 1951 brought the suburban starlings into the central London roost at least two hours earlier than usual. Fog can also upset the departure of birds to their roosts. Starlings have several times stayed on the roof of my house rather than go off to their distant roost.

During a fog in 1950 birds that usually roosted at Lade were held up in Cambridge and roosted on Jesus College, the Roman Catholic Church and around the Market Square. At the Brent blackbird roost Leo Batten found that when visibility was down to fifty to sixty yards there was a drop in the number of birds coming to the roost. In conditions of thick fog hundreds of blackbirds were forced to spend the night in gardens rather than attempt the journey to the roost with visibility down to only forty feet. Birds often roost with their heads turned and resting on their backs with the bills under the scapular feathers but others may leave the beak pointing forward. Those birds that spend the night on perches remain securely on their twigs and branches through a special arrangement that, as the tarsal joint is bent, tightens the toes and so, as the muscles of the leg go limp and relaxed the greater becomes the grip by the toes on the perch. In this way birds can remain safely perched in even quite high winds.

Those of us who live in suburbia, if we glance up, may be able to observe birds actually travelling to and from their roosts since some species use regular and often unchanging routes or flyways. The persistence of these routes will depend on the degree of permanence of the roost itself. Over the last 150 years there has been an increase in the urban roosting habits of the starling, especially in northern industrial England. Around London many of its suburban flyways to the compact central roost have been known for probably forty years being extended over the period to at least fourteen miles to the north-west and south-west to accommodate the outward suburban sprawl. Three such flyways affect the study area in which I live and, as can be seen in figure 10, one of them passes over my house and has done so to my knowledge for at least thirty years. In all there are perhaps thirteen major flight lines of starlings over suburban London. Birds from Bushey, Harrow and Kingsbury travel over Dollis Hill and, after being joined by my local starlings, pass on across Cricklewood, St John's Wood, Regent's Park and Broadcasting House. Starlings coming from Stanmore and Hendon tend to follow a more easterly flyway along the course of the Edgware Road and birds from Northwood and west Harrow a route just along the western border of my study area.

The starlings collect in the late afternoon at such local gathering points as tall trees like the elms by the Brent Reservoir, cooling towers, steel masts and the roofs of buildings like those of the Post Office Research Station. Then they set off in flocks, small groups or even single birds to join other parties as they go. Twenty or thirty often assemble in my fruit trees and then take off to follow one of the parties flying overhead. In calm weather or with a tail wind they may fly quite high and be easily missed. With a head wind, poor visibility and rain the starlings travel quite low often dropping down from rooftop height to seek shelter from buildings and lines of trees and passing close to the

LAPWING and SPOTTED CRAKE. *Above*, lapwing, a migrant and winter visitor to grasslands, mudflats, sewage farms and marshes; *below*, spotted crake, a very rare winter visitor to sewage farms and reservoirs. This marsh bird may sometimes breed where the aquatic vegetation is very thick.

COMMON SANDPIPER and PECTORAL SANDPIPER, wetland wader species. *Above*, common sandpiper, a regular spring and autumn passage bird to lowland rivers, lakes and sewage farms; *below*, pectoral sandpiper, an annual transatlantic vagrant recorded from sewage farms and even rubbish-tip pools.

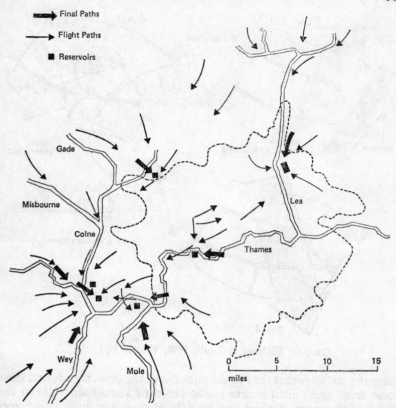

Final Paths

Flight Paths

■ **Reservoirs**

Gade

Misbourne

Colne

Lea

Thames

Wey

Mole

0   5   10   15
miles

FIG. 9 Gull flight lines in the London area (mainly after Sage 1970).

ground over open spaces, gardens and roadways. They fly purposefully and steadily with rapidly beating wings and glides made with extended and more rarely closed wings. In Warwickshire I have used my car speedometer to time flocks of starlings as they flew to roost alongside a road parallel to their flight line and I found that their speed ranged between 45 and 48 m.p.h. Some eight minutes after leaving my home the birds arrive at the central roost. Similar routes or flyways exist around all starling roosts and it is possible by obtaining compass bearings on two or more of the flightlines to plot them on an Ordnance Survey map and so find the location of the roost itself. The noise and concentration of birds at the roost site usually corrects any errors in the 'fixes' obtained in this way. Some suburban starlings may roost in their nestholes, others in small local gatherings and others in plantations and coverts in the countryside outside. At Peterhead in Aberdeen-

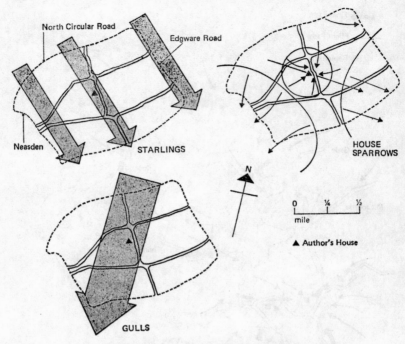

FIG. 10 Flylines at Dollis Hill. Winter 1973–74.

shire the starlings that feed in the suburbs of the town transferred their roost from some giant cranes to the sea-cliffs some four miles to the south of the town. Several regular flylines pass over suburban Peterhead on their way to the coast. Birds will use the same routes in the morning when vacating the roosting site but they generally travel in the dark and are less easily seen. The biggest numbers in London, Huddersfield and Dublin occur in late summer, but in Newcastle, Manchester, Birmingham, Liverpool and Bristol the peaks are reached in winter. Enthusiastic suburban bird watchers might be interested in plotting the starling flyways in their own areas and counts of birds using them each month or week would reflect the total at the roost itself.

House sparrows tend to change their roosts more frequently than the starlings and so they may employ many flightlines in the course of a year to reach a variety of different sites. I live in a catchment area for three possible roosting places but one of these is occupied for about seventy-five per cent of the year and the flyline to it passes over my house. Birds gather in noisy chirping assemblies in my trees and then set off singly or, more regularly, in small flocks to fly a distance of just over half a mile to the roost. The birds nearly always fly at rooftop level but, if they are using an alternative roost a mile away, they may climb up to a height of one hundred feet before setting course. I have never seen a pre-roost assembly larger than about fifty sparrows and very rarely does the whole flock set off together. They are not so easy to spot on the move as starlings. Most sparrow flightlines are only a few hundred yards long but some may stretch for a mile or more. In Athens in April 1973 I saw suburban house sparrows travelling for more than two miles to their roost and J. D. Summers-Smith reported an Egyptian roost that drew birds up to four miles from their feeding areas. In the evenings the house sparrows are noisy both at their pre-roost assemblies and the roosts themselves and there are sometimes social choruses in the mornings which all help to pinpoint roosts and gathering points. The flying birds may give themselves away by a 'churrip' flight call.

Finches also reach their roosting places by direct paths perhaps over several miles but the evidence is rather scanty for the size of the catchment areas. I came across a chaffinch roost in Worcestershire which was drawing birds from a distance of about two and a half miles and Ian Newton has described how a greenfinch was caught at a roost nearly two miles from where it had been ringed and released a few hours earlier. Thrushes and blackbirds will follow flyways to their communal roosts and I counted seventeen blackbirds passing singly over my garage on their way to a clump of hawthorns about a hundred yards away. We have already seen how woodpigeons will spend the night in tall trees in parks and gardens and in winter these too can be seen making for the roost each night along the same flight path. The woodpigeons that fed in St James's Park had a flightline over London's Victoria Station to some trees on an island in the lake in Battersea Park. Richard Fitter has described how they performed a reverse journey to that of the starlings and 'the two species could be seen passing each other at Chelsea Bridge, the starlings flying high, but the pigeons at roof-top level'. My local birds have a somewhat vague route to the nearby park but there are more firm tracks in many suburban districts where large roosts may be involved. There are no pied wagtails roosting in flocks at Dollis Hill but other suburban areas may witness the growth of large roosts outside the breeding season. The factory roost at Sparkhill, Birmingham, drew pied wagtails from a ten-mile radius around the city and a tree roost at Thornton Heath in south London was occupied by birds coming some two miles from their feeding grounds at Beddington Sewage Farm.

The outer suburbs may contain roosts of carrion crows and it is often possible to see birds flying in twos and threes or loose flocks along the same nightly paths to the roost. Some of the crows that feed near the Brent Reservoir and the Hendon rubbish dump fly about a mile to an elm tree roost at the top of Dollis Hill while over a hundred have been watched leaving the reservoir in a westerly direction probably for a roost on Barn Hill. Many of the crow roosts are old and well established and they may be occupied all the year round. Flyways to these are often traditional and small groups of black birds can be seen flapping slowly across the streets and gardens in the evenings. The closely related rooks and jackdaws live generally in more rural habitats where their roosts can number several thousand birds. From a big roost at Gatton Park in Surrey which held some five thousand birds there were flylines from Kingswood in the north-west, Walton Heath and Reigate Hill in the west and Redhill in the south, while jackdaws were traced on another route from Richmond Park across Motspur Park and Banstead to the north-north-west, a distance of some thirteen miles.

Mallard which spend the day in my local park fly at dusk in a direct line over my garden to spend the night on the nearby reservoir and they can be seen travelling over at most times of the year. They sometimes fly over in the dark and I can hear the rush of wings as they pass low and fast above the trees. For me it is always a special delight to hear over a suburban estate a sound so evocative of remote coastal marshes.

One of the most noticeable of all bird movements in many suburban districts is that of large numbers of gulls following regular flyways to their roosts on reservoirs, lakes, rivers and estuaries away from their daytime feeding grounds. In London birds may travel up to twenty miles and I used to watch black-headed gulls flying west over Ladbroke Square from the Royal Parks out to the western reservoirs. Movements started in September and I saw hundreds of birds going west in the afternoon and east in the morning. For example, on 22 January 1937, almost a thousand birds were involved. Col. Richard Meinertzhagen in a letter to me in March of the same year also noted that 'almost every morning from my bedroom window' – in Kensington Park Gardens – 'in the winter I see gulls passing west in the evening and passing east soon after dawn. Starlings and woodpigeons do the reverse, the great roosting place of the former being Trafalgar Square and Charing Cross and of the latter the Island on the Serpentine'. At Dollis Hill a regular flightline has run over my house from Kingsbury and the Brent Reservoir and thence to Willesden, Harlesden, Wormwood Scrubs, Hammersmith and finally Barn Elms reservoirs. On this pathway birds sometimes pass at the rate of 1700 birds an hour. In the valley of the River Lea B. S. Meadows found that 90% of the roosting gulls generally used two flyways – one north-east to north from the valleys of the Stort and Lea and the other south-west to east from the direction of the Thames estuary. He also found that although some birds of the common five gull species arrived from all directions 'there was a tendency for each species of gull to arrive in greater numbers from one direction than from another'. The gull flyways around

London have been described by Bryan Sage, including the early morning broad-front dispersals just before dawn and the regular afternoon flights to the roosts. Figure 9 summarizes the regular routes around London used by the gulls. One flyway in north London carried 2500 gulls on a January afternoon and of these 1800 were black-headed and all passed between 1645 hours and 1715 hours BST. Some of the Lea Valley flightlines could be traced for distances of up to thirty miles and more. The flyways to the Tring and Hilfield Park reservoirs averaged from twelve to thirteen miles in length. Radar observations that were made at London Heathrow Airport have confirmed a heavy flyway along the Thames Valley to Staines from the west-north-west.

When gulls are on their routes I have found that, like starlings and other birds, they tend to fly higher with the wind behind them, whereas a head wind will force them to travel much closer to the ground. I have watched gulls leaving the Brent Reservoir on a front perhaps some five hundred or six hundred yards wide, gathering height slowly and making off towards Neasden and Willesden to the south. Numbers are at their highest in mid-winter and I do not normally see birds between mid-May and late June when the first black-headed and lesser black-backed gulls may return. After passing over my garden the birds reach the great built-up mass of the Post Office Research Station on the summit of the hill. This great block, full of generators and electrical equipment, is able to produce a small-capacity, man-made thermal in which heated air begins to rise and form a local upcurrent. The gulls break off their line and begin to soar in circles above the station, reaching a considerable height before setting off again for their roost. Birds sometimes stay soaring for as long as ten minutes. The local topography of the hill is not steep enough for a slope current to form and the birds must be taking advantage of a true thermal and enjoying it. Gulls have been increasing very fast in Britain in recent years and a high proportion of them roost at night on reservoirs. Many of their flyways have not been plotted and there is considerable scope here for those who are interested in birds and have a liking for maps.

CHAPTER 10

Birds on the Move

FOR the birdwatcher who lives in suburbia there are two seasons – spring and autumn – when the comparative sameness of the local bird community is temporarily enhanced and relieved by the arrival of migrants which may pass overhead or even drop down to feed, drink and rest before resuming their migratory journey. It is also possible to hear bird migrants calling at night as they fly over our suburban homes and on moonlit nights I have occasionally seen birds crossing the silver disc of the moon. Then birds may turn up that have 'irrupted' from their distant breeding grounds and spread to new regions. These are irregular voyagings and lack the annual and rhythmic pattern of true migration and the same can be said of 'weather movements' when birds are forced by severe cold and snow in the winter to travel in search of more open regions where food is available There is a vast literature on the subject of bird migration and so I am restricting myself to some of the observational aspects in suburban areas.

I would like first of all to deal with those irregular, irruptive invasions that take place from time to time. At the outset it is necessary to make it clear that irruptive movements are only so in those regions that receive the birds; they are, of course, eruptive in their countries of origin. These irregular movements generally start in one of two kinds of environment or biotope which both experience considerable extremes of climate – northern forest and steppe. Big fluctuations can also occur in the production of fruit by the trees in the forest belt and such factors as extremes of weather, uncertain and irregular fruit crops and specialized feeding habits in birds can all bring about an imbalance in the populations of those species. If there is a failure in a staple food supply after a good breeding season then birds are forced to begin foraging movements which can easily be extended to areas beyond the normal range. Crossbills are fond of spruce seeds and a shortage in the supply of them can be offset only by a move away in search of new woods and plantations. After the 1962 invasion of Britain most of the crossbills recorded were seen feeding in pines and European larches. After such invasions a few birds may stay to nest erratically among conifers, even in suburban areas, while small parties of non-breeding birds often appear in widely scattered localities.

The European slender-billed nutcracker which is found among Arolla pines is another eruptive species and J. Dorst has shown that invasions of these forest birds occur 'when an abundant crop (during which the population has increased, due in part to lower mortality in the winter) is followed by a poor year when the birds are driven to seek food elsewhere'. During the autumn of 1968 some three hundred and fifteen nutcrackers were reliably reported in Britain. Many of these chocolate-brown birds with white spots were seen in pine trees near the sea but others frequented roadsides, churchyards and public parks and more than a hundred visited gardens where some of them even fed on bread.

Another irregular visitor to our shores is the waxwing whose principal food here is made up of berries such as those of rowan, hawthorn, dog-rose, guelder rose and various exotic shrubs including Berberis, Cotoneaster and Pyracantha. In some years the numbers are quite considerable and in the winter of 1946–7 birds were reported in many places, including quiet residential roads as well as busy streets in the outer suburbs of many towns. Some penetrated the centre of Norwich, Rugby and other towns and there were at least five hundred in the region of London. After examining the records of these five hundred birds, *The Birds of the London Area* reported that the waxwings were not seen in central London or the closely built inner suburbs 'but from the middle and outer suburbs . . . where the berries of rowan, privet, cotoneaster, hawthorn and other fruiting shrubs could be obtained so freely the records outnumbered those from the open spaces by four or five to one'. Birds were seen in Brixton, Herne Hill, Hampstead and St John's Wood. During a later invasion in 1965 waxwings were also seen in the suburbs of Birmingham, Coventry, Bedworth, Loughborough, Solihull, Warwick and Rugeley. In many invasions birds are very regularly reported from suburbs and towns in the east and north-east of Britain.

There are other bird species which were perhaps once regarded as rather sedentary which have revealed behaviour rather similar to that found in the better-known eruptive birds. In 1957 large numbers of great and blue tits were seen on the move in Western Europe and Britain. These movements followed a previous rather mild winter with a high rate of survival among the tits. Similar movements may also take place among siskins, redpolls and bramblings and irregular wanderings of this kind may be more common than is generally supposed. In the autumn of 1959, after a very successful nesting season, bearded tits began to erupt from their breeding grounds in East Anglia. These rare and attractive birds left their homes and discovered other reedbeds in England where, like the crossbill, they temporarily colonized new areas or reoccupied old deserted sites. Dr David Lack suggested that overcrowding in the normal breeding areas was the proximate stimulus for the invasion type of irregular migration, where a raised level of excitement and restlessness among the birds brought about an emigration before food came into really short supply. I have often watched bearded tits at Minsmere in Suffolk rising high above the reeds, calling noisily and swooping down again, demonstrating in this way their autumnal nervousness. On several occasions in October I have also seen parties climb steeply, turn south into wind and move off on their true eruptive flight. Birds may then appear, often in pairs, in unaccustomed localities like the two which were seen at the Brent Reservoir in October 1965. Leo Batten later saw seventeen together in the reeds by the reservoir; he trapped six and released them again with rings on their legs and two of these marked birds were later caught in the area of Manea in Cambridgeshire. Bearded tits have also been seen at gravel pits, sewage farms and other reservoirs and are worth looking for in autumn in these habitats.

There are sometimes rare vagrants that may turn up in suburban situations which cannot be looked upon as true migrants. They could better be described as vagrants or lost birds. Such rarities include the Leach's petrels at Staines in 1949, the rough-legged buzzard at Mill Hill in 1946, the yellow-billed cuckoo found dead in an Eastbourne garden in 1952 and whose corpse was sent to me by a radio listener, the ortolan bunting, greenish warbler and hoopoe which I have seen in Brent in the last few years and the black-eared wheatear and red-breasted flycatcher which I watched less than five miles from St Paul's Cathedral. County Bird Reports and Avifaunas diligently list these perhaps 'once-in-a-lifetime' birds which may be seen by the bird-watcher who regularly and systematically works over the same ground. They form part of that diversity of birds which can elude the less regular watcher.

In its true sense migration has a regularity, a purposive character and definite quality of direction which distinguish it from eruptive move-ments. There is a transfer of the breeding population from its summer home to its winter quarters. The actual movements of birds can be conveniently divided into two – unseen and seen. The former consist of passage at night or in daylight far above the range of vision while the latter are revealed by flights of birds in daylight and by the appearance of migrant birds in areas where they do not breed. Night migration is regular among many of our smaller birds which may be diurnal in their habits for the rest of their lives but migrate at night when they are not so vulnerable to attack by predators. Other birds travel by day and some migrants may choose to do both. In *Bird Migrants* I con-sidered that 'the question of day and night movement cannot be answered by dividing all birds into two categories, as some species may travel sometimes in the hours of daylight and sometimes in the hours of darkness. Wading birds, which as a rule migrate at night, are largely nocturnal by nature and night travel is not so surprising in their case. An additional factor which may be directly related to the night migration of birds which are used to finding their food in daylight, is that such birds need light to feed by and so the spending of the night hours in travel leaves the hours of day for finding food – an essential prerequisite for long and sustained travelling'.

A number of the night-flying wading birds can be recognized by their calls although some species appear on occasion to use special and unfamiliar notes on their migratory flights. The species which are most likely to be recognized are curlew, whimbrel, redshank, greenshank, dunlin, green sandpiper, golden and ringed plover, turnstone, oyster-catcher and stone curlew. I have three times heard bar-tailed godwits calling at night over Dollis Hill as well as the commoner species of wader. I am afraid that today whimbrels no longer occur in the numbers that Charles Dixon reported in 1909 when 'For nights, together they may be heard passing, uttering their unmistakable cries especially in the vicinity of Harlesden, Kilburn and Hampstead.' These nocturnal migrations were also reported by Gilbert White in 1788 when he described how these 'aquatic and gregarious birds, especially the nocturnal, that shift their quarters in the dark, are very noisy and loquacious'. Various ducks, wild geese and quail call at night and red-wings, which may move in the day as well, are very typically night migrants, passing over countless suburban areas in September, October and during the spring months. When I was living in Rugby I noted 106 redwing calls in just over an hour on one October night and I counted more than two thousand between 1830 and 2310 hours GMT over Dollis Hill in October 1958. Sometimes the peak of calls at night seems to be reached between 0200 and 0400 hours. Song thrushes and blackbirds also travel by night but J. N. Hollyer has suggested that the flight call of the Continental song thrush may be mistaken for that of the redwing. After visually identifying many night migrant thrushes calling in daylight I consider that the redwing's contact call is both longer and 'wavier' in pattern or form than the corresponding call of the song thrush. After spending nights and days at the old Dungeness Lighthouse on the South Coast of England where I experienced a number of good passage movements I reported in *Voices of the Wild*; 'The air around the lighthouse was full of sound; I could hear dis-tinctly the thin "See-ip" of redwings and the shorter "Sipp" of song thrushes, the "Tzeeerk" of blackbirds and, above all other sounds, the clear, plaintive "Tleeee" of passing golden plover.' Subsequent observations of other Continental song thrushes in north-west London confirmed this difference but I believe that it may require very careful listening and discrimination.

Before the coming of radar it was very difficult to make any kind of study of night migrants especially as some movements took place on the darkest nights. However, I have seen waders crossing the surface of the moon – a type of observation made as long ago as 1888 by F. M. Chapman. On several nights in late August 1961 up to twenty small birds an hour were observed over London flying across the moon's disc. No satisfactory method has been worked out for obtaining the height of migrants observed with a telescope against the moon. Only with the advent of radar did it become possible to find out the real altitudes at which migration was taking place. Writing in 1959, Dr David Lack expressed the opinion that the first time 'radar echoes were definitely identified as coming from birds was in the spring of 1940, when an experimental equipment on a wavelength of 50 cm at Christchurch, Hampshire, detected gulls'. With more sophisticated apparatus radar studies were able to show that the common small birds coming to Britain for the winter tended to fly higher in spring than in autumn and also at a greater height by night than by day. Much of the detected migration occurred below 5000 feet but a few small passerines were recorded up to 14,000 feet and even 21,000 feet. Waders such as lapwings seemed to travel at a more constant height, usually somewhere between 3000 and 6000 feet but with the highest echo at 11,000 feet. Watching migration by radar also proved that all night movements were taking place on a broad front and there was no evidence that night migrants were using coastlines as guides. It was possible to assess, in addition to height, the speed, direction, density and distribution of the night migrants involved, to link their movements with wind and weather, and to measure the extent of the inland broad-front migrations that were taking place. The study was carried out with high-powered long-range radars in the Outer Hebrides, Shetland, Aberdeenshire, Northumberland, Norfolk, Essex and Hampshire. Radar measurements still need to be supplemented by field work with binoculars and notebooks and we who live in suburbia can still see and hear something of the birds' seasonal travels across the British Isles.

The ways in which we can most easily tell that migration is taking place are of two kinds. The first is the direct and visible movement of birds overhead (what we now call visible migration), and the second is the seasonal change in the kinds and numbers of birds that we can trace day by day during the spring and autumn months. I propose to deal with the second phenomenon first which is revealed to us by the birds, strangers to us, that arrive one day and may be gone the next. We may walk round our suburban park one evening and see nothing but familiar resident birds. The next morning there may be birds of unfamiliar species about that could only have arrived overnight. Ian Wallace has shown that the appearance of migrants at inland localities such as parks is identical in manner to that of their arrival at the coast. Birds like warblers and chats usually 'arrive suddenly overnight and while the "falls" are not often large, the similarity of the birds' behaviour (a short rest on arrival followed by very active feeding through the day) leaves little doubt that they came by night flight'. They come in a much less spectacular way than those taking part in visible diurnal movements, although some migrants can actually be seen dropping down in daylight – wheatears, redwings and hedge-sparrows, for example. At Dollis Hill I have kept a watch on some allotments which have provided a small but regular oasis for some passerine migrants. One September evening in 1951 I toured this area and found that only resident birds were present. Early the next morning I found scores of chiffchaffs in the currant bushes and these could have only come in overnight. Some of the warblers remained for the next seven days. Parks, gardens and allotments in suburban areas are worth watching for migrants and even small gardens with a few grimy raspberry canes or bean poles can provide shelter for a tired migrant willow warbler, whitethroat or goldcrest perhaps. In spring when the passage is more urgent and rushed birds tend not to stay so long.

Many parts of the suburbs can prove attractive to migrants – not only gardens but parks, street trees, cemeteries, reservoirs, sewage farms, gravel pits, playing fields and waste ground. All of them are worth investigating and regular visits will soon show the arrivals and departures. Even the inner suburbs are worth looking at. When I lived in Ladbroke Square in west London I recorded willow warblers, chiffchaffs and jackdaws on both spring and autumn migration. The spring visitors included whitethroats, lesser whitethroats, garden warblers, blackcaps, grey wagtails, and cuckoos, while the purely autumn migrants were made up of a few warblers and siskins, pied wagtails, pied flycatchers, goldcrests and wheatears. With some additional thrushes, redstarts, whinchats, pipits and a few more warblers such a variety of migrants could be reproduced in many parks and open spaces in the inner suburbs of many towns.

For many years I have kept a watch for migrants on the summit of Dollis Hill and here of the 47 migrant species that I have observed about half could be regarded as fairly regular. Since this area is typical of a great deal of British suburbia it may be of interest to trace the passage movements that occur there during the course of a year. The first true migrants appear in February and these are redwings whose migration in the spring lasts into April. Between 1952 and 1962 there were rooks and jackdaws as well. There is often a sprinkling of willow warblers and fieldfares in April, but chiffchaffs are rather scarce in spring and the cuckoo is now very rare. There are occasional wheatears, whinchats and redstarts and many suburbs may witness a trickle of tree pipits, yellow wagtails and warblers – blackcaps, garden warblers, whitethroats, lesser whitethroats and wood warblers. The suburban bird watcher who visits the banks of rivers and lakes may also add a migrant reed or sedge warbler at this time. Spring passages at Dollis

Hill, as in other areas, may be rather thin in many years but at the Brent Reservoir there have sometimes been quite heavy falls of migrants after cloudy wet nights like those of 2 May 1965 and 6 May 1967. For me it is often the presence of an unaccustomed song or call that warns me first that a bird of a new species is passing through. An appreciation of bird songs and calls is of great advantage in keeping a check on migratory movements. Two companion LP records which I prepared for BBC Radio Enterprises – *Back Garden Birds* and *Woodland Birds* may be of help in the recognition of many of the songs and calls.

Reservoirs are important attractions for swallows, martins, swifts, gulls, terns, duck and wading birds. E. R. Parrinder has described how a visit in May to a small area of reservoir, flooded gravel pit, sewage farm and water meadows in Middlesex produced the following migrant species – white wagtail, Sandwich tern, black tern, shelduck and such waders as black-tailed godwit, greenshank, common and green sandpipers, sanderling, ringed plover, turnstone, dunlin and ruff. Apart from the scarce black-tailed godwit the waders were all regular spring migrants to the London area, although not as common as during the autumn passage. In many years it is often possible to see curlew, whimbrel, wood sandpiper, redshank, spotted redshank, little ringed plover, curlew sandpiper, little stint and knot. At Blithfield Reservoir in Staffordshire oystercatchers, golden plover and bar-tailed godwits were also well known as spring migrants. At Cambridge Sewage Farm Ian Nisbet found that the average date of spring migration among the waders ranged from 26 March for redshank to as late as 24 May for little stint. The average dates for the other species of wader at Cambridge were black-tailed godwits 17 April, green sandpipers 26 April, bar-tailed godwits 1 May, whimbrels 10 May, and greenshanks, common sandpipers, ruffs, turnstones, wood sandpipers, grey plover, sanderlings, Temminck's stints and knot between 12 and 21 May. There can, of course, be annual deviations in these dates of several days. It was considered that the common spring waders at Cambridge were Arctic or British breeding birds. Between 1941 and 1967 the spring movements in Leicestershire of grey plover, turnstones, sanderlings, black, common or Arctic terns were more extensive than in autumn but the autumn passage involved many more species. The counting of birds of all these species occurring inland can provide an index of population for the wading birds passing through Britain each year. May is one of the best months in which to see black terns on migration and as many as a hundred and twenty-one have been seen at Staines on a single day in that month. In May 1973 a little gull and a Mediterranean gull were seen fishing with terns on the River Thames at West Thurrock.

Lapwings are also regular migrants and, if I look up at the sky in summer, I sometimes see parties of these plover flying overhead. These passages may begin in late May, become rather more frequent in June and quite common in July. In some years I noticed only a few birds passing but in others I have observed flocks containing one hundred and fifty birds or more. Even in Kensington I used to see half a dozen or so in most summers. It is very likely that these mid-summer birds of passage are juveniles from the Continent, making their way into England, and a young bird which was ringed in Bohemia in May and recovered the following August in north London gives some support to this theory.

After a summer lull the waders are beginning to turn up again at the reservoirs, sewage farms and other wetland habitats which can provide them with the necessary mud, water, food and shelter. A great deal of this wader migration is on a broad front, often in conditions of easterly wind and rain, but westerly gales may bring in American birds such as pectoral and Baird's sandpipers. The broad front migrants turn up in many different localities at about the same time and so a visit in late summer and autumn to the wetlands and even any stretch of water with a natural feeding edge is well worthwhile. Besides the commoner birds of passage there may be much rarer birds such as great snipe, lesser yellowlegs, spotted sandpiper, white-rumped sandpiper, broad-billed sandpiper and grey phalarope. One September there were a hundred curlew sandpipers and some forty little stints at Nottingham Sewage Farm, and in the autumn of 1953 a very large passage of ruffs and both these species was reported in many places. It was estimated that in late August and early September 1969 there were at least three thousand five hundred juvenile curlew sandpipers present in Britain. There is a regular autumn migration route for these birds from the Baltic down the Continental seaboard to Africa and this remarkable westward movement was attributed to unusual and persistent cyclonic weather over the Baltic and Russia which coincided with the evacuation of the nesting grounds by the young sandpipers.

July and August are also marked by strong passages of lesser black-backed gulls and I sometimes see early birds at Dollis Hill in the middle of June. In eight of the last twelve years – up to 1973, that is – I have observed the first of these passage gulls between 1 and 8 July. Flocks gather on playing fields, in parks, on reservoir banks, golf courses and other open spaces. About a thousand were recorded on 1 September 1971 near Harefield Moor gravel pit in Middlesex while autumn flocks of 500 are not unknown at rubbish tips and reservoirs in the London area. At this time of the year there may also be common gulls, common and Arctic terns, black terns, cormorants and such duck as teal, garganey, shoveler, pintail and pochard making their appearance on inland waters. It is also possible to see an occasional bird of prey – a buzzard, harrier, osprey, hobby or peregrine – that on passing through the region finds a good hunting area and stays for a short time before moving on.

The smaller passerine birds also begin to appear. The autumn migration of the willow warbler takes place near my home between mid-July and late August, with generally two peaks – about the 6th and between 22 and 29 August. I regularly see birds not only on the allotments and in the local park but in small suburban gardens and even in street trees such as sycamores, planes and whitebeams. They sometimes sing a quieter version of their typical song – shorter and more hesitant. The autumn passage of the chiffchaff is rather later and lasts from about 1 August to early October and this warbler very much favours the brambles, currants and bean poles on the allotments. I often surprise linnets and whitethroats on the allotments and quite expect to see the occasional blackcap, garden warbler, whitethroat and lesser whitethroat, pied flycatcher, tree pipit, redstart and whinchat. Yellow wagtails may appear on the suburban grasslands and grey wagtails turn up by lakes, fountains, waterfalls and even on the banks of the sealion pool in the London Zoo. Besides these easily recognizable migrants there may also be parties of nomadic great and blue tits moving across the region and even a goldcrest or two.

As autumn moves on, the possibility of finding the first winter visitors begins to grow. These include various ducks, perhaps coot and moorhens, water rails, gulls, jack snipe and woodcock, fieldfares, redwings, meadow pipits, siskins, redpolls, chaffinches and bramblings. Sometimes the first comers can be seen arriving across the sea, if you live on the coast, while others may be spotted dropping down to feed and rest after their journey is over. At other times we come upon them just after they have completed their descent. And this ability to see birds actually on the move brings us to the subject of visible migration itself – a study that has fascinated me ever since 1948 when I traced a migration route which I called 'the Cotswold corridor' across the south Midlands of England.

Today it is known that a vast amount of broad-front bird migration takes place over Europe and the British Isles and that sometimes a column of birds with a lateral spread of several hundred miles is on the move. In autumn great immigrations of Continental birds strike the eastern and southern seaboards along many miles of coast and radar has shown how widespread these invasions, as well as emigrations, can be over Britain. Under certain conditions migration can take place at a low enough altitude for us to see it from the ground. It may still be on a wide front or, in certain situations, along narrow routes such as coasts, rivers and hill scarps but these are not fully understood or have not been worked out for many parts of the country. Figure 11 gives a broad indication of some of the directions taken by migrants in autumn. It seems clear that this visible migration over the London

FIG. 11 Directions taken by autumn migrants inland.

suburbs is best seen when there is a north-westerly flow of air. However, in the south Midlands I recorded migration that was clearly visible in a wide variety of wind conditions: 'Birds passed over on completely still mornings, with south-east and south-south-east breezes, with strong north-east and west winds, and with south-east or south-south-west winds of variable strength.' The heaviest passages appeared to take place with moderate east-north-east or north-east winds but some birds then passed too high and above the range of vision. In north-west London tail winds tended to induce the migrants to fly high as well.

The first description of this kind of inland visible migration in the London area was given by F. D. Power who watched birds between 1874 and 1909 flying over his suburban garden in Brixton. Here he observed chaffinches, which were in fact the commonest birds, as well as skylarks, starlings, rooks, greenfinches and bramblings flying over in a westerly direction especially with north-west winds. Not until the late 1920s were there any more significant observations of this kind reported from London's urban spread. On 6 October 1948 W. G. Teagle noticed chaffinches flying north-west over central London and he counted 525 going in the same direction over the London parks in a period of half an hour on 15 October. In 1949 Leslie Baker and E. R. Parrinder began regular watches from the centre of London and in September 1951 I began to study the movements over suburban north-west London, after three years studying the Cotswold migrations. More extensive co-operative migration watches were organized in London and its suburbs in 1960. Migrations over the heart of London are still recorded and on 23 October 1973 I counted 1500 chaffinches passing north-west at rooftop level over Bush House in the Strand over a period of an hour.

For me one of the recurring and pleasant experiences that I look forward to each year is the arrival of autumn when I can begin my search for visible migrants passing over my home and nearby allotments. The spring movements that I am able to see are small. A few chaffinches move north in late March and April and I have also seen birds at this time over Handsworth Wood and Bristol as well as coasting near Hythe and Minsmere. Martins and swallows can be seen making their way in ones and twos over my house. Swifts are influenced by rivers and water courses and a series of cycle patrols by mobile watchers in May along the courses of the Rivers Cam and Great Ouse showed that these birds could be traced on their northward journey through Cambridgeshire. Many thousands of swifts were observed along the waterways but the largest numbers were along the rivers and their tributaries. The bird movements in autumn are generally more spectacular but in good weather birds may pass beyond the range of our vision. I remember Herbert Axell, the warden at the Royal Society for the Protection of Birds reserve at Minsmere in Suffolk, remarking to me that 'a good migration season for birds is a bad one for *birdwatchers*!'

In many years in September and October I have seen movements over suburban Brent of lesser black-backed gulls, lapwings, woodpigeons, jays, starlings, pied and grey wagtails, skylarks, meadow pipits, greenfinches, bramblings, chaffinches, siskins, redpolls, tree sparrows, swallows and house martins. From 1952–63 rooks and jackdaws were regular in small numbers in autumn and from 1951–60 there were also small parties of stock doves, but all movements of these three species appear to have ceased. The swallow is a regular passage bird in the autumn months generally flying into the wind even when it finds itself travelling north. Birds travel in a narrow route over the top of Dollis Hill. Several hundred birds may be involved in a single passage movement and on 24 September 1964 I counted 2250 swallows flying to the south. Swallow movements may be resumed in the evening and birds can still be seen on passage as the starlings and house sparrows are going to roost. The heaviest house martin migration I ever recorded was on 4 October 1952 when 700 birds went through but

REDSHANK and SNIPE, further wetland wader species. *Above,* redshank, a passage visitor to wetland habitats that may also nest in marshes, sewage farms and wet pastures; *below,* snipe – mainly a winter visitor and a regular bird at sewage farms.

WILLOW WARBLER and BLACKCAP, autumn migrants. *Above,* willow warbler in honeysuckle, a very common autumn migrant through suburban parks and gardens; *below,* blackcap eating ivy berries. Another autumn passage bird in suburbia that sometimes overwinters as well.

there are always some passage movements every autumn. The sand martin is very scarce.

Blackbirds and song thrushes sometimes pass over in small numbers but the truly impressive migrants in daylight are the fieldfares and redwings. Each autumn I see fieldfares passing over but the strongest passages were of 2500 flying west-north-west over a period of 100 minutes on 26 October 1966 and of 1050 flying north-west in November 1961. Leo Batten reported more than a thousand over the Brent Reservoir on 1 November 1959. Fieldfares that I watched passing over my house in October 1955 were part of a larger migration that was also observed at the same time in Essex, Kent and Surrey. The largest redwing migrations have been in October and these have sometimes involved up to a thousand birds.

The movements of skylarks begin in mid-September and continue until the end of October and I have a single passage record of the woodlark. Most meadow pipit migrations take place in the early morning and the passage itself lasts from about the middle of September to the middle of October, often with a peak around 21 September. Most of the birds that I have watched have been flying south-west or west. In 1972 I also recorded rock pipits for the first time. There are many flocks of starlings about in the autumn months but it is always possible to separate the true migrants from the birds coming from their roosts by their times of movement which are later than those of the local birds. The biggest starling passage that I ever saw was on 26 October 1966 – a heavy day of general migration – when at least ten thousand birds moved steadily west-north-west between 0755 and 0925. Another quite heavy movement took place on 16 October 1960 which involved some 3290 birds. Grey wagtails go over in very small numbers but the total numbers like those of pied wagtails, the scarcer finches and tree sparrows vary a great deal from year to year. In fact, no single autumn visible passage is ever like any of those that have gone before and this gives interest and variety to the pursuit of migrant tracking.

The chaffinch is one of the most regular of the diurnal autumn migrants in my part of suburbia and the period of its passage stretches from about 19 September to late October or early November. In some years this bird can be seen in hundreds flying over suburban areas and my most noteworthy morning was that of 19 October 1964 when my wife and I counted 7500 flying north-west over the house. There have been quite a number of October days on which the tally has exceeded the thousand. In November 1959 perhaps 60,000 chaffinches passed through the northern radius of the London area on one day alone. In October 1966 I also counted some 500 bramblings with smaller numbers of greenfinches, siskins, redpolls and tree sparrows.

I have carried out many of my migration watches either from my house or from a small group of allotments not far away; these were closed in 1973 to accommodate an underground reservoir bearing light-weight houses. They have proved in the past to be a very good vantage point with a lot of open sky all round so that I have been able to pick up birds early in spite of the compass direction from which they were coming. The allotments are more than two hundred and fifty feet above sea level and command a very wide view. The watches have been carried out in the early morning but nothing much happens until an hour or so after first light. If the movements are fairly light they tend to occur from an hour after light to three hours after first light but if the passage is a heavy one then migration may go on to the afternoon. The migrants may well have set off from the Continent the same morning especially those that pass over suburban north London a little later. The distance from the French coast to Dollis Hill is less than a hundred miles. With a flying time of between two and three hours for most migrant species and aided by a tail wind these birds can be expected in mid-October to arrive in north-west London from France about half past eight. A head wind will, of course, delay their arrival.

The 12 October 1973 dawned overcast and with a 10–15 m.p.h. wind blowing from the south-east. By 0815 redwings and chaffinches from Scandinavia and starlings from North Germany and the Baltic were moving north-north-west over the allotments, having probably left the coast of France earlier that same morning. I recorded in my log: 'By 1100 hours about 1500 chaffinches and 250 starlings had gone through.' The next day the rush of early morning migrants went on and this time I counted 2000 chaffinches as well as smaller numbers of redwings, fieldfares, tree sparrows and four species of finch. As the bulk of the migrants from the Continent flew north, so swallows were making their way into the wind on their journey to Africa. On 14 October the movement of chaffinches weakened but more redwings were moving overhead and some of them were dropping down to rest on the allotments. This comparative rush of migrants had been brought about by strong winds and fog which had resulted in a build-up of migrants on the Continent waiting to cross to Britain. This hold-up had taken place on 11 October. On the previous day – the 10th – I was on the roof of Broadcasting House in central London watching for migrants and introducing a Radio 4 *Living World* programme to mark the 50th Anniversary celebrations of the BBC. Dilys Breese, Derek Jones and I saw small numbers of chaffinches and pied wagtails flying north-west at a fair height above the awakening heart of London. Previous watches that I had carried out from the roof of that very functional building had revealed quite considerable passages in the autumn over central London.

Although swallows and house martins in the autumn and chaffinches in the spring appear to use the conspicuous top of Dollis Hill as a landmark and to travel on a fairly narrow route, all the regular movements have been of the broad front kind. For example, on 16 October 1960, between 0715 and 1145 I counted 5889 birds of seven different species flying either north or north-west over my house. This passage was also observed and recorded in other parts of the London area that day and it seemed possible that a column of perhaps four hundred thousand birds flew over London. I have described in some detail the migrations that I have watched in north-west London since they serve to indicate how much one watcher can see in the suburbs if he is regular and systematic in his observations. There are many suburban areas awaiting their chroniclers. When co-operative studies are possible then the apparently isolated and unconnected notes from individual observers can perhaps be seen to fit into a wider and more significant pattern. From 24 September to 13 November 1964 some forty watchers studied the visible migrations in the London area. A. Gibbs and Ian Wallace have described how many new diurnal passage species were recorded and they concluded that perhaps almost four million birds could have passed over the region during the period of the survey.

I have also seen swallows, house martins, pied wagtails, linnets and siskins migrating over Ladbroke Square in Kensington and there are other parts of London and its suburbs where passage movements can be seen. Ian Wallace has described passages in Regent's Park in 1959 in which 'the species passing included three Corvids, Woodlark, all the common Thrushes, seven Finches, Yellowhammer and both Sparrows'. Over Clapham and Wandsworth Commons John Gooders reported movements of chaffinches, linnets, starlings, meadow pipits and skylarks as well as 'the grouping of all migrant swallows in autumn along an aerial path no more than 50 yards wide'. I have already referred to this phenomenon of a narrow route for Dollis Hill and Ian Wallace found a similar one in Regent's Park. Narrow flyways have also been seen in the Lea Valley, along the Thames and some of the downland scarps. P. J. Strangeman reported a 'westerly passage of diurnal migrants' in autumn over Bishop's Park in Fulham and P. J. Grant watched cormorants, skylarks, redwings, meadow pipits, starlings and chaffinches on the move across Greenwich Park. Over the years the *London Bird Reports* have recorded a number of localities in which visible migration has been observed.

Outside London the records of diurnal passages are sometimes rather sketchy but they undoubtedly do occur. I have described elsewhere in detail the migrants of the Cotswold scarp and watches that I made in Rugby showed that song and mistle thrushes, fieldfares, redwings, meadow pipits, yellow and pied wagtails, house martins and black-headed gulls were flying south-west, some of them perhaps to join the 'corridor' farther down. Lesser black-backed gulls were one of the most interesting and conspicuous of the Cotswold migrants and they

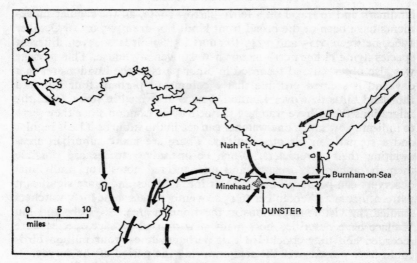

FIG. 12 Autumn movements on north Somerset coast.

were also frequent near Stratford-upon-Avon with other gulls, pipits, larks, finches, yellow wagtails, greenfinches and swallows. In the neighbourhood of Birmingham autumn movements of chaffinches, skylarks, redwings, fieldfares, meadow pipits and wagtails all flying west or south-west have been recorded especially in Erdington, Hall Green, Wylde Green, Selly Oak, Sutton Coldfield, Handsworth Wood, Edgbaston Park and near Bartley Reservoir. At Barr Beacon, just to the north of Birmingham, there have been broad front passages of starlings, skylarks, chaffinches, linnets, meadow pipits and lapwings. Similar types of visible passage have also occurred in the Trent Valley near Nottingham, near Alvecote in Warwickshire and in the vicinity of Gainsborough. Woodpigeons have been seen flying in flocks of fifty or so over Earlswood in November and I have seen large parties travelling across the London area, along the South Coast and near Porlock in Somerset. In figures 12 and 13 it is possible to see plotted some of the autumn movements of birds along the Somerset coast. In spring the visible migration is smaller and less obvious.

It is the broad front migrations then that we are most likely to see but for inland birdwatchers living in the open country these movements may be difficult to recognize since it is not always easy to separate migrants from local breeding birds. In urban and suburban districts birds passing overhead which are not local breeders are obviously strangers and migrants. These daytime passages, as radar studies have shown, are extremely complicated and not restricted to fixed weather conditions. A north-westerly airstream across the London area seems

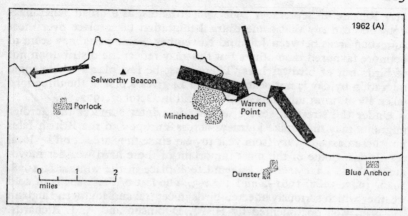

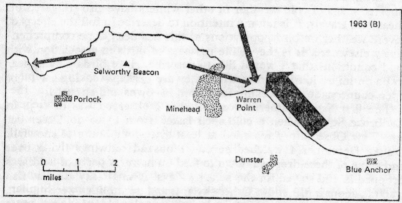

FIG. 13 Directions taken by passerine migrants near Minehead, Somerset, in September. (A) 1962; (B) 1963. The breadth of the arrows is in direct proportion to the number of migrants.

to be an important factor but smaller visible migrations can occur with tail or cross winds. Birds that take advantage of guide lines or landmarks are able to adjust for the effects of wind but those moving at night or travelling over the sea or above cloud may be subject to lateral 'drift' by the wind. Birds that leave the Continent in good weather may fly into overcast skies and heavy rain borne on easterly or south-easterly winds which carry them westward to Britain. Conditions such as these can lead to 'falls' of birds even in such inland areas as suburban allotments, sewage farms, parks and gardens. Birds may then appear in places that are not within their normal or regular range like the yellow-browed warbler from Siberia that appeared in a garden near Reigate in September 1960. Nevertheless, as a broad generalization, one can say that some diurnal migration takes place over most suburban areas between July and November. Some parts may seem to be more favoured than others but this may reflect the distribution not of birds but of birdwatchers. There must be few places where some migration by day is not visible. Figure 14 gives a plot of the directions taken by autumn migrants at Dollis Hill in October 1972.

Under the stress of severe weather in winter some of the hardier migrants may undertake journeys across Europe and the British Isles but these passages vary from year to year since they are set off by local conditions. Some of the most important of these hard weather movements that I have seen in England took place in the winters of 1938, 1940, 1947, 1960, 1961–2 and 1962–3. The last of these spells of cold weather which seriously affected birds in central and southern England has been well documented by H. M. Dobinson and A. J. Richards. Shorter snaps of cold weather in other winters have also triggered off these bird travels. It is not my intention to describe in full the effects of severe weather on bird populations as this has been done comprehensively elsewhere. It is the visible passages of birds in association with cold conditions that I would like to describe, since birds may appear to be on migration in winter when they are perhaps looking for more open countryside and seeking food even in towns and suburbs.

The first hard weather movement that I observed was in 1938 in Ladbroke Square when a cold spell lasted from 17 to 26 December and Kew Observatory recorded at least sixty-four hours of snowfall. On 22 December I watched several thousand redwings flying over and some of these dropped down to feed on haws. A party of fieldfares dropped in and stayed for the next six days. A single skylark was also walking about in the snow. Other skylarks and bramblings were passing overhead to the west. Some of the bramblings also landed in the square and many of the larks came down in London streets and some of them were taken by kindly passers-by into the warmth of local police stations. In St John's Wood at this time the bird visitors to one garden included black-headed gull, great spotted woodpecker, blackbird, song thrush, redwing, robin, skylark, great, blue and coal tits, greenfinch, chaffinch and brambling. There were reports also of wild geese and waders and the numbers of ducks in the London area grew considerably. Smew were seen in central London and on a pond at Beddington, and Slavonian, black-necked and red-necked grebes visited several London waters.

During the cold weather in early 1940, including the ice storm of 27 and 28 January, I was in Oxford but saw little visible movement although Port Meadow attracted white-fronted geese, shoveler and goldeneye. The very severe weather in 1947 lasted from late January to early March with temperatures of 25 degrees of frost Fahrenheit.

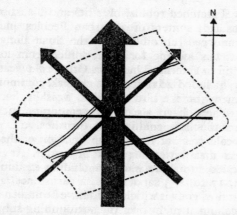

FIG. 14 Directions of 3599 migrants over Dollis Hill, 8 Oct., 12-16 Oct., 10-20 Oct., 1972. The breadth of the arrows is in direct proportion to the number of migrants.

Over Rugby's suburbs I noticed quite large passages of thrushes and skylarks while movements of starlings took place in Warwickshire and other Midland counties as well. Many ducks and grebes left the area but the unfrozen river basin at Abbey Park in Leicestershire became a refuge for grebes and both the common and scarcer species of duck. During the long frost fieldfares and redwings flew into many towns and suburbs while woodpigeons also streamed in looking for green crops in allotments and gardens. Owls, driven by hunger to change their habits, began to hunt in daylight. Waxwings also appeared in Rugby gardens at this time and all the records of this handsome bird in the nearby county of Leicestershire were 'within, or in close proximity to, the City'.

During the cold snap of January 1955 two fieldfares visited my Dollis Hill garden for the day. On 20 February in the same year another very hungry fieldfare arrived and fed for five hours without stopping on some of the apples that I had put out to help the blackbirds over the bad weather. It stayed until 13 March, roosting in my garden and regularly chasing blackbirds up to a hundred and fifty yards away from the food. Another bird arrived in snow on 7 January 1963 and stayed until the end of the month during which time it was filmed for the BBC television news programme *Town and Around*. There were a few redwings in my garden as well and I also obtained film shots of these thrushes eating cotoneaster berries within a few feet of passing Central Line underground trains at White City station in suburban west London. Redwings even foraged for food 'beneath the stalls at Norwich fruit market'. After a heavy snowfall and frost in

November 1973 I watched robins, blue tits and blackbirds scrabbling about in the roadside gutters of suburban Peebles and in the same period rooks could be seen dibbling in the slush along the roads in Aberdeenshire towns looking for grain spilled from lorries carrying cereals from a ship in Peterhead harbour. Other cold weather visitors to my garden have included 40 redpolls, a skylark, common gulls on the lawn, a tree sparrow on the bird table and a siskin that remained for three months. There have also been temporary increases in the numbers of greenfinches, goldfinches, thrushes, tits and gulls. In February 1956 cold weather brought an invasion of the London area by diving ducks and various species of wader. At Beddington a single visit revealed 170 shore waders including 82 dunlin, 57 ringed plover, 23 knot, 17 ruffs, 5 sanderlings, 2 turnstones, a purple sandpiper and a bar-tailed godwit which could have been seen on the wing or perhaps heard calling at night over the surrounding suburbs.

During the 23 years that I have lived in north-west London I have observed hard weather movements among birds in six of the Decembers, fourteen of the Januaries and one of the Februaries. During a short cold spell in 1958 which lasted from 22 to 27 January I watched passages of lapwings, chaffinches, fieldfares, stock doves and white-fronted geese with smaller movements involving other birds such as redwings, skylarks and woodpigeons. The January 1960 movement was much more spectacular and I recorded that 'The weather of 10 January that year was very cold indeed and the skies were clear. At 3.25 p.m. a party of 40 lapwings flew SSW some thirty minutes in advance of a snow-storm which soon brought visibility down to less than a hundred yards. Two days later I watched redwings flying by day over Willesden and the BBC Television Centre in Wood Lane and there were more on the following day. Then on the 14th a strong movement took place from 8.50 a.m. Redwings were passing over at the rate of 600 an hour until 1.30 p.m. and with them were scores of fieldfares, skylarks, lapwings, greenfinches and linnets, all moving SW. This was the peak day for hard weather movements in England and large numbers of these species were seen passing through Sussex and Hampshire where the total was described as "terrific".' This same period of cold weather probably accounted for the presence at Dollis Hill of a glaucous gull from the Arctic.

There was another strong passage one January day in 1962 when 4900 skylarks travelled south-west with redwings, fieldfares and tree sparrows, and on that same day Leo Batten reported some 1250 larks flying over the Brent Reservoir a half mile or so away. On 5 January in the following year some 1600 fieldfares and 700 redwings flew west over the reservoir while I observed passages not only of these two species but of woodpigeons and white-fronted geese as well. The heaviest cold weather movements in 1963 took place between 7 and 9

January and at this time the resident blackbirds at Dollis Hill evacuated the area, almost certainly driven out by wind chill – the dry convective cooling of the atmosphere which was at its worst on the 7th. Skylarks and lapwings were again on the move in January 1964 while in January 1968 and 1972 I watched parties of the two immigrant thrushes, skylarks and chaffinches flying south. February has not proved so spectacular a month but on the 8th in 1969, in addition to the expected birds of passage, I saw bramblings flying south as well. These birds will sometimes appear in suburban gardens and they have been known to take shelled peanuts from suspended mesh containers as well as to visit bird tables.

Some periods of cold weather may begin as early as November or December and involve all the species that I have mentioned so far. In north-west London end-of-year movements have taken place in snowy weather among lapwings, woodpigeons, pied wagtails, linnets, house sparrows and on 27 December 1962 snow buntings. The cold at this time was quite exceptional in the Midlands and southern England and at the Brent Reservoir there were reports of 'a glaucous gull, four shelduck, three shags, several teal, wigeon and shoveler, single goosander, merganser, Lapland bunting and lesser spotted woodpecker'. In this same period pink-footed geese, whooper and Bewick's swans, reed and corn buntings also joined the movement away from the snow and frost. It is interesting to note that on the whole the species involved in these hard weather passages remain fairly constant. In 1912 W. Eagle Clarke reflected that 'as soon as frost sets in, particularly if it be accompanied by snow, mistle-thrushes, song-thrushes, redwings, fieldfares, blackbirds, greenfinches, linnets, starlings, skylarks, meadow-pipits, ring-doves, lapwings, golden plover, woodcock, snipe, dunlin, curlew, etc. (and in some seasons rooks, magpies and snow buntings), remove themselves from its baneful influence'.

Many of these cold weather movements are set in action by the tracking of a cold front which pushes the birds in front of it. If this weather originates in the north then the birds generally move to the south-west but when, as in the winter of 1962–3, this region is itself under snow and ice then random and 'trial and error' movements may follow. H. M. Dobinson and A. J. Richards found that passage during that winter was very widespread, as was made clear by the radar evidence, but large-scale immigration, especially from Cap Gris Nez and Cherbourg, made the picture complicated and many species were involved for the first time, including 'herons, white-fronted geese, woodlarks, greenfinches, bramblings and snow buntings'. Many birds flew to the south-west but at Dollis Hill the direction was mainly between north-north-west and north-north-east and this corresponded with that of birds observed near the south coast of England. At this time East Anglia was still comparatively open and free from snow.

Unfavourable weather in north-eastern Britain often triggers off movements to the south-west. An interesting example of this is provided by an invasion of southern Warwickshire in 1962 by fieldfares which having left the cold countryside of the north found a remarkable supply of food in the apple orchards; a local roost of these birds held at least five thousand birds. And, as we have already seen, bad weather on the Continent can also bring passerines coasting or moving inland into Britain in their struggle for survival. I have watched redpolls, linnets and twites moving south along the Lincolnshire coast as snow storms began to drive in from the North Sea. Some of our birds also emigrate to Ireland as a result of deteriorating conditions in Britain with thrushes, starlings, chaffinches and skylarks joining those of their fellows that may be already there. Writing of the skylark the ornithologists R. J. Ussher and R. Warren recorded that 'in snow a fresh immigration (from beyond the sea) sometimes takes place en masse, a tide of birds pouring into Ireland in tens, hundreds and thousands'.

As a suburban birdwatcher I have all my study material conveniently at hand. In spite of many rewarding ornithological expeditions in recent years to Spain, the Camargue, Italy, the Alps and East Africa, I still look forward to picking up once again the threads that form the web of my suburban birdlife. I have been interested for many years now in bird populations and their changing dynamics, but visible migration and hard weather movements have added spice to the daily routine counts and observations. I have, of course, derived an almost schoolboy-like pleasure from seeing uncommon migrants in my garden or watching flocks of birds, strangers to the suburban area over which they fly, on their journeys to and from Europe or Africa. For a birdwatcher, isolated as he may feel in his flat or small semi-detached home, there is no better way to compensate for the absence of tidal estuary, northern floe or forest than to look more closely at the birds around him. Suburbia is just one of the habitats that birds have occupied and it is as worthy of investigation as any other. It is itself composed of differing ecosystems which hold a varied, hardy and adaptable flora and fauna. The watchful eye and alert, discriminating ear will help to show how the migrants 'keep their appointed times and season'. There is no lack of stimulus or variety even in suburbia for birds are extraordinarily vital and attractive animals. While I can continue to derive pleasure from studying their behaviour, considering the problems that they pose and just having them around I shall be quite satisfied.

The Birds of Ladbroke Square, Kensington, West London, 1927-40

Birds which stay the summer

B regular breeder   O former or occasional breeder
P non-breeder but present

Mallard O	Song Thrush B
Woodpigeon B	Blackbird B
Swift P	Robin B
Carrion Crow P	Spotted Flycatcher B
Jay O	Hedgesparrow B
Great Tit B	Starling B
Blue Tit B	Greenfinch P
Coal Tit P	Chaffinch P
Wren P	House Sparrow B
Mistle Thrush B	

Winter visitors and passage migrants

W winter visitor   M passage migrant

Kestrel W	Wheatear M
Lapwing M	Blackcap M
Great Black-backed Gull W	Garden Warbler M
Lesser Black-backed Gull MW	Whitethroat M
Herring Gull W	Lesser Whitethroat M
Common Gull W	Willow Warbler M
Black-headed Gull W	Chiffchaff M
Turtle Dove M	Pied Flycatcher M
Barn Owl W	Pied Wagtail W
Tawny Owl W	Grey Wagtail M
Cuckoo M	Yellow Wagtail M
Swallow M	Siskin M
House Martin M	

Vagrants and hard weather visitors

Heron	Marsh Tit
Mute Swan	Long-tailed Tit
Sparrowhawk	Fieldfare
Stock Dove	Redwing
Green Woodpecker	Goldcrest
Great Spotted Woodpecker	Red-breasted Flycatcher

Skylark
Rook
Jackdaw
Magpie

Goldfinch
Linnet
Bullfinch
Brambling

The Breeding Birds of Five Inner Suburban London Parks 1959–67

Regent's Park (1959)	Bishop's Park Fulham (1964)	Clapham Common (1961–3)	Wandsworth Common (1964)	Greenwich Park (1967)
Mallard	Mallard	Mallard	Mallard	Mallard
Tufted Duck		Tufted Duck		
Pochard				
		Mute Swan		Mute Swan
Moorhen		Moorhen	Moorhen	Moorhen
		Coot	Coot	
Stock Dove				Stock Dove
Woodpigeon	Woodpigeon	Woodpigeon	Woodpigeon	Woodpigeon
Tawny Owl		Tawny Owl	Tawny Owl	Tawny Owl
			Swift	
				Great Spotted Woodpecker
Carrion Crow	Carrion Crow	Carrion Crow	Carrion Crow	Carrion Crow
				Jackdaw
Jay	Jay	Jay	Jay	Jay
Great Tit	Great Tit		Great Tit	Great Tit
Blue Tit	Blue Tit	Blue Tit	Blue Tit	Blue Tit
				Coal Tit
Wren	Wren			Wren
Mistle Thrush	Mistle Thrush	Mistle Thrush	Mistle Thrush	Mistle Thrush
Song Thrush	Song Thrush	Song Thrush	Song Thrush	Song Thrush
Blackbird	Blackbird	Blackbird	Blackbird	Blackbird
Robin	Robin			Robin
				Blackcap
Spotted Flycatcher		Spotted Flycatcher		Spotted Flycatcher
Hedgesparrow	Hedgesparrow	Hedgesparrow	Hedgesparrow	Hedgesparrow
Pied Wagtail			Pied Wagtail	
Starling	Starling	Starling	Starling	Starling
Greenfinch	Greenfinch		Greenfinch	Greenfinch
Goldfinch				Goldfinch
Bullfinch				Bullfinch
Chaffinch	Chaffinch			Chaffinch
House Sparrow	House Sparrow	House Sparrow	House Sparrow	House Sparrow

Species Total 25	16	17	18	27

The sources for this Appendix are Wallace, D. I. M. (1961). *Lond. Bird Rept.* 24:81–107; Strangeman, P. J. (1966). *Lond. Bird Rept.* 30:80–102; Gooders, J. (1965). *Lond. Bird Rept.* 29:73–88; Grant, P. J. (1967). *Lond. Bird Rept.* 31:64–92. For fuller details, see the Bibliography for chapter 2.

The Birds of Dollis Hill,
An Outer London suburb, 1951–74

Birds which stay the summer

B regular breeder   O occasional breeder   F former breeder

Mallard B	Great Tit B	Spotted Flycatcher B
Kestrel O	Blue Tit B	Hedgesparrow B
Stock Dove F	Wren B	Pied Wagtail B
Feral Pigeon B	Mistle Thrush B	Starling B
Woodpigeon B	Song Thrush B	Greenfinch B
Tawny Owl F	Blackbird B	Goldfinch B
Swift O	Robin B	Bullfinch O
Skylark F	Blackcap O	Chaffinch B
Carrion Crow B	Whitethroat O	House Sparrow B
Jay B	Willow Warbler O	Tree Sparrow B

Winter visitors and passage migrants

W winter visitor   M passage migrant

Pintail W	Turtle Dove M	Garden Warbler M
Hobby M	Cuckoo M	Lesser Whitethroat M
Peregrine W	Woodlark M	Greenish Warbler M
Lapwing M	Swallow M	Chiffchaff M
Golden Plover M	House Martin M	Goldcrest MW
Curlew M	Sand Martin M	Pied Flycatcher M
Whimbrel M	Rook M	Meadow Pipit MW
Bar-tailed Godwit M	Jackdaw M	Tree Pipit M
Green Sandpiper M	Treecreeper M	Rock Pipit M
Greenshank M	Fieldfare M	Grey Wagtail M
Great Black-backed Gull W	Redwing MW	Yellow Wagtail M
Lesser Black-backed Gull MW	Wheatear M	Siskin M
Herring Gull W	Stonechat M	Linnet MW
Common Gull MW	Whinchat M	Redpoll M
Black-headed Gull W	Redstart M	Brambling M
Sandwich Tern M	Nightingale M	Yellowhammer

Vagrants

Heron	Little Owl
Bittern	Kingfisher
White-fronted Goose	Great Spotted Woodpecker
Canada Goose	Lesser Spotted Woodpecker

Mute Swan
Buzzard
Sparrowhawk
Pheasant
Moorhen
Woodcock
Redshank
Glaucous Gull
Collared Dove

Magpie
Coal Tit
Hawfinch
Twite
Serin
Crossbill
Reed Bunting
Snow Bunting

The Birds of Four Outer Suburban London Parks and Open Spaces, 1970

B bred   b probably bred

Species	Bushey Park Hampton Court	Richmond Park	Kew Gardens	Osterley Park
Great Crested Grebe		B		B
Little Grebe	B		B	
Mandarin				b
Mallard	B	B	B	B
Tufted Duck		B	B	
Pochard			B	
Canada Goose	B			
Kestrel	B	B	b	B
Partridge	b	B		B
Pheasant	b	B	B	
Moorhen	B	B	B	B
Coot	B	B	B	B
Lapwing	b			b
Stock Dove	b	B		B
Woodpigeon	B	B	B	B
Cuckoo		b		
Barn Owl		B		
Little Owl	b	B	b	B
Tawny Owl	B	B	B	B
Swift				b
Green Woodpecker	B	B	B	B
Great Spotted Woodpecker	B	B	b	B
Lesser Spotted Woodpecker	b	B		b
Skylark	b	B		B
Swallow	B	b		B
House Martin		b		
Carrion Crow	B	B	B	B
Jackdaw		B		
Magpie	B	B		B
Jay	B	B	B	B
Great Tit	B	B	B	B
Blue Tit	B	B	B	B
Coal Tit	B	B	B	B
Long-tailed Tit	B	b	B	
Nuthatch	B	B	B	B
Treecreeper	B	B	B	B
Wren	B	B	B	B
Mistle Thrush	B	B	B	B
Song Thrush	B	B	B	B
Blackbird		B	B	B
Redstart		B		

Robin	B	B	B	B
Reed Warbler		B		
Blackcap	B	B	B	B
Garden Warbler		B		
Whitethroat		B		
Willow Warbler	B	B		
Chiffchaff	B	B		B
Goldcrest	b		B	B
Spotted Flycatcher			B	B
Hedgesparrow	B	B	B	B
Meadow Pipit	B			
Pied Wagtail	B		B	B
Starling	B	B	B	B
Hawfinch			B	
Greenfinch	B		B	
Goldfinch	B		B	b
Linnet			B	b
Bullfinch	B	B	B	B
Chaffinch	B	B	B	B
Yellowhammer			B	
Reed Bunting	b	B		
House Sparrow	B	B	B	
Tree Sparrow	B	B		B

From *Bird Life in the Royal Parks 1969–70*. Report by the Committee on Bird Sanctuaries in the Royal Parks (England and Wales). 1971.

APPENDIX 5

The Regular Duck Carrying Capacity of the Fifteen Most Important Reservoirs in England and Wales

Reservoir	No. of Years Counted	Mallard	Teal	Wigeon	Shoveler	Pochard	Tufted Duck	Golden-eye
ABBERTON (Essex)	13	1410	3245	1790	200	1250	295	180
CHEW VALLEY (Somerset)	8	690	605	1190	245	355	350	10
BLITHFIELD (Staffs.)	8	1130	585	945	75	225	295	40
PITSFORD (Northants.)	6	675	325	1525	20	40	200	20
HOLLOWELL (Northants.)	3	975	125	900	10	125	50	5
HANNINGFIELD (Essex)	6	510	365	265	35	330	335	15
BLAGDON (Somerset)	14	385	360	375	50	315	230	10
EYEBROOK (Leics.)	14	700	235	800	10	115	15	5
STAINES (Midd'x)	9	300	25	100	15	250	550	10
BARN ELMS (Surrey)	12	200	50	10	—	350	650	—
CROPSTON (Leics.)	11	375	325	425	5	25	40	—
DURLEIGH (Somerset)	13	105	270	185	40	160	70	5
KING GEORGE VI (Midd'x)	9	600	200	100	60	10	75	5
CHEDDAR (Somerset)	14	120	150	25	25	580	80	5
QUEEN MARY (Midd'x)	9	425	25	20	25	50	325	10

(The figures are calculated from the three highest counts in each year for which ful data are available.) Reproduced with the kind permission of H.M.S.O. and the Nature Conservancy.

APPENDIX 6

The Birds of the Brent Reservoir and Vicinity, Middlesex, 1833-1970

Birds which stay the summer

B regular breeder   **O** occasional breeder

Mute Swan O	Grasshopper Warbler O	Blue Tit B
Mallard B	Sedge Warbler B	Great Tit B
Kestrel B	Reed Warbler B	Reed Bunting B
Moorhen B	Garden Warbler O	Chaffinch B
Coot B	Blackcap B	Greenfinch B
Woodpigeon B	Whitethroat B	Goldfinch B
Feral Pigeon B	Lesser Whitethroat B	Linnet B
Tawny Owl B	Willow Warbler B	Bullfinch B
Swift B	Spotted Flycatcher B	House Sparrow B
Skylark B	Robin B	Tree Sparrow B
House Martin B	Blackbird B	Starling B
Yellow Wagtail O	Song Thrush B	Jay B
Pied Wagtail O	Mistle Thrush B	Magpie B
Wren B	Willow Tit B	Carrion Crow B
Hedgesparrow B	Coal Tit B	

Former breeding species

Great Crested Grebe	Wryneck	Chiffchaff
Red-legged Partridge	Green Woodpecker	Whinchat
Corncrake	Great Spotted Woodpecker	Long-tailed Tit
Lapwing	Lesser Spotted Woodpecker	Nuthatch
Stock Dove	Woodlark	Cirl Bunting
Little Owl	Swallow	Hawfinch
Nightjar	Red-backed Shrike	

Winter visitors and passage migrants

w winter visitor   **M** passage migrant

Little Grebe M	Green Sandpiper M	Tree Pipit M
Teal M	Common Sandpiper M	Meadow Pipit MW
Gadwall M	Curlew M	Rock Pipit W
Shoveler MW	Snipe MW	Grey Wagtail M
Pochard W	Jack Snipe MW	Goldcrest W
Tufted Duck W	Black-headed Gull W	Stonechat MW
Smew W	Lesser Black-backed Gull MW	Wheatear M
Water Rail W	Great Black-backed Gull W	Redstart M

Ringed Plover M	Herring Gull MW	Fieldfare MW
Golden Plover M	Common Gull MW	Redwing MW
Dunlin MW	Black Tern M	Brambling MW
Ruff M	Common Tern M	Siskin W
Spotted Redshank M	Arctic Tern M	Redpoll W
Redshank M	Cuckoo M	Jackdaw W
Greenshank M	Sand Martin M	Rook W

Vagrants and rare visitors

Red-throated Diver	Garganey	Little Stint	Collared Dove
Black-throated Diver	Red-crested Pochard	Temminck's Stint	Turtle Dove
Great Northern Diver	Ferruginous Duck	White-rumped Sandpiper	Barn Owl
Black-necked Grebe	Scaup	Pectoral Sandpiper	Long-eared Owl
Slavonian Grebe	Mandarin	Curlew Sandpiper	Short-eared Owl
Red-necked Grebe	Eider	Knot	Alpine Swift
Leach's Petrel	Common Scoter	Sanderling	Kingfisher
Storm Petrel	Velvet Scoter	Wood Sandpiper	Hoopoe
Cormorant	Long-tailed Duck	Black-tailed Godwit	Richard's Pipit
Shag	Goldeneye	Bar-tailed Godwit	Great Grey Shrike
Bittern	Red-breasted Merganser	Whimbrel	Waxwing
Little Bittern	Goosander	Woodcock	Dipper
Night Heron	Osprey	Great Snipe	Aquatic Warbler
Squacco Heron	Kite	Black-winged Stilt	Wood Warbler
Heron	Sparrowhawk	Avocet	Firecrest
Spoonbill	Buzzard	Grey Phalarope	Pied Flycatcher
Canada Goose	Hen Harrier	(Stone Curlew)	Black Redstart
Barnacle Goose	(Marsh Harrier)	Great Skua	Nightingale
Brent Goose	Hobby	Pomarine Skua	Ring Ouzel
Grey Lag Goose	Merlin	Arctic Skua	Bearded Tit
White-fronted Goose	Peregrine	Little Gull	Marsh Tit
Pink-footed Goose	Partridge	Iceland Gull	Crested Tit
Whooper Swan	Quail	Glaucous Gull	Treecreeper
Bewick's Swan	Pheasant	Kittiwake	Corn Bunting
Ruddy Shelduck	Spotted Crake	White-winged Black Tern	Ortolan Bunting
Shelduck	Oystercatcher	Sandwich Tern	Lapland Bunting
Wigeon	Little Ringed Plover	Roseate Tern	Snow Bunting
Pintail	Dotterel	Little Tern	Twite
	Grey Plover	Pallas's Sand Grouse	Crossbill
	Turnstone		Chough
			Hooded Crow
			Raven

Reproduced from *The London Naturalist*, No. 50, by kind permission of L. A. Batten.

The Birds of Rye Meads Sewage Purification Works, Hertfordshire, 1957-62

Breeding community (*numbers of pairs in brackets*)

Little Grebe (13)
Mallard (20)
Shoveler (1)
Tufted Duck (8)
Mute Swan (1)
Red-legged Partridge (2+)
Partridge (2+)
Pheasant (8)
Water Rail (1)
Moorhen (16+)
Coot (15)
Lapwing (2)
Little Ringed Plover (1)
Snipe (8)
Redshank (5)
Stock Dove (1)
Woodpigeon (1)

Collared Dove (+)
Cuckoo (2)
Little Owl (1)
Tawny Owl (1)
Kingfisher (1)
Skylark (9)
Swallow (2)
Carrion Crow (3)
Great Tit (1)
Blue Tit (2)
Wren (4+)
Song Thrush (10)
Blackbird (12)
Robin (5)
Reed Warbler (11)
Marsh Warbler (5)
Sedge Warbler (34)

Garden Warbler (1)
Whitethroat (2)
Willow Warbler (2)
Chiffchaff (1)
Hedgesparrow (8)
Meadow Pipit (5)
Yellow Wagtail (8)
Pied Wagtail (2)
Starling (13)
Greenfinch (4)
Goldfinch (2)
Linnet (2+)
Bullfinch (2)
Chaffinch (3)
Reed Bunting (c. 30)
House Sparrow (?)
Tree Sparrow (15)

Visitors (*recorded on more than 10 occasions*)

Great Crested Grebe
Shag
Heron
Teal
Garganey
Wigeon
Scaup
Pochard
Goldeneye
Common Scoter
Kestrel
Ringed Plover
Golden Plover
Jack Snipe
Curlew
Green Sandpiper
Wood Sandpiper
Common Sandpiper
Greenshank
Dunlin

Ruff
Great Black-backed Gull
Herring Gull
Common Gull
Black-headed Gull
Black Tern
Common Tern
Turtle Dove
Barn Owl
Swift
Green Woodpecker
Great Spotted Woodpecker
House Martin
Sand Martin
Rook
Jackdaw
Magpie
Jay
Willow Tit
Long-tailed Tit

Nuthatch
Treecreeper
Mistle Thrush
Fieldfare
Redwing
Wheatear
Stonechat
Whinchat
Blackcap
Lesser Whitethroat
Spotted Flycatcher
Tree Pipit
Grey Wagtail
Siskin
Redpoll
Brambling
Yellowhammer
Corn Bunting

Vagrants (*recorded on fewer than* 10 *occasions*)

Black-throated Diver	Grey Plover	Wryneck
Slavonian Grebe	Turnstone	Woodlark
Black-necked Grebe	Great Snipe	Hooded Crow
Cormorant	Whimbrel	Coal Tit
Bittern	Black-tailed Godwit	Marsh Tit
Gadwall	Spotted Redshank	Bearded Tit
Pintail	Knot	Redstart
Red-crested Pochard	Little Stint	Black Redstart
Goosander	Temminck's Stint	Nightingale
Smew	Pectoral Sandpiper	Grasshopper Warbler
Shelduck	Curlew Sandpiper	Melodious Warbler
White-fronted Goose	Sanderling	Wood Warbler
Canada Goose	Broad-billed Sandpiper	Goldcrest
Bewick's Swan	Grey Phalarope	Firecrest
Buzzard	Red-necked Phalarope	Pied Flycatcher
Sparrowhawk	Stone Curlew	Rock Pipit/Water Pipit
Hobby	Little Gull	Great Grey Shrike
Peregrine	Short-eared Owl	Twite
Merlin	Lesser Spotted Woodpecker	Snow Bunting

Reproduced from *The London Bird Report*, No. 26, by kind permission of T. W. Gladwin.

APPENDIX 8

The Breeding Community of Birds at two Gravel Pit Sites in Southern England, 1968

Waterside Birds (Number of pairs)

	Sevenoaks	Nursling Gravel Pit
Great Crested Grebe	8 (7)	—
Little Grebe	—	5
Mallard	65 (85)	4
Teal	—	1
Gadwall	3 (4)	—
Tufted Duck	6 (12)	4
Pochard	—	2
Grey Lag Goose	3 (4)	—
Canada	4 (2)	—
Mute Swan	—	1
Water Rail	—	1
Coot	12 (26)	12
Moorhen	17 (32)	7
Little Ringed Plover	2 (4)	—
Lapwing	— (1)	1
Snipe	— (1)	—
Redshank	—	2
Kingfisher	1 (4)	—
Reed Warbler	—	18
Sedge Warbler	1 (6)	7
Reed Bunting	9	5

Resident Birds (other than waterside: numbers of pairs)

Kestrel	2	—
Partridge	1	—
Pheasant	5 (1)	2
Stock Dove	1 (2)	1
Woodpigeon	6 (22)	3
Tawny Owl	1	—
Little Owl	3 (1)	—
Skylark	6 (12)	2
Carrion Crow	2 (8)	1
Magpie	3 (1)	—
Jay	2 (1)	2
Great Tit	20 (19)	4
Blue Tit	28 (36)	4
Marsh Tit	—	1
Willow Tit	1 (2)	—

	Sevenoaks	Nursling Gravel Pit
Long-tailed Tit	2 (5)	2
Treecreeper	4 (7)	1
Wren	23 (62)	20
Mistle Thrush	3 (9)	1
Song Thrush	16 (47)	8
Blackbird	46 (89)	19
Robin	20 (39)	17
Goldcrest	—	2
Hedgesparrow	33 (49)	13
Pied Wagtail	3	—
Starling	31	1
Greenfinch	9	3
Goldfinch	8	1
Linnet	6	—
Bullfinch	3	3
Chaffinch	16	9
Yellowhammer	1	—
House Sparrow	28	—
Tree Sparrow	8	—

Summer Visitors (other than waterside birds: numbers of pairs)

	Sevenoaks	Nursling Gravel Pit
Turtle Dove	1 (8)	1
Cuckoo	1 (2)	—
Swallow	1	—
Sand Martin	772 (220)	—
House Martin	—	4
Nightingale	—	1
Blackcap	10	8
Garden Warbler	1	4
Whitethroat	20	8
Lesser Whitethroat	1	1
Willow Warbler	13	13
Chiffchaff	4	11
Spotted Flycatcher	2	1

The unbracketed figures are reproduced from *Bird Study*, vol. 17; those for Sevenoaks are by kind permission of Dr Jeffery G. Harrison, who also supplied privately the updated figures (in brackets) for 1972, and those for Nursling Gravel Pit, near Southampton, by kind permission of David E. Glue.

Bibliography

CHAPTER 1.   The Rise of Suburbia

BRIGGS, A. (1963). *Victorian Cities*. London.

BRYANT, A. (1940). *English Saga*. London.

CLARK, P. and SLACK, P. (1971). ed. *Crisis and Order in English Towns, 1500–1700*. London.

CLARKE, G. (1946). *The Wealth of England 1496–1760*.

COLLINS, W. (1861). *Hide and Seek*. London.

DYOS, H. J. (1967). *The Victorian Suburb. A Study of Camberwell*. Liverpool.

GILLETT, J. (1964). *The History of Willesden*. Unpublished MS, Willesden Public Library, Brent.

H.M.S.O. (1918). Local Government Board. *Report of the Committee on Building Construction in Connection with the Provision of Dwellings for the Working Classes. The Tudor Walters Report.*

(1940). *Royal Commission on the Distribution of Industrial Population: The Barlow Report. Cmd. 6513.*

HOWARD, E. (1898). *Tomorrow, a Peaceful Path to Real Reform*. London.

(1965). *Garden Cities of Tomorrow*. A reprint with introductory essay by Lewis Mumford. London.

JACKSON, A. A. (1973). *Semi-detached London*. London.

JOHNSON, J. H. (1964). The suburban expansion of housing in Greater London, 1918–1939. In *Greater London*, ed. by J. T. Coppock and H. C. Prince. London.

JONES, E. (1970). *Towns and Cities*. London.

KELLETT, J. R. (1969). *The Impact of Railways on the Victorian City*. London.

MUMFORD, L. (1961). *The City in History*. London.

PEVSNER, N. (1970). *An Outline of European Architecture*. London.

RASMUSSEN, S. (1951). *London the Unique City*. New York.

SCHAFFER, F. (1970). *The New Town Story*. London.

SIMMS. T. H. (1949). *The Rise of a Midland Town. Rugby. 1800–1900* Rugby.

TAYLOR, N. (1973). *The Village in the City*. London.

THOMAS, D. (1970). *London's Green Belt*. London.

THORNS, D. C. (1972). *Suburbia*. London.

WELLS, H. G. (1909). *Ann Veronica*. London.

CHAPTER 2.   The Nearer Suburbs

ALEXANDER, W. B. (1933). A census of house martins; are their numbers declining? *Journ. Min. Agric.* 40:8–12.

BROWN, E. P. (1963). The bird life of Holland Park. The effect of human interference. *London Bird Report* 26:60–87.

(1964). The bird life of Holland Park, 1962–1963. *London Bird Report* 28:69–78.

(1972). Studying wildlife in Holland Park. *Lond. Nat.* 51:7–19.

CRAMP, S. (1950). The census of swifts, swallows and house martins. *London Bird Report* 14:49–57.

(1960). The irruption of tits and other species in the London area. 1957–1958. *London Bird Report* 23:62–69.

CRAMP, S. and GOODERS, J. (1967). The return of the house martin. *London Bird Report* 31:93–8.

GARDINER, S. (1972). Oxford's enigma. *The Observer.* 5 November 1972.

GOMPERTZ, T. (1957). Some observations on the feral pigeon in London. *Bird Study* 4:2–13.

GOODERS, J. (1965). The birds of Clapham and Wandsworth Commons. *London Bird Report* 29:73–88.

(1968). The swift in central London. *London Bird Report* 32:93–8.

GOODWIN, D. (1952). The colour varieties of feral pigeons. *London Bird Report* 16:35–6.

(1958). The existence and causation of colour-preferences in the pairing of feral and domestic pigeon. *Bull. B.O.C.* 78:136–9.

(1960). Comparative ecology of pigeons in inner London. *Brit. Birds* 53:201–12.

GRANT, P. J. (1967). The birds of Greenwich Park and Blackheath. *London Bird Report* 31:64–92.

(1970). Birds of urban areas cleared for redevelopment. *London Bird Report* 33:65–6.

GREATER LONDON COUNCIL. (1973). *Survey of London.* Vol. XXXVII. North Kensington. ed. F. H. W. Sheppard.

HARRISON, C. J. O. (1960). The food of some urban tawny owls. *Bird Study* 7:236–40.

HARRISON, H. J. (1949). Remarkable accumulation of nest material by starling. *Brit. Birds* 42:119.

HUDSON, R. (1972). Collared doves in Britain and Ireland during 1965–70. *Brit. Birds* 65:139–55.

LACK, D. (1956). *Swifts in a tower.* London.

(1956). Further notes on the breeding biology of swifts *Apus apus Ibis* 98:606–19

(1958). The return and departure of swifts *Apus apus* at Oxford. *Ibis* 100:477–502.

LACK, D. and LACK, E. (1952). The breeding behaviour of the swift. *Brit. Birds* 45:186–215.

LACK, D., and OWEN, D. F. (1955). The food of the swift. *J. Anim. Ecol.* 24:120–36.

MURTON, R. K. (1965). *The Woodpigeon.* London.

(1971). *Man and Birds.* London.

MURTON, R. K., and WESTWOOD, N. J. (1966). The foods of the rock dove and feral pigeon. *Bird Study* 13:130–46.

PEAL, R. E. F. (1965). Woodpigeons in a London suburb. *London Bird Report* 29:89–90.

PERRINS, C. (1971). Age of first breeding and adult survival rates in the swift. *Bird Study* 18:61–70.

SALFELD, D. (1963). Jay learning to feed from nutholder. *Brit. Birds* 56:221.

—— (1969). Jays recovering buried food from under snow. *Brit. Birds* 62:238–40.

SEEL, D. C. (1968). Breeding seasons of the house sparrow and tree sparrow *Passer* Spp. at Oxford. *Ibis* 110:29–44.

—— (1968). Clutch-size, incubation and hatching success in the house sparrow and tree sparrow *Passer* Spp. at Oxford. *Ibis* 110:270–82.

—— (1969). Food, feeding rates and body temperature in the nestling house sparrow *Passer domesticus* at Oxford. *Ibis* 111:36–47.

SETH-SMITH, D. (1937). Winter gathering of pied wagtails in London suburb. *Brit. Birds* 30:319.

STRANGEMAN, P. J. (1966). The bird life of Bishop's Park, Fulham, and its vicinity. *London Bird Report* 30:80–102.

WALLACE, D. I. M. (1961). The birds of Regent's Park and Primrose Hill, 1959. *London Bird Report* 24:81–107.

CHAPTER 3. *The Outer Ring. i. Estates and Factories*

ARMSTRONG, E. A. (1955). *The Wren.* London.

BARRINGTON, R. (1971). *The Bird Gardener's Book.* London.

BARTLETT, T. L. (1964). Bird gardening in the suburbs. *Bird Notes* 31:156–160.

BATTEN, L. A. (1971). Blackbird mortality. *Ibis* 113:414–15.

—— (1972). The past and present bird life of the Brent Reservoir and its vicinity. *Lond. Nat.* 50:8–62.

—— (1972). Breeding bird species diversity in relation to increasing urbanization. *Bird Study* 19:157–66.

BEVEN, G. (1965). The food of tawny owls in London. *London Bird Report* 29:56–62.

BLACKETT, A. (1970). Blue tits and gulls feeding by artificial light. *Brit. Birds* 63:136–7.

BOULDIN, L. E. (1968). The population of the house martin *Delichon urbica* in East Lancashire. *Bird Study* 15:135–46.

CARR, D. (1967). Blue tits nesting in bus stop indicator. *Brit. Birds* 60:52–3.

COMMITTEE OF THE LONDON NATURAL HISTORY SOCIETY. (1964). *The Birds of the London Area.* A new revised edition. London.

COULSON, J. C. (1960). A study of the mortality of the starling based on ringing recoveries. *J. Anim. Ecol.* 29:251–70.

CRAMP, S., and TOMLINS, A. D. (1966). The birds of inner London. *Brit. Birds* 59:209–32.

CRAMP, S., PETTET, A., and SHARROCK, J. T. R. (1960). The irruption of tits in autumn. *Brit. Birds* 53:49–77.

DIXON, C. (1909). *The Bird Life of London.* London.

DOWSETT, R. J. (1960). Starlings affected by smog. *Brit. Birds* 53:33–4.

FERGUSON-LEES, I. J. (1964). Studies of less familiar birds. 127. Collared dove. *Brit. Birds* 57:170–5.

FITTER, R. S. R. (1945). *London's Natural History*. London.

FLEGG, J. J. M., and GLUE, D. E. (1971). *Nestboxes*. A publication of the British Trust for Ornithology.

GOODWIN, D. (1949). House sparrows pursuing pigeons. *Brit. Birds* 42:64.

HARDY, E. (1971). Pigeons, crows and other species building nests of wire. *Brit. Birds* 64:77–8.

HARRISON, C. J. O. (1964). 'Industrial' discoloration of house sparrows. *Brit. Birds* 57:85.

HARTLEY, P. H. T. (1954). Back garden ornithology. *Bird Study* 1:18–27.

HUDSON, R. (1972). Collared doves in Britain and Ireland during 1965–70. *Brit. Birds* 65:139–55.

HUGHES, S. W. M. (1972). Brambling feeding from a suspended nut-basket. *Brit. Birds* 65:445.

KING, B. (1966). Nocturnal singing and feeding by robins in winter. *Brit. Birds* 59:501.

(1967). Spotted flycatchers catching insects after dark by artificial lighting. *Brit. Birds* 60:255–6.

MCCLINTOCK, D. (1972). What the birds don't eat. Article in *New Scientist* 17 August 1972.

MEADOWS, B. S. (1970). Breeding distribution and feeding ecology of the black redstart in London. *London Bird Report* 34:72–9.

MONTIER, D. (1968). A survey of the breeding distribution of the kestrel, barn owl and tawny owl in the London area, 1967. *London Bird Report* 32:81–92.

MORRIS, D. (1954). The snail-eating behaviour of thrushes and blackbirds. *Brit. Birds* 47:33–49.

NICHOLSON, E. M. (1951). *Birds and Men*. London.

PARSLOW, J. (1973). *Breeding Birds of Britain and Ireland*. Berkhamsted.

PEET, W. M. (1959). Starlings affected by smog. *Brit. Birds* 52:238.

ROSE, S., and PEARCE, L. (1972). Sulphur dioxide – a UK snapshot view. Article in *New Scientist*, 17 February 1972.

ROYAL SOCIETY FOR THE PROTECTION OF BIRDS. (n.d.) *Pesticides and the Gardener. The Birds in your Garden*.

SEEL, D. C. (1960). The behaviour of a pair of house sparrows while rearing young. *Brit. Birds* 53:303–10.

SIMMS, E. (1962). A study of suburban bird-life at Dollis Hill. *Brit. Birds* 55:1–36.

(1971). *Woodland Birds*. London.

(1972). Unpublished MS of Hindson Memorial Lecture given to the London Natural History Society, 25 October 1972, entitled *Wildlife in a London Suburb*.

SLADE, B. E. (1963). Starlings eating putty. *Brit. Birds* 56:113.

SOPER, T. (1966). *The Bird Table Book*. London.

SPENCER, R., and GUSH, G. H. (1973). Siskins feeding in gardens. *Brit. Birds* 66:91–9.

SUMMERS-SMITH, J. D. (1963). *The House Sparrow*. London.

THOMAS, A. (1972). Blackbird taking flatworm from underside of waterlily leaves. *Brit. Birds* 65:82.

WILLIAMS, P. L. (1967). Sand martins nesting in drainage holes by main road. *Brit. Birds* 60:167–78.

CHAPTER 4. *The Outer Ring.* ii. *The Open Spaces*

BARKER, G. (1972). *Wildlife Conservation in the Care of Churches and Churchyards.* London.

BATTEN, L. A. (1972). The past and present bird life of the Brent Reservoir. *Lond. Nat.* 50:8–62.

BATTEN, L., *et al.* (1973). *Birdwatchers' Year.* Berkhamsted.

COLLINS, H. E. (1964). The restoration of excavated land. Paper 16. The Countryside in 1970. *Proceedings of the Study Conference, November* 1963:250–2.

COMMITTEE ON BIRD SANCTUARIES IN THE ROYAL PARKS (ENGLAND). (1928–70). Reports published by H.M.S.O. with later issues entitled *Birds in London,* 1939–47, 1948, 1949, and *Bird Life in the Royal Parks,* 1950, 1951–2, 1953–4, 1955–6, 1957–8, 1959–60, 1961–2, 1963–4, 1965–6, 1967–8, 1969–70. London.

COMMITTEE OF THE LONDON NATURAL HISTORY SOCIETY. (1964). *The Birds of the London Area.* A new revised edition. London.

CONDRY, W. M. (1966). *The Snowdonia National Park.* London.

CORNELIUS, L. W. (1971). Yellow wagtails breeding in inner London. *London Bird Report* 35:92.

DIXON, C. (1909). *The Bird-life of London.* London.

FITTER, R. S. R. (1945). *London's Natural History.* London.

FITTER, R. S. R., and LOUSLEY, J. E. (1953). *The Natural History of the City.* London.

GIBBS, A. (1963). The bird population of rubbish dumps. *London Bird Report* 26:104–10.

GLUE, D. E. (1973). Adaptation by predators to urban life. *Brit. Birds* 66:411.

GRANT, P. J. (1971). Birds at Surrey Commercial docks. *London Bird Report* 35:87–91.

GRAY, D. B. (1973). Whinchats on disused railway. *Bird Study* 20:81–82.

GREENHALGH, M. E., and P. A. (1968). Oystercatchers nesting on rubbish tip. *Brit. Birds* 61:528.

HARTING, J. E. (1866). *The Birds of Middlesex.* London.

HEY, T. (1972). For the birds, sanctuary in the churchyards. Article in *The Times,* 28 October 1972.

HICKLING, R. A. O. (1954). The wintering of gulls in Britain. *Bird Study* 1:129–48.

JEFFERIES, R. (1905). *Nature near London.* London.

JOHNSTON, R. F., and SELANDER, R. K. (1963). Further remarks on discoloration in house sparrows. *Brit. Birds* 56:469–70.

JONES, B. W. (1958). Survey of birds in the Brookvale district of Erdington, Birmingham. *West Midland Bird Report* 24:19–22.

LORD, J., and MUNNS, D. J. (1970). ed. *Atlas of Breeding Birds of the West Midlands.* London.

MIRAMS, D. R. (1951). West Bromwich area. *West Midland Bird Report* 16:9–10.

NEWTON, I. (1967). The adaptive radiation and feeding ecology of some British finches. *Ibis* 109:33–96.

(1972). *Finches*. London.

NOBLE, K. (1972). Oystercatchers breeding at Rainham Marsh, Essex. *London Bird Report* 36:91–2.

PARR, D. (1972). ed. *Birds in Surrey. 1900–70*. London.

PLANT, J. W., and ROBINSON, L. K. (1970). *Programme for derelict land reclamation. City of Stoke-on-Trent*. Stoke-on-Trent.

RUTTLEDGE, R. F. (1963). Whooper swans feeding on refuse dump. *Brit. Birds* 56:340.

SAGE, B. L. (1963). The breeding distribution of the tree sparrow. *London Bird Report* 27:56–65.

SIMMS, E. (1974). *The Wild Life of the Royal Parks*. H.M.S.O. London.

WEST MIDLAND BIRD CLUB. (1957–65). *Annual Reports 23–31*.

WILLIAMSON, K. (1968). The importance of managing scrub as a breeding habitat for birds, from *1968 Handbook of the Society for the Promotion of Nature Reserves*.

(1973). The wildlife of the church. *Comment*. Magazine of Tring Anglican and Methodist Churches, January 1973.

WOOD, R. F., and THIRGOOD, J. V. (1955). Tree planting on colliery spoil heaps. *Forestry Commission. Forest Research B. Paper, No. 17*.

CHAPTER 5. *The Edge of the Countryside*

BEST, R. H., and COPPOCK, J. T. (1962). *The Changing Use of Land in Britain*.

BRIDGMAN, C. J. (1962). Birds nesting in aircraft. *Brit. Birds* 55:461–70.

BUSNEL, R. G., and GIBAN, J. (1965). Le problème des oiseaux sur les aérodromes. *Colloque tenu à Nice les 25,26 et 27 novembre, 1963*. Institut national de la recherche agronomique.

CROOKS, S. E., and MOXEY, P. A. (1966). Study of a lapwing population in north-west Middlesex. *London Bird Report* 30:60–79.

DUNBALL, A. P. (1972). Landscape treatment of trunk roads and motorways. *Journ. Devon Trust Nat. Cons.* 4:120–3.

FINNIS, R. G. (1960). Road casualties among birds. *Bird Study* 7:21–32.

(1968). Blackbirds persistently feeding on ripening tomatoes. *Brit. Birds* 61:85.

HODSON, N. L., and SNOW, D. W. (1965). The road deaths enquiry, 1960–1. *Bird Study* 12:90–9.

HOSKINS, W. G., and STAMP, L. D. (1963). *The Common Lands of England and Wales*. London.

HUDSON, W. H. (1900). *Nature in Downland*. London.

LANCUM, L. H. (1948). *Wild Birds and the Land*. H.M.S.O. London.

LINK, T. C. E. (1964). House martins nesting on new bridge over motorway. *Brit. Birds* 57:82.

LOCKLEY, R. M. (1936). *Birds of the Green Belt*. London.

MAGEE, J. D. (1971). Birds of Cassiobury Park, the west Hertfordshire golf course and Whippendell Woods, Watford. *London Bird Report* 36:67–74.

MINISTRY OF HOUSING AND LOCAL GOVERNMENT. (1962). *The Green Belts*. H.M.S.O. London.

MURTON, R. K. (1971). *Man and Birds*. London.

NEWTON, I. (1964). Bud-eating by bullfinches in relation to the natural food supply. *J. Appl. Ecol.* 1:265–79.

(1972). *Finches*. London.

NICHOLSON, E. M., and COLLING, A. W. (1964). Chart of human impacts on the countryside. *Proceedings of the Study Conference for the Countryside in 1970*: 106–10.

PAHL, R. E. (1965). Urbs in rure. *London School of Economics and Political Science, Geographical Papers, No. 2.*

PARKER, A. (1970). The decline of the rook as a breeding species at Hainault, Essex. *London Bird Report* 33:87–95.

SCOTT, R. E., ROBERTS, L. J., and CADBURY, C. J. (1972). Bird deaths from power lines at Dungeness. *Brit. Birds* 65:273–86.

SIMMS, E. (1963). A July journey through the Cotswolds. *BBC Book of the Countryside*. ed. Arthur Phillips. London.

(1971). *Woodland Birds*. London.

SNOW, D. W., and MAYER-GROSS, H. (1967). Farmland as a nesting habitat. *Bird Study* 14:43–52.

STAMP, L. D. (1955). *Man and the Land*. London.

(1969). *Nature Conservation in Britain*. London.

SUMMERS-SMITH, J. D. (1963). *The House Sparrow*. London.

THOMAS, D. (1970). *London's Green Belt*. London.

VERNON, J. D. R. (1970). Food of the common gull on grassland in autumn and winter. *Bird Study* 17:36–38.

(1972). Feeding habits and food of the black-headed and common gulls. *Bird Study* 19:173–86.

WAY, M. (1970). Wildlife on the motorway. Article in *New Scientist*, 10 September 1970.

WILLIAMSON, K. (1967). The bird community of farmland. *Bird Study* 14:210–26.

WRIGHT, E. N. (1965). A review of bird scaring methods used on British airfields. In *Busnel and Giban*, 113–19.

(1972). Bird strikes and the new London airport. Article in *Animals*, April 1972: 151–5.

WRIGHT, E. N., and BROUGH, T. (1966). Bird damage to fruit. Fruit present and future. *Roy. Hort. Soc.* 1966:168–80.

WRIGHT, E. N., and SUMMERS, D. D. B. (1960). The biology and economic importance of the bullfinch. *Ann. Appl. Biol.* 48:415–18.

CHAPTER 6. *Rivers, Lakes and Reservoirs*

ATKINSON-WILLES, G. L. (1963). ed. Wildfowl in Great Britain. *Monographs of Nature Conservancy, 3.* H.M.S.O. London.

BATTEN, L. A. (1972). The past and present bird life of the Brent Reservoir and its vicinity. *Lond. Nat.* 50:8–62.

BOYD, A. W. (1951). *A Country Parish*. London.

CRAMP, S., and TEAGLE, W. G. (1955). A comparative study of the birds of two stretches of the Thames in inner London, 1951–3. *London Bird Report* 18:42–57.

FITTER, R. S. R. (1945). *London's Natural History*. London.

(1949). *London's Birds*. London.

(1963). *Wildlife in Britain*. London.

GLADWIN, T. W. (1972). Lemsford springs nature reserve *Grebe* 2:47–51.

GRANT, P. J. (1970). Duck on the River Thames at Woolwich. *London Bird Report* 34:80–5.

(1971). Birds at Surrey Commercial Docks. *London Bird Report* 35:87–91.

(1973). The past and present bird life of the Brent reservoir and its vicinity – an amendment. *Lond. Nat.* 52:70–1.

HARRIS, M. P. (1970). Rates and causes of increases of some British gull populations. *Bird Study* 17:325–35.

HASTINGS, A. B. (1937). Biology of water supply. *Brit. Mus. (Nat. Hist.) Econ. Ser.* 7a:1–48.

HICKLING, R. A. O. (1957). The social behaviour of gulls wintering inland. *Bird Study* 4:181–92.

HOMES, R. C. (1949). Winter duck population of the London area. *London Bird Report* 13:46–56.

(1958). A ten-year review of duck counts in the London area. *London Bird Report* 22:36–49.

(1964). The reservoirs and other large waters. In *The Birds of the London Area*. 42–56. London.

JOHNSON, I. G. (1966). Water pipits wintering on watercress beds. *Brit. Birds* 59:552–4.

(1970). The water pipit as a winter visitor to the British Isles. *Bird Study* 17:297–319.

LORD, J. (1965). Some birds of Blithfield reservoir 1952–63. *West Mid. Bird Report* 31:8–15.

MACAN, T. T., and WORTHINGTON, E. B. (1951). *Life in Lakes and Rivers*. London.

MURTON, R. K. (1971). *Man and Birds*. London.

MURTON, R. K., THEARLE, R. J. P., and THOMPSON, J. (1972). Ecological studies of the Feral Pigeon *Columba livia* var. I. Populations, breeding biology and methods of control. *J. appl. Ecol.* 9:835–74.

MURTON, R. K., COOMBS, C. F. B., and THEARLE, R. J. P. (1972). Ecological studies of the Feral Pigeon *Columba livia* var. II. Flock behaviour and social organization. *J. Appl. Ecol.* 9:875–89.

NATURE CONSERVANCY. (n.d.) *Tring Reservoirs. National Nature Reserve.*

ODDIE, W. E. (1963). Birds in the Bartley reservoir area 1931–62 (Part 1). *West Mid. Bird Report* 29:9–14.

(1964). Birds in the Bartley reservoir area 1931–62 (Part 2). *West Mid. Bird Report* 30:9–14.

OSBORNE, K. C. (1971). Water pipits in the London area. *London Bird Report* 35:68–73.

PEARSALL, W. H., GARDINER, A. C., and GREENSHIELDS, F. (1946). Freshwater biology and water supply in Britain. *Freshw. Biol. Assoc. Brit. Emp. Sci. Pub.* 11:1–90.

ROGERS, M. J. (1951). Notes on the birds of Bellfields reservoir. *West Mid. Bird Report* 17:9–15.

— (1955). The birds of Cannock reservoir. *West Mid. Bird Report* 21: 20–7.

SAGE, B. L. (1970). The winter population of gulls in the London area. *London Bird Report* 33:67–80.

SHEPHERD, M. R. (1967). Radipole lake, Dorset, urban sanctuary. *Birds* 1:130–3.

SIMMS, E. (1957). *Voices of the Wild.* London.

— (1957). Hordes of squabbling neighbours. Article in *John Bull,* 10 August 1957

— (1957). Ortolan bunting in Middlesex. *Brit. Birds* 50:118–19.

— (1972). Bird life along the waters of Brent. Article in *The Willesden and Brent Chronicle,* 1 December 1972.

STRANGEMAN, P. J. (1971). Birds of the River Thames at Westminster, Inner London, 1968–70. *London Bird Report* 35:73–80.

TANSLEY, A. G. (1968). *Britain's Green Mantle.* London.

WALLACE, D. I. M. (1957). Little buntings in Middlesex. *Brit. Birds* 50:208–209.

CHAPTER 7. *Marshes, Sewage Farms and Gravel Pits*

ANDREWS, H. *et al.* (1966). Birds trapped by sludge or mud. *Brit. Birds* 59:161–2.

BEVEN, G. (1966). Kestrel temporarily trapped by sludge on a sewage farm. *Brit. Birds* 59:45.

BOYD, A. W. (1951). *A Country Parish.* London.

— (1957). Sewage-farms as bird-habitats. *Brit. Birds* 50:253–63.

BRADNEY, R. J. (1963). Birds of Blackbrook sewage farm. *West Mid. Bird Report* 28:9–12.

CLEGG, M. (1972). Carrion crows feeding on marine molluscs and taking fish. *Bird Study* 19:249–50.

CROOK, J. H. (1953). An observational study of the gulls of Southampton Water. *Brit. Birds* 46:385–97.

DIXON, C. (1909). *The Bird-life of London.* London.

GILLHAM, E. H. (1956). Short-eared owls and some other birds-of-prey on the north Kent marshes. February 1 to June 6, 1955. *Kent Bird Report* 4:32.

GILLHAM, E. H., and HOMES, R. C. (1950). *The Birds of the North Kent Marshes.* London.

GLADWIN, T. W. (1963). A short account of Rye Meads, Herts., and its ornithology. *London Bird Report* 26:88–99.

— (1972). Lemsford springs nature reserve. *Grebe* 1:47–51.

GLUE, D. F. (1970). Changes in the bird community of a Hampshire gravel pit 1963–8. *Bird Study* 17:15–27.

— (1971). Saltmarsh reclamation stages and their associated bird life. *Bird Study* 18:187–98.

GREENHALGH, M. E. (1971). The breeding bird communities of Lancashire saltmarshes. *Bird Study* 18:199–212.

HARRISON, J. M. (1970). Creating a wetland habitat. *Bird Study* 17:111–22. (1972). *A Gravel Pit Wildfowl Reserve*. WAGBI: Redland.

HARRISON, J., HUMPHREYS, J. N., and GRAVES, G. (1973). *Breeding Birds of the Medway Estuary*. Kent Orn. Soc.: WAGBI. Chester.

HAWKINS, K., and KING, B. (1966). Birds trapped by sludge or mud. *Brit. Birds* 59:45.

HOMES, R. C., SAGE, B., and SPENCER, R. (1960). Breeding populations of lapwings, coot and meadow pipits. *London Bird Report* 23:54–61.

HUTSON, A. M. (1970). Possible breeding of the spotted crake in the London area. *London Bird Report* 34:86–8.

INTERNATIONAL UNION FOR CONSERVATION OF NATURE AND NATURAL RESOURCES. (n.d.) *Liquid Assets*. Morges and Le Sambuc.

KEYWOOD, K. P., and MELLUISH, W. D. (1953). A report on the bird population of four gravel pits in the London area, 1948 to 1951. *London Bird Report* 17:43–72.

LAPWORTH, H. (1949). Alvecote pools. *West Mid. Bird Report* 15:7.

LEES, H. T. (1963). Little ringed plovers in Warwickshire. *West Mid. Bird Report* 29:15–16.

MELLUISH, W. D. (1957). The census of great crested grebes 1946 to 1955. Final report and summary of results. *London Bird Report* 21:48–57.

MILNE, B. S. (1956). A report on the bird population of Beddington sewage farm 1954–5. *London Bird Report* 20:39–54.

NAU, B. S. (1961). Sand martin colonies in the London area. *London Bird Report* 25:69–81.

NOBLE, K. (1971). Birds of Rainham marsh. *London Bird Report* 35:56–68.

OAKELEY, R. G. (1957). Bishop's Stortford sewage farm. *Coturnix*. 7th Report. 35–7.

PARR, D. (1963). Bird life on a sewage disposal works. *London Bird Report* 27:66–90.

PARRINDER, E. R. (1964). The gravel pits. In *The Birds of the London Area*. 57–60. London.

PARRINDER, E. R., and PARRINDER, E. D. (1969). Little ringed plovers in Britain in 1963–7. *Brit. Birds* 62:219–23.

PARSLOW, J. (1973). *Breeding Birds of Britain and Ireland*. Berkhamsted.

RICHARDS, A. J. (1961). The birds of Brandon. *West Mid. Bird Reports* 27:9–16.

RYALL, R. H. (1973). Spotted crakes taking food from anglers. *Brit. Birds* 66:118–19.

SAGE, B. L. (1959). *A History of the Birds of Hertfordshire*. London. (1963). The breeding distribution of the tree sparrow. *London Bird Report* 27:56–65.

SIMMS, E. (1957). *Voices of the Wild*. London.

STEAD, P. J. (1964). Unusual numbers of sea-birds at Teesmouth in August 1962. *Brit. Birds* 57:76–78.

TANSLEY, A. G. (1968). *Britain's Green Mantle*. London.

WEBBER, G. L. (1965). Birds trapped by sludge on a sewage farm. *Brit. Birds* 58:296–7.

WILSON, J. (1973). Wader populations of Morecambe Bay, Lancashire. *Bird Study* 20:9–23.

WINSOR, C. E. (1951). Minworth sewage works. *West Mid. Bird Report* 16:8.

CHAPTER 8. *Birds and the Pursuit of Sport*

BROWN, R. S. (1963). Carrion crows attacking starlings. *London Bird Report* 26:112.

BUCKNILL, J. A. (1900). *The Birds of Surrey.* London.

EDLIN, H. L. (1956). *Trees, Woods and Man.* London.

FITTER, R. S. R. (1945). *London's Natural History.* London.

HARRISON, J., and WARDELL, J. (1962). WAGBI. duck rearing in 1961. *Rept. Wildfowlers' Association of Great Britain and Ireland, 1961–62:* 21–8.

KIRKMAN, F. B., and HUTCHINSON, H. G. (1936). *British Sporting Birds.* London.

MIDDLETON, A. D., and ASH, J. S. (1964). The conservation of game as a natural resource. *Proc. Countryside in 1970 Study Conference, November 1963:*241–9.

MOORE, N. W. (1957). The past and present status of the buzzard in the British Isles. *Brit. Birds* 50:173–97.

MURTON, R. K. (1971). *Man and Birds.* London.

PARSLOW, J. L. F. (1967–8). Changes in status among breeding birds in Britain and Ireland. *Brit. Birds* 60:2–47, 97–123, 177–202, 261–85, 396–404, 493–508; 61:49–64, 241–55.

PAYN, W. H. (1962). *The Birds of Suffolk.* London.

POTTS, G. R. (1971). The partridge survival project. *Ibis* 113:419.

ROWBERRY, E. C. (1934). Gulls in the London area. *Lond. Nat.* 1933:45–8.

SIMMS, E. (1963). September migration in North Somerset. Unpublished MS.

TANSLEY, A. G. (1968). *Britain's Green Mantle,* London.

VERNON, J. D. R. (1970). Food of the common gull on grassland in autumn and winter. *Bird Study* 17:36–38.

YOUNG, J. G. (1972). The pheasant and the sparrowhawk. *Birds,* Vol. 4. No. 4:94–9.

CHAPTER 9. *Suburban Roosts and Flyways*

ARMSTRONG, E. A. (1955). *The Wren.* London.

BATTEN, L. A. (1972). The past and present bird life of the Brent Reservoir and its vicinity. *Lond. Nat.* 50:8–62.

BOSWALL, J. (1966). Pied wagtails roosting inside greenhouses. *Brit. Birds* 59:100–6.

— (1966). The roosting of the pied wagtail in Dublin. *Bull. Brit. Orn. Cl.* 86:131–40.

BRACKBILL, H. (1972). Starlings grounded by drenched plumage in cold weather. *Brit. Birds* 65:82–3.

BUNYARD, P. F. (1936). Roosting of pied wagtails (*Motacilla alba lugubris*) in commercial glass-houses. *Bull. Brit. Orn. Cl.* 56:108–9.

CARR, D. (1965). Wakefulness of blue tit roosting in street lamp. *Brit. Birds* 58:220–21.

COHEN, E. (1960). Unusual roosting site of pied wagtails. *Brit. Birds* 53:315.

COMMITTEE ON BIRD SANCTUARIES IN THE ROYAL PARKS. (1957). *Bird Life in the Royal Parks* 1955–6:16.

CORNISH, C. J. (1902). *The Naturalist on the Thames.*

COX, R. A. F. (1953). Swift roosting in a tree. *Brit. Birds* 46:414.

CULLEN, R. M. (1964). Article 'Roosting' in Thomson, A. L. (ed.), *New Dict. Birds.* London and New York.

DICKINSON, B. H. B., and DOBINSON, H. M. (1957). A study of a greenfinch roost. *Bird Study* 16:135–46.

DRINNAN, R. E., and RIDPATH, M. G. (1957). Counting flocks of roosting birds by photography. *Bird Study* 4:149–59.

ELMS, N. E. G. (1972). House martins settling and roosting in reedbeds. *Brit. Birds* 65:126.

FITTER, R. S. R. (1943). The starling roosts of the London area. *Lond. Nat.* for 1942:3–23.

(1949). *London's Birds.* London.

FLOWER, W. U. (1969). Over 60 wrens roosting together in one nestbox. *Brit. Birds* 62:157–8.

FORSTER, G. H. (1955). Thermal air currents and their use in bird-flight. *Brit. Birds* 48:241–53.

FROST, R. A. (1971). Starlings grounded after bathing in very cold weather. *Brit. Birds* 64:321.

GLUE, D. E. (1968). Bird predators feeding at autumn roosts. *Brit. Birds* 61:526–7.

GOMPERTZ, T. (1957). Some observations on the feral pigeon in London. *Bird Study* 4:2–13.

GRIFFITHS, J. (1955). Jackdaw roost continuing throughout breeding season. *Brit. Birds* 48:139.

HICKLING, R. A. O. (1957). The social behaviour of gulls wintering inland. *Bird Study* 4:181–92.

(1967). The inland wintering of gulls in England, 1963. *Bird Study* 14:104–13.

HODGSON, N. L. (1966). Swallows living inside engineering works until late December. *Brit. Birds* 59:153–4.

HOMES, R. C. (1955). Gull roosts of the London area. *London Bird Report* 18:37–9.

LORD, J., and MUNNS, D. J. (1970). ed. *Atlas of the Breeding Birds of the West Midlands.* London.

LYNN-ALLEN, E., and ROBERTSON, A. W. P. (1956). *A Partridge Year.* London.

MACKENZIE, J. M. D. (1957). Treecreepers roosting in wellingtonias. *Bird Study* 4:94–7.

(1959). Roosting of treecreepers. *Bird Study* 6:8–14.

MEADOWS, B. S. (1961). The gull roosts of the Lea Valley reservoirs. *London Bird Report* 25:56–60.

NEWTON: I. (1972). *Finches.* London.

NICHOLSON, E. M. (1951). *Birds and Men.* London.

POTTS, G. R. (1967). Urban starling roosts in the British Isles. *Bird Study* 14:25–42.

ROLLS, J. C. (1972). Redwings roosting in reedbeds. *Brit. Birds* 65:126–7.

RUTTLEDGE, W. (1972). Goldfinch roost in inner London. *Brit. Birds* 58:442–3.

SAGE, B. L. (1958). A new gull roost in the London area. *London Bird Report* 22:50–1.

(1964). The gull roosts of the London area. *Lond. Bird Report* 28:63–8.

(1970). The winter population of gulls in the London area. *London Bird Report* 33:67–80.

SEAGO, M. J. (1967). *The Birds of Norfolk.* Norwich.

SIMMS, E. (1957). *Voices of the Wild.* London.

(1973). Evensong among the sparrows. Article in *The Willesden and Brent Chronicle*, 12 October 1973.

SMITH, S. (1950). *The Yellow Wagtail.* London.

SNOW, D. W. (1958). *A Study of Blackbirds.* London.

SUMMERS-SMITH, J. D. (1963). *The House Sparrow.* London.

WYNNE-EDWARDS, V. C. (1959). The control of population-density through social behaviour: a hypothesis. *Ibis* 101:436–41.

(1962). *Animal Dispersion in Relation to Social Behaviour.*

ZAHAVI, A. (1971). The function of pre-roost gatherings and communal roosts. *Ibis* 113:106–9.

CHAPTER 10. *Birds on the Move*

AXELL, H. E. (1966). Eruptions of bearded tits during 1959–65. *Brit. Birds* 59:513–43.

BATTEN, L. A. (1972). The past and present bird life of the Brent Reservoir and its vicinity. *Lond. Nat.* 50:8–62.

BATTEN, L., et al. (1973). *Birdwatchers' Year.* Berkhamsted.

BROWNE, P. W. P. (1953). Nocturnal migration of thrushes in Ireland. *Brit. Birds* 46:370–4.

CHAPMAN, F. M. (1888). Observations on the nocturnal migration of birds. *Auk* 1888:37.

CHITTENDEN, D. E. (1973). Bramblings taking peanuts from suspended mesh containers. *Brit. Birds* 66:121.

CLARKE, W. E. (1912). *Studies in Bird Migration.* 2 vols. London and Edinburgh.

COMMITTEE ON BIRD SANCTUARIES IN THE ROYAL PARKS. (1962). *Report* for 1959–60. H.M.S.O. London.

CORNWALLIS, R. K., and TOWNSEND, A. D. (1968). Waxwings in Britain and Europe during 1965/6. *Brit. Birds* 61:97–118.

DARLINGTON, A. (1951). The use of mobile observers in the study of patterns of migration. *Brit. Birds* 44:152–7.

DAVIS, P. (1964). Crossbills in Britain and Ireland in 1963. *Brit. Birds* 57:477–501.

DIXON, C. (1909). *The Bird-life of London.* London.

DOBINSON, H. M., and RICHARDS, A. J. (1964). The effects of the severe winter of 1962/3 on birds in Britain. *Brit. Birds* 57:373–434.

DORST, J. (1956). *The Migrations of Birds*. Paris.

EASTWOOD, E. (1967). *Radar Ornithology*. London.

EASTWOOD, E., and RIDER, G. C. (1965). Some radar measurements of the altitude of bird flight. *Brit. Birds* 58:393–426.

GIBBS, A., and WALLACE, D. I. M. (1961). Four million birds? *London Bird Report* 25:61–8.

GOODERS, J. (1965). The birds of Clapham and Wandsworth Commons. *London Bird Report* 29:73–88.

GRANT, P. J. (1967). The birds of Greenwich Park and Blackheath. *London Bird Report* 31:64–92.

HARTHAN, A. J., and SMOUT, T. C. (1963). A fieldfare invasion in south Warwickshire. *West Mid. Bird Report* 29:18.

HOLLYER, J. N. (1970). The invasion of nutcrackers in autumn 1968. *Brit. Birds* 63:353–73.

—— (1972). Flight call of continental song thrush. *Brit. Birds* 65:170.

HOLME, H. C., and SIMMS, E. (1953). Black-eared wheatear in London. *Brit. Birds* 26:42–5.

HOMES, R. C. (1957). Wildfowl and wader movements in the London area in the severe weather of February, 1956. *London Bird Report* 21:41–7.

LACK, D. (1954). *The Natural Regulation of Animal Numbers*. London.

—— (1959). Watching migration by radar. *Brit. Birds* 52:258–67.

—— (1960). The height of bird migration. *Brit. Birds* 53:5–10.

—— (1960). The influence of weather on passerine migration. A review. *Auk* 77:171–209.

MASON, C. F. (1969). Waders and terns in Leicestershire and an index of relative abundance. *Brit. Birds* 62:523–33.

NISBET, I. C. T. (1957). Wader migration at Cambridge sewage farm. *Bird Study* 4:131–48.

NISBET, I. C. T., and VINE, A. E. (1956). Migration of little stints, curlew sandpipers and ruffs through Great Britain in the autumn of 1953. *Brit. Birds* 49:121–34.

PARRINDER, E. R. (1964). On Migration in *The Birds of the London Area*, 92–106. London.

POWER, F. D. (1910). *Ornithological notes from a London suburb*. London.

RAYNER, G. W. (1951). Visible migration. *West Mid. Bird Report* 16:4–7.

SEAGO, M. J. (1967). *The Birds of Norfolk*. Norwich.

SIMMS, E. (1938). Curlew sandpiper in Surrey. *Brit. Birds* 32:239.

—— (1949). An overland migration route. *West Mid. Bird Report* 15:10–11.

—— (1950). Autumn bird migration across the south midlands of England. *Brit. Birds* 43:241–50.

—— (1952). *Bird Migrants*. London.

—— (1953). Yellow-billed cuckoo in Sussex. *Brit. Birds* 46:218.

—— (1957). Ortolan bunting in Middlesex. *Brit. Birds* 50:118.

—— (1957). What is the mystery behind migration? Article in *John Bull*, 21 September 1957.

—— (1962). A study of suburban bird life at Dollis Hill. *Brit. Birds* 55:1–36.

—— (1964). September migration in north Somerset. Unpub. MS.

—— (1965). Effects of the cold weather in 1962/3 on the blackbird population at Dollis Hill. *Brit. Birds* 58:33–43.

(1972). Wings over Brent. Article in *The Willesden and Brent Chronicle*, 27 October 1972.

(1973). Autumn features the pattern of bird migration, Article in *The Willesden and Brent Chronicle*, 9 November 1973.

(1974). *Wild Life in the Royal Parks*. H.M.S.O. London.

SNOW, D. W. (1953). Visible migration in the British Isles. A review. *Ibis* 95:242–70.

STANLEY, P. I., and MINTON, C. D. T. (1972). The unprecedented westward migration of curlew sandpipers in autumn 1969. *Brit. Birds* 65:365–80.

STRANGEMAN, P. J. (1966). The bird life of Bishop's Park, Fulham. *London Bird Report* 30:80–102.

THOMSON, A. L. (1964). Article 'Migration' in Thomson, A. L. (ed.). *New Dict. Birds*. London and New York.

USSHER, R. J., and WARREN, R. (1910). *The Birds of Ireland*. London

WALLACE, D. I. M. (1961). The birds of Regent's Park and Primrose Hill, 1959. *London Bird Report* 24:81–107.

(1964). On Migration in *The Birds of the London Area*, 314–22. London.

WHITE, G. (1788). *The Natural History of Selbourne*.

WILLIAMSON, K. (1952). Migrational drift in Britain in autumn 1951. *Scot. Nat.* 64:1–18.

(1955). Migrational drift. *Acta XI Int. Orn. Cong.* 179–86.

(1959). The September drift-movements of 1956 and 1958. *Brit. Birds* 52:334–77.

FOOD PARASITISM AMONG BIRDS AT DOLLIS HILL, NORTH-WEST LONDON, 1951–73

Parasite	*Victim*
Mallard	Feral pigeon, woodpigeon, blackbird, house sparrow, black-headed gull
Herring gull	Black-headed gull, common gull
Common gull	Black-headed gull
Black-headed gull	Mallard, feral pigeon, woodpigeon, starling
Woodpigeon	Feral pigeon, blackbird, starling, house sparrow
Great tit	Blue tit, house sparrow
Blue tit	Great tit, robin, hedgesparrow, house sparrow
Fieldfare	Blackbird, starling
Blackbird	Song thrush, great tit, hedgesparrow, house sparrow
Robin	Great tit, hedgesparrow, siskin, house sparrow
Starling	Blackbird, song thrush, hedgesparrow, house sparrow
Greenfinch	Blue tit, house sparrow
House Sparrow	Blackbird, hedgesparrow, greenfinch, chaffinch

Index

K 6